Contents

FOREWORD

At a recent technology literacy forum in Seattle, Washington, one would-be contributor left the meeting in disgust. "We want action, not talk," he declared. Yet to me, action without talk is unthinkable. As is talk without action. The two are inseparable, and a successful book about online communities will give ample consideration to both: Communities are the birthplace of talk and action.

Jenny Preece's new book strikes a rare and much-needed balance between talk and action. It accomplishes much more than that; it also addresses the more rigorous cousins of talk and action—theory and evidence. Too often, books focus on one without the other. People of action claim not to have time for "armchair theorizing"; theorists don't want the gritty details of reality fouling their pristine theory. But action without theory can be pointless toil; theory without a grounding in reality can be empty academicism. When theory, evidence, talk, and action are gracefully combined, as they are in this book, something truly useful and compelling emerges. This book clarifies why it is important to look at online communities. And, why, especially, is it important to do so right now.

Communication technology, historically, has come in one of two flavors. In the first, individuals communicate with other individuals (using the telephone or letters, for example). In the second, small groups of people, who are often elite, "broadcast" their messages to very large groups of people (using, say, newspapers, television, or radio). The Internet, as everybody knows, is changing all of that. New modes of communication are now possible. We are seeing the rise of new forums, where large numbers of people can communicate with others as equals or peers in a way that is far more symmetric than that of the broadcast models to which we've been accustomed. The Internet has given rise to a new community model of communication.

The question of what we should do with these new species of forum naturally arises. A combination of factors is necessary for a new communication venue to become a communication institution that is more or less permanent. To endure means having an audience, producers, sufficient development resources to support it, and the mobilized organization and infrastructure behind it. The forum itself becomes institutionalized (and sustainable, more or less) when these factors become stabilized. This is what's happening now on the Internet. Thousands of experiments are currently underway; a thousand flowers are blooming, but how many of these will sprout next spring or the following one? And how many of them are weeds?

That's where this book comes in. It's both a guide to current efforts and a solid foundation from which to think about, build upon, and participate in virtual communities.

Who should read this book? Clearly, developers of next-generation virtual community tools, services, and applications should adopt this as their bible. It will force them to see these systems as important new social environments where people exchange information, get to know one another, deliberate, work together, conduct economic transactions, and discuss the past—and the future.

Educators and researchers in information systems, computer science, sociology, political science, psychology, and many other disciplines will of course also benefit greatly from the book. However, a great number of other people need to study it and think about its implications as well; policymakers, journalists, businesspeople, and citizens alike need to confront the issues that Jenny Preece brings up in this book.

How the Internet is used, who makes the decisions, and why are at the core of what's important in the development of the Internet. Unfortunately, these questions rarely are asked. Too often it's assumed that corporations can now take over (once the initial investment from the taxpayers who paid for the Internet's early development has paid off). These questions are everybody's business! Therefore, opening up that process in any real way is to be congratulated.

The struggle for the soul of cyberspace has begun, and Professor Preece goes a long way toward opening up this process. Without playing favorites (as I would have done!), she outlines opportunities for business, health, education, government, and the civic sector alike to build new communities online. Communities, after all, are ultimately at the core of virtually everything we do. Let's do it right!

Doug Schuler
Seattle, Washington

Preface

There is no doubt whatever about the influence of architecture and structure upon human character and action. We shape our buildings, and afterwards our buildings shape us.

—Winston Churchill (as quoted in Brand, 1994, p. 3)

Everyone, it seems, is enthralled by online communities, and everyone has a story or has a friend with a story; generating a buzz of excitement. No doubt about it: Fresh experiences await us online—new people, new stories, comfort from fellow-travelers, insights from different cultures. In short, it's a new world online. There are communities for shopping, investing, sending greetings, learning, finding information of all kinds, sharing passions, discussing any and all topics under the sun, or just for chatting with friends.

When in 1996 I told colleagues that I was teaching a graduate class in online communities they looked askance. Some thought online communities were a passing fad, and that the class would disappear in short order; but it has not. In fact, each year, this class attracts more students from commercial organizations, government, and the social sciences, as well as from information systems and computer science. Online community fever has hit the Internet, and my class has caught it, too. Already there are many dot-com companies promising to create or teach the secrets of building successful online communities. Academia, too, is being drawn in; during the next five years, many courses will be launched across the globe.

Yes, the Web provides terabytes of information, but information alone lacks the human connection that online communities can provide. E-health offers patients databases of medical information, but patients also want to hear about treatments and how to deal with problems from other patients. E-education enables students to study in the comfort of their armchairs, but sitting alone isn't fun, especially when a homework assignment is due next week and you need help. Team projects also are greatly facilitated by shared development of Web pages. Members can exchange ideas, help one another, and develop rewarding partnerships. In these ways, learning becomes exciting and takes on a social dimension.

Of course, as with any technology, there can be dangers. Health information if submitted by amateurs may be wrong or inaccurate, and could, literally, endanger life; similarly, financial guidance can be misleading, causing monetary losses. Worse is that the Internet is being used to spread racial hatred and pornography. And online scams trick people just as in "real life." The online world, in short, offers all the advantages and disadvantages as the offline world.

Why do some online communities entertain, inform, and provide support while others wither and disappear? Rich, informed descriptions of social interaction online come from keen-eyed sociologists and communication studies experts who pay little attention to software; technical experts often ignore social issues, and instead focus on software and usability. But understanding the complexity of online communities requires study into both social and technical issues. That is the aim of this book:

to erect the framework in which to bring together discussions of social and technical issues, and to integrate theory and practice. Supporting sociability and designing usability lays the firm foundation on which online communities can grow and thrive. Both these undertakings can be achieved using community-centered development techniques that encourage active and focused participation in the development process. Involving the community motivates a sense of ownership, early, which is important for its success. Design guidelines and checklists also help developers as they design for good sociability and usability.

In this time of technological turbulence and increasing social isolation we still can construct technologies that shape communities across the world and draw people together in a positive way. Whether you are a developer, moderator, researcher or participant, there is a role for you in online communities.

Who Should Read This Book?

This is an interdisciplinary book appropriate for a number of audiences. The primary audiences are students learning about online communities and cyberspace human-computer interaction, and online community developers, and moderators. It will also appeal to enthusiasts, who want to know more about online communities, and new researchers, who want an overview of the multidisciplinary issues that influence the way online communities develop.

Primary readership

This book is intended for community developers of all kinds, including professionals developing large commercial communities. Likewise, people developing homespun online communities, such as for a local parent-teacher association, an environmental action group, a local political discussion group, a health support group, or a women's group will also benefit from reading this book. *Part Two* is particularly interesting, as this is where readers learn how to adapt and augment their existing skills. Readers with experience of online communities may wish to skim *Chapter 2, Community Tours*; practically oriented readers may be tempted to skip the whole of *Part One*, but this is discouraged. Understanding the basics, which includes a background of the psychology and sociology that underpins online behavior, is important because it informs community development.

Moderators and those with special leadership roles will learn more about interpersonal behavior online from *Part One*. *Chapters 7, 9*, and *11* of *Part Two* contain useful information about sociability and how to develop and manage social interaction. *Chapter 8* will interest readers involved in software selection, and *Chapter 10* will appeal to those who plan to evaluate online communities.

This book has been tried and tested by students in university-level courses. It is most appropriate for graduate students, who are encouraged to read the whole book. Undergraduates may skip *Chapters 5* and *6* on research. *Chapter 11* contains case studies of online communities developed by teams of graduate students. Students may wish to read both parts in parallel, as suggested by my students, who are professionals in information systems. This approach is particularly useful for classes that center on a semester-long project, because students develop foundational knowledge at the same time they exercise practical skills in their projects.

Secondary readership

Online community enthusiasts and participants will gain a broad understanding of criteria that influence social interactions in online communities. They will learn what to look for in online communities and how to contribute knowledgeably to software selection, sociability, and usability design in online communities. They will learn about the kind of behavior that is expected online and the dangers to look out for. *Part One* and *Chapters 9, 10* and *11* of *Part Two* are most relevant.

New researchers will learn about the underlying principles of online community development, and will read about key areas of research. They will gain a multi-disciplinary perspective of the field, which will enable them to fairly judge the contributions of different fields and to identify key contributors. The book will also help this readership to determine which directions to follow and how their work can influence this exciting, rapidly developing field.

How Readers Benefit from This Book

This book addresses the development of new online communities and the improvement of existing ones. It is divided into two parts, plus the Preface and a chapter that explores the future of online communities. Annotated suggestions for further reading appear at the end of each chapter.

Part One, Getting Acquainted with Online Communities, does just that, gets you acquainted with online communities. *Chapter 1* introduces the key issues and terminology of the book, and suggests a definition for the term *online community*. *Chapter 2* is a tour of a rich selection of health, e-commerce, education and other interesting online communities. The next four chapters cover the basics of sociability and usability and introduce key research findings. After reading *Part One*, readers will have the fundamental knowledge necessary to begin learning about community-centered development. Readers will be able to:

- Discuss what an online community is and why online communities are becoming so important.

- Identify sociability and usability characteristics in health, e-commerce, and education communities, and generalize this understanding to other types of communities.

- Discuss research findings that inform understanding of social interaction online, including social presence, networking, empathy, trust, collaboration, and more.

- Describe the features of current software that support online communities.

Part Two, Developing Online Communities assumes an understanding of topics discussed in *Part One. Part Two* describes how these concepts are used in community-centered development. After reading *Part Two*, readers will be able to:

- Describe community-centered development and start to practice it.

- Identify software with suitable functionality for different types of online communities based on a community's purpose and participants.

- Give examples of good sociability and usability and be able to explain why they are good.

- Identify examples of poor sociability and usability and describe what needs to be done to improve them.

- Select and use appropriate methods for collecting information about user needs (i.e., requirements).

- Apply sociability and usability heuristics for online community development.

- Select and use appropriate methods and metrics for evaluating online communities.

- Know how to welcome and nurture a new community.

Parts One and *Two* are peppered with a rich collection of examples. Though these examples may become dated, the underlying messages associated with them will endure. Keep in mind, the book focuses on sociability and usability; it is not intended to teach software skills. Many other books and Web sites do this. Knowing how to apply sociability and usability principles in community-centered development will enable readers to harness state-of-the-art products to develop successful online communities.

The Web site

The *Online Communities* accompanying Web site, containing pointers to example communities, software for developers, articles and books, and other interesting, relevant Web sites, is available at www.ifsm.umbc.edu/onlinecommunities. Also available is the John Wiley & Sons Web site, www.wiley.co.uk/preece.

Acknowledgments

Like a community, the ideas in this book evolved over time and were nourished by interaction with colleagues, students, and friends. I have enjoyed the enthusiasm of graduate students who generously pooled their expertise to develop online communities that lived on after the students moved on.

Jonathan Lazar's enthusiasm for learning and teaching this topic knows no bounds. Dick Seabrook's enthusiasm for MOOs is memorable. Ronald Tsao's technical skill and aesthetic sensibility are a pleasure to experience. "Sam" Zhensen Huang tracked down figures for this book, and helped in many ways that will not be forgotten. Blair Nonnecke has been a good friend and colleague; working with him to uncover the secrets of "lurking" online has been a thrilling experience. The discussion of lurkers in *Chapter 3* draws on Blair's work. There are many more, though unnamed, to whom I owe thanks.

I also thank the following people who generously read drafts of this book and offered helpful suggestions for improvements: Dorine Andrews, Tom Eriksson, Jean Gasen, Caroline Haythornthwaite, Michael Harrison, Roxanne Hiltz, Amy Lee, Judy Olson, Ron Rice, Doug Schuler, Ben Shneiderman, Marc Smith, David Squires, and Barry Wellman.

Jonathan Lazar, Ronald Tsao, Judah Buckwater, Beth Hanst, Dick Seabrook, and Ross Malaga contributed case studies for *Chapters 2* and *11*. The discussion of digital questionnaires in *Chapter 10* is adapted from a jointly authored paper in which Jonathan Lazar was lead author. Many ideas in *Chapter 12* were influenced by colleagues at the workshop on Human-Centered Computing, Online Communities and Virtual Environments, at Bonas, France in June 1999. *Chapter 6* is strongly based on work by Barry Wellman and his colleagues Laura Garton, Maria Gulia, and Caroline Haythornthwaite. Barry and Caroline also supplied references and made many suggestions that improved the chapter. Ron Rice and Judy Olson helped me to gain a deeper understanding of some of the theories discussed in *Chapters 6* and 7. Ron generously read and then reread these chapters, provided references, and made suggestions for improvements. I thank you all.

My colleagues at the University of Maryland, Baltimore County, provided a stimulating work environment. I particularly thank Barbara Morris; I could not have written this book and chaired the Information Systems Department without her goodwill and support. I also thank Jay Liebowitz for his encouragement, and Dean Welch and his staff.

My colleagues at John Wiley & Sons helped to make this book happen. I thank Dawn Booth, Simon Plumtree, Gaynor Redvers-Mutton, Lyn Udall, Bill Zobrist, and my talented editor Janice Borzendowski. Also Mark and Sally Spedding of O.O.M.B., Salisbury, UK, for their excellent page design.

I thank Mark Kostabi for allowing me to include his art in the chapter headings. Mark's art captures the spirit of this book in its colorful blend of humans and technology. For color versions of these pictures see book web site at www.ifsm.edu/onlinecommunities/.

Finally, I thank Ben Shneiderman for many insightful discussions that helped me formulate the concept of sociability more clearly, and understand its relationship with usability. Ben's suggestions, comments on drafts, and enthusiastic support have been a source of inspiration.

Reference

Brand, S. (1994). *How Buildings Learn: What Happens after They're Built*. New York: Penguin.

For Ben

Part One

Getting Acquainted with Online Communities

It is very rare that a relationship of belonging exists. . . . [M]y aim is to construct a situation where a deep, profound belonging exists. That has proved incredibly hard to do.

—Alexander, Ishikawa, Silverstein, Jacobson, Fiksdahl-King & Angel, *A Pattern Language* (1977)

The purpose of this part is to discuss the nature of online community, in particular, to answer the question What is an online community? The way relationships form online, how people behave, and the role social policies play all affect how an online community functions. The design of supporting software also impacts the community. Part One provides background information to enable you to understand the interrelationships between people's behavior online, sociability, and usability. People's interactions create online communities, and developers can influence their success by how they design policies and software.

Note: *Chapter 1*, *Introduction*, sets the scene. *Chapter 2*, *Community Tours*, takes you on a guided tour of online communities for health, education, and e-commerce. Like any guided tour, of, say, an art museum or historic site this guide points out interesting features along the way. This chapter is for newcomers to online communities. It provides the foundation for understanding sociability and usability. Experienced users may wish to skim this chapter.

Chapters 3 and *4*, *Sociability: Purpose, People, and Policies*, and *Usability: Tasks, People, and Software*, discuss sociability and usability, building on *Chapter 2*. Why people behave as they do is extremely complex. Even after years of research by psychologists and sociologists, our knowledge of behavior in the physical world is limited, so it is not surprising that we have much to learn about behavior online. Pieces of the puzzle are being put in place, but the picture is incomplete. Though each of these chapters uses a simple framework for discussing components of sociability and usability, like most frameworks, they hide a web of complexity. Nevertheless, the frameworks are valuable for categorizing key concepts so that they can be applied to online community development. The aim of *Chapters 3* and *4* is to prepare you for *Part Two*, *Developing Online Communities*.

Chapters 5 and *6*, *Research Speaks to Practice: Interpersonal Communication* and *Research Speaks to Practice: Groups*, introduce research from psychology, sociology, and communications studies that explains aspects of online behavior discussed in previous chapters. These chapters are enlightening, but developers eager to get to *Part Two* may wish to skim over them.

After reading *Part One, Getting Acquainted with Online Communities*, you will have the necessary background to develop or contribute to developing an online community using ready-made software and HTML, or more sophisticated techniques, if you have these skills.

Contents

1 Introduction

We are made for conversation with our kind. ... [and to] communicate and share in the communications of others.

—John Dewey, *Characters and Events*, Vol. I (as quoted in Murphy, 1978, p. 181)

The term *online community* is used for many kinds of Internet social interactions. This chapter examines the meaning of the term, suggests a definition, and raises some key issues regarding its use. The chapter also introduces the terms *sociability* and *usability*, the key themes running through the book.

Contents

The Rhythm of Inspiration
Mark Kostabi 1995 © Kostabi World

Internet communities are here! In fact, they're everywhere. From New York to London, Singapore, and beyond, trillions of email messages bounce from screen to screen, every second of every day. Millions of people send messages or type *www.something.com*; entrepreneurs pan for Internet gold; children play games and talk with friends; teenagers dream of fame and fortune as they program feverishly in basements; women meet new friends in iVillage.com; sports fanatics around the world "meet" to relive the thrill of recent games. In the wild west of the Internet, everyone can stake a claim. In corporate boardrooms, high-level managers quake at the prospect of their markets being stolen. In short, if you are not on the Internet, you don't exist.

But what's after Amazon, eBay, Travelocity, TheGlobe, Xoom? What will it be? Web sites crammed with page after page of unchanging information are out. Pioneers driven by passion and power strive to settle the Internet, gambling on promising URLs and patenting what they hope are unique ideas. Entrepreneurs spawn communities hoping that customers will emerge from the cacophony of chatting. Software developers design software, believing they are designing communities. Meanwhile, keen-eyed, reflective sociologists describe the emergence of communities. But communities are neither designed nor do they just emerge. How software is designed affects community development just as the architecture of a house affects those who live in it. How people interact in a community shapes its long-term evolution. And though people's behavior cannot be controlled, it can be influenced. Social behavior is complex, whether it occurs on- or offline. Theories from sociology and psychology help to explain social behavior online, but there is much that is unpredictable (Wallace, 1999).

This book focuses on the development of online communities. Two concepts that help amateur and professional developers alike understand this process are *sociability* and *usability*. Moderators, managers, and participants also benefit from becoming familiar with these concepts. Sociability and usability form a bridge linking knowledge about human behavior to appropriate social planning, policies, and software design for successful online communities.

The collective purpose of a community, the goals and roles of the individuals in a community, and policies generated to shape social interaction all influence social interaction in the community. Sociability is concerned with all these issues. A community's purpose could be, for example, to exchange information about rare plants, to discuss local government, to chat about the latest football game, to support those suffering from rheumatism, to aid students studying via distance education or to support business practices (i.e., a community of practice). Millions of different communities exist on the Internet, and all the people participating in them have goals, whether to find information, make new friends, find best buys, learn about the stock market, have fun, or get advice. Within the social framework defined by the community's purpose and policies, people strive to satisfy their own needs. Whether they contribute to the good of the community or are just there to indulge themselves depends on the community's policies and individual personalities. Thus, the purpose, the people, and policies comprising a community determine what it is like. Each community is unique, and there is no guaranteed recipe for a successful community. However, developers *can* influence the way a community develops by carefully communicating its purpose and policies. Clearly communicated, easily understandable, socially acceptable, and logistically feasible policies can help to produce successful communities.

Usability is well-established in human–computer interaction design (Preece, 1993; Nielsen & Mack, 1994; Preece, Rogers, Sharp, Benyon, Holland & Carey, 1994; Preece, Rogers & Sharp, 2001; Hackos & Redish, 1998; Shneiderman, 1998a; Mayhew, 1999). Usability is concerned with developing computer systems to support rapid learning, high skill retention, and low error rates. Such systems support high productivity; they are consistent, controllable, and predictable, which makes them pleasant and effective to use (Shneiderman, 1998a). The implication for online communities is that users are able to communicate with each other, find information, and navigate the community software with ease.

Pioneers who want to develop or manage online communities also need to know some psychology and sociology, in addition to being familiar with currently available software. This knowledge is distilled and operationalized via sociability and usability. These two concepts then provide a framework for developing and evaluating online communities.

What Is an Online Community?

Online community means different things to different people. For some, it conjures warm, fuzzy, reassuring images of people chatting and helping each other. For others, it generates dark images of conspiracy, subversive and criminal behavior, and invasion of privacy. Still others see a future in which physical communities are undermined or replaced by online communities.

Not surprisingly, our experiences in physical communities lead us to infer what an online community is. Dictionary definitions, for example, talk of groups with common interests, shared goals, activities, and governance; groups and individuals who cooperate to share resources and satisfy each other's needs. Some include enjoyment and pleasure, while others strongly associate community with a physical locale, such as a village or town. The need to respect the feelings and property of others is also mentioned, along with the importance of governance systems to ensure that this happens. All these attributes appear in descriptions of online communities, but their relative relevance is debated.

Superficially, the term online community isn't hard to understand, yet it is slippery to define. In a multidisciplinary field such as this, some definitions reflect a disciplinary perspective. Further complications also arise when a topic suddenly becomes popular and the term takes on buzzword status. Widespread use by e-commerce entrepreneurs has in fact made the term a buzzword.

A working definition of online community

Developing online communities is a complex practical activity, and developers need a definition that guides practice. To that end, the following definition is used in this book:

An online community consists of:

- *People*, who interact socially as they strive to satisfy their own needs or perform special roles, such as leading or moderating.

- A shared *purpose*, such as an interest, need, information exchange, or service that provides a reason for the community.

- *Policies*, in the form of tacit assumptions, rituals, protocols, rules, and laws that guide people's interactions.

- *Computer systems*, to support and mediate social interaction and facilitate a sense of togetherness.

The reasons for identifying these four high-level criteria are revealed more fully in *Chapters 3* and *4*. This definition provides a framework to guide developers in making operational decisions, as will be seen throughout the book. Furthermore, it is sufficiently general to apply to a range of different communities, including physical communities that have become networked (Schuler, 1996; Lazar & Preece, 1998), communities supported by a single bulletin board, listserver or chat software, those that are embedded in Web sites, multiuser dungeons or domains (MUDs) and object-oriented MUDs (MOOs), and others. (If you are totally unfamiliar with online communities, take a look at some of the communities in *Chapter 2* before reading on.)

Other ways of defining online community

We can't move on to examine the components of the working definition without first discussing how others have characterized online community. This discussion exemplifies the difficulty of agreeing to a single definition. It will also reveal the complexity of the issues underlying online communities, issues that will be aired here, then discussed in more depth in later chapters.

In 1994, cyberspace guru Howard Rheingold wrote: "... virtual communities are cultural aggregations that emerge when enough people bump into each other often enough in cyberspace. A virtual community is a group of people who may or may not meet one another face to face, and who exchange words and ideas through the mediation of computer bulletin boards and networks' (Rheingold, 1994, pp. 57–58). His definition resulted from his seven-year involvement in the WELL (Whole Earth 'Lectronic Link), an early online community developed in the San Francisco Bay area (Rheingold, 1993). He went on to paint a larger picture composed of the activities that people engaged in, their reasons for participating, and the way they communicated. In a single paragraph, Rheingold captured the essence of online community in a way that endures today. He wrote: "In cyberspace, we chat and argue, engage in intellectual discourse, perform acts of commerce, exchange knowledge, share emotional support, make plans, brainstorm, gossip, feud, fall in love, find friends and lose them, play games and metagames, flirt .... We do everything people do when people get together, but we do it with words on computer screens, leaving our bodies behind. ... our identities commingle and interact electronically, independent of local time or location" (Rheingold, 1994, p. 58).

Rheingold's description of his experience in the WELL is almost as relevant today as in 1994. Lack of physical presence online is still seen as a problem for communication (*Chapter 5*). Attempts to solve this problem occupy technologists and produce generations of ever more sophisticated avatars, video images, virtual environments, and ingenious graphical representations. Despite these efforts, textual communication is still the dominant default medium of communication. As important as solving the many technical issues is to understand social interaction online, develop appropriate social procedures, and support them with good human-computer interfaces.

The most significant changes since 1994 are the availability of greater processing power at lower prices, coupled with the widespread expansion of the Internet. Consequently, millions more people have access to online communities, compared with just a few thousand in the early 1990s. However, despite this huge surge in participation in online communities, fundamental questions remain unanswered: How are online communities changing people's lives? What kind of people are becoming participants? What is the relationship between online communities and physical communities? How are they impacting each other? Are online communities really communities, or are they pseudo-communities in which people swap pleasantries, exchange information, make uncommitted gestures of support, and develop ephemeral friendships? Why do some communities endure and others are here today and gone tomorrow? Can deep friendships develop from instant access to thousands of people, scattered across the globe?

Attempts to characterize and define the concept of an online community are steps toward answering these questions, because they identify salient characteristics; they lay the foundations for insightful observation, followed by carefully planned research studies. But when a topic, like online communities, captures the enthusiasm of different groups with different expertise and goals, inevitably, a range of definitions emerge that reflect these differences. In 1996, a multidisciplinary group of human-computer interaction professionals met to identify key characteristics of online communities. The outcome of their brainstorming sessions provides a basis for examining definitions that reflect particular perspectives.

Multidisciplinary brainstorm perspective

The report from the brainstorming workshop held at an ACM CHI (Computer Human Interaction) Conference on the theory and practice of physical and network communities identified the following core attributes (Whittaker, Issacs, & O'Day, 1997, p. 137):

1. Members have a shared goal, interest, need, or activity that provides the primary reason for belonging to the community.

2. Members engage in repeated, active participation; often, intense interactions, strong emotional ties, and shared activities occur among participants.

3. Members have access to shared resources, and policies determine the access to those resources.

4. Reciprocity of information, support, and services among members is important.

5. There is a shared context of social conventions, language, and protocols.

Some of these criteria are explicitly recognized in the working definition—specifically, the first and fifth attributes. Others are discussed as lower-level attributes (three and four) later in the book. The need for repeated, active participation mentioned as part of the fourth attribute is more controversial. Some people feel strongly that this is essential, that without this repeated engagement there is no community. But what does this mean? If some percentage of participants post on a bulletin board twice, three times, five times, or ten times, do they constitute a community? Emotions can run high over this issue. Conference and journal reviewers have been known to reject papers because they felt use of the term community had been trivialized. However, as the discussion that follows indicates, these purist notions of community are being replaced by definitions based on fewer and more superficial social interactions. Commercialization of the Internet is sweeping online communities along in its wake, thereby diluting the potency of the concept.

The working group also identified seven noncore attributes: different roles and the reputations of people in those roles; awareness of membership boundaries and group identity; initiation criteria for joining; community history and long duration of existence; notable events or rituals, shared physical environments; and voluntary membership (Whittaker et al., 1997, p. 137). Most of these attributes also appear in other definitions, several of which speak of continuing relationships cemented by rituals. As in the core criteria, the notion of belonging over time is strong. "Shared physical environment" evokes images of villages, towns, and local gathering places. It is a strong component in many definitions, and developers must consider what it means for their online communities. For example, the way software supports different types of communication and online activity is addressed later in this book.

Sociology perspective

Even sociologists struggle to define community. For years, sociologists have defined and redefined the concept (Wellman, 1982). Initially, communities were defined by physical features such as size, location, and the boundaries that confined them. In later years, when commuting became a way of life for many urban dwellers, identifying, defining, and measuring physical characteristics of populations in continual transit became a problem. Furthermore, cheaper transportation made it easier for people to join multiple communities to satisfy different needs. Subsequently, the strength and type of relationships among people seemed more promising criteria for defining communities (Wellman, 1997; Haythornthwaite & Wellman, 1998). Relationships that developed to satisfy strong identifiable needs were particularly potent indicators of community.

Sociologists can map and determine the strength of these relationships using established techniques, such as network analysis, as discussed in *Chapter 6*. Though applying techniques from sociology to online communities appears promising, research on online communities is still at an early stage, compared with geographically based communities, and more time is needed for a consensus to emerge.

The focus on social interaction that sociologists bring to this new field is a welcome counterbalance to the intense technological hype often associated with the Internet. Unfortunately, many researchers studying online communities seem unfamiliar with the long history of studying community by sociologists (Wellman & Gulia, 1998). Consequently, there is a real danger of wasting time reinventing the wheel.

Technology perspective

At the opposite end of the social-technical spectrum are the technology-oriented definitions. The software that supports online communities is a frequently used shorthand way of defining them. It is very common to hear "techies" refer to chat, bulletin board, listserver, UseNet News or Web-based community. Such terms are concise and instantly meaningful to these insiders. They know immediately the basic structure of the supporting software and how it functions. They know, for example, that a listserver delivers email messages to participants and that bulletin board participants must go to the board. They know that the listserver community will not benefit from messages being structurally related (known as *threading*), as is possible in the bulletin board community; and much more. The point is, "geek speak" is of value to those in the know about technology-related issues, but says little or nothing about social organization and interaction.

Virtual worlds perspective

Participants in MOOs and other virtual worlds are keenly aware of technology. Many are eager to push the limits of 3D virtuality. They seek immersive experiences, with the ultimate goal to represent themselves as 3D objects moving around a 3D world with realistic perspective. Not surprisingly, their perspective on online communities involves a sense of immersion that mimics reality. Many virtual worlds portray *fantasy* environments, i.e. where players participate in games or social interactions in which they disguise their true identities. Participation generally occurs regularly over long periods, of weeks or months, so there is opportunity for relationship building. Consequently, prolonged, repetitive interaction is seen as a criterion for an online community by participants and researchers. So-called MOOers and MUDers think the term online community has been usurped to describe less intense social interaction such as occurs in typical bulletin boards.

E-commerce perspective

E-commerce entrepreneurs take a very broad view of community. Any chat or bulletin board or communications software can be regarded as an online community.

For them, the important issue is what draws people to and holds people in a Web site, a concept known as *stickiness*, so that they will buy goods or services. Entrepreneurs know that email is the "killer app" of the Internet. The success of America Online (AOL) has proved that chatting online to friends, family, and new acquaintances is big business. E-commerce entrepreneurs anticipate that online communities not only will keep people at their sites, but will also have an important role in marketing, as people tell each other about their purchases and discuss banner ads, and help and advise each other. Consequently, online communities are spawning by the dozen on dot-com sites. Owners of these sites believe that online communities serve the same function as the sweet smell of baking cakes does in a pastry shop. Both evoke images of comfort, warmth, happiness and maybe even trust.

This highly commercial perspective devalues the concept of community. But as Steve Jones points out, the Internet, and particularly the Web, is a market-driven social space (Jones, 1999a). In other words, business shapes and dictates social interaction. The Internet is to business what 747 jumbo jets are to transportation. It provides fast, inexpensive communication and information transfer for businesses and their professional and customer communities throughout the world. But many researchers and online community advocates resent the implication that any online communication among people constitutes a community. They believe that an online community is more than just a stream of messages.

Special interest groups (SIGs) and networks

Online community has also become a blanket term to describe any collection of people who communicate online. This book accepts the current, broad, and nondiscriminating definition of community. But not everyone takes this view, as this discussion indicates, and readers should be aware of these different attitudes. Sociologists make clear distinctions between groups, networks, and communities (Wellman, 1997). Broadly speaking, a group has clear boundaries that determine membership. Departments in companies and universities and officially designated neighborhoods in cities are examples of groups. In contrast, networks involve relationships that can cross these boundaries. The term community connotes the strength of relationships.

There are many examples of groups, such as special interest groups (SIGs) for education, professional issues and hobbies. SIGs fulfill a specific, narrowly defined purpose, and aim to draw only members sharing that interest. According to Lee Sproull, "Groups benefit their members and vice versa by providing physical, economic, cognitive, and emotional resources. Electronic groups do not provide direct physical or economic resources but they frequently offer information that may lead to them— for example, medical advice, sales opportunity etc." (Sproull & Faraj, 1997). Andrew Feenberg points out that "online groups need not form a community to work effectively together so long as the members have well-defined roles in performing a shared task" (Feenberg, 1993, p. 188).

Similarly, the term online community is often used to include community networks (Schuler, 1996), also known as networked communities (Cohill & Kavanaugh, 1997). An increasing number of physical communities, such as Seattle, Washington, and Blacksburg, Virginia, have community networks to link and support community members. These networks, like the WELL (Rheingold, 1993), typically focus on local services and community issues. Citizens can link to the Internet, but there is a strong focus on the local community.

Douglas Schuler, author of *New Community Networks*, advocates the role of community networks as a resource that should be built by the community (Schuler, 1996). He claims that new communities should combine aspects of the old and the new, because history is an important part of community: "They must rest on the solid foundations of principles and values and be flexible and adaptable, intelligent, and creative. They must be inclusive. Everyone must be allowed to participate. They will have to engage both governments and business because they both exist to provide services for people. These institutions must be accountable to the people, and not the reverse" (Schuler, 1996, p. xi). Schuler proposes the following core values for building community networks: conviviality and culture, education, strong democracy, health and human services, economic equity, opportunity and sustainability, and information and communication. They imply long-term relationships, acknowledging the past and the importance of governance (as discussed later in *Chapter 3*). But they go beyond mere attributes; they are values to guide developers and inspire participants. Schuler reminds us that technology can have a special role in promoting these values via online communities. Developers, managers, students, and users are advised to keep one eye on these core values while they strive to map human needs with technology.

Bright and Dark Sides of Online Communities

From birth to death, we shape and are shaped by the communities to which we belong. For better or worse, these communities influence our vocabulary, what we talk about, how we spend our time, what we consider important, with whom we interact, and the nature of those interactions. Some communities enable strong social interactions, while others are weak networks of associates; some support, nurture, and care for their members, while others are mean-spirited, uncaring, and destructive.

As with the advent of the telephone and television, the introduction of computers into the home is changing how people interact socially (Anderson, Bikson, Law, & Mitchell, 1995). The incredible growth of companies like Amazon.com indicates that it is quicker, easier, and cheaper for many people to buy their books and other commodities via the computer than to go to a store. Greater numbers of people are communicating via email and joining bulletin board communities. Adoption of the term online community in e-commerce supports the belief that the term conveys strong positive associations for customers. Yet physical communities do not always function well and to the advantage of all, or even the majority, of their members. So why assume that online communities will do any better? It's easy, but dangerous, to assume that all communities are good. There will be many different types of online and networked communities, just as there are all kinds of face-to-face communities.

A threat to personal relationships?

As more people gain Internet access, will the distinction between online and face-to-face community blur? People use the Internet to connect with family and friends (Kraut, Patterson, Lundmark, Kiesler, Mukhopadhyay, & Scherlis, 1998), but, what will be the effect of bringing people together who have never been connected before? Anecdotes tell of people traveling across the world to meet new Internet friends, building strong relationships, and even marrying. Conversely, numerous reports chronicle disappointments, even danger and fraud. Often, the relationship is just not what was expected. One reason is that people represent themselves more favorably in their email descriptions, representations not borne out in real life. Seemingly trivial, but potentially devastating examples include people lying about age or weight.

So how do online relationships affect individuals, their families, and their local communities? Perhaps, "rather than creating new kinds of communities, this technology often just creates a false sense of connection and intimacy" (Friedman, 1997, p. 377). Can people really develop strong ties with strangers they have never met face to face? Or is the Internet merely enabling us to reach further into the world while we neglect to build relationships with next-door neighbors and our local community?

In the mid-1990s, researchers from Carnegie Mellon University investigated the impact of the Internet on 169 people in 73 households over a two-year period (Kraut et al., 1998; Kraut, Scherlis, Mukhopadhyay, Manning, & Kiesler, 1996). Findings from this study suggest that "greater use of the Internet was associated with small, but statistically significant declines in social involvement as measured by communication within the family and the size of people's local social networks, and with increases in loneliness, a psychological state associated with social involvement. Greater use of the Internet was also associated with increases in depression" (Kraut et al., 1998, p. 1025). A survey of 4113 adults in 2689 households, done by researchers at Stanford, also raises concerns that people who spend a lot of time online do so at the expense of face-to-face relationships, particularly with friends and family (Nie & Ebring, 2000).

A possible explanation is that time spent using the Internet may substitute for time that would otherwise be spent engaged in social activities. A similar explanation has been suggested to account for the negative effects of television (Robinson & Godbey, 1997). However, there is a paradox. Many participants reported that the Internet enabled them to communicate more easily with friends and family. It seems possible that the Internet supports existing strong ties developed from frequent social contact and a strong sense of commitment (Granovetter, 1973, 1982), whereas developing strong ties with friends met online is rarer (Kraut et al., 1998). Converting weak ties to strong ties may require periods of frequent or prolonged face-to-face social interaction.

Because many kinds of relationships are possible, does it matter that the Internet supports strong ties associated with already existing relationships and weak ties associated with meeting new people via the Internet? Aren't both valuable? Certainly, weak ties contribute to information exchange. But problems occur when people mistake weak ties for strong ties or give up strong ties in order to develop lots of weak ties. Strong ties support people in times of crisis and encourage richer social interactions (Wellman, 1992).

A threat to social capital and society?

In the last thirty years, Americans' participation in social societies, such as parent teacher associations, local civic groups, political organizations, choral societies, local sports clubs and even church-related societies has been declining dramatically (Putnam, 1995, p. 66). For example, between 1960 and 1990, voter turnout declined by a one-fourth. Most startling, Robert Putnam reports that "more Americans are bowling today than ever before, but bowling in organized leagues has plummeted in the last decade or so" (Putnam, 1995, p. 69). That is, more Americans are choosing to bowl alone rather than socialize with others. Even apparent countertrends turn out not to be as optimistic as they might at first appear. For instance, though membership in environmentally oriented societies, such as Sierra Club, and women's groups is on the increase, analysis reveals that activity is confined to paying fees. Few people take part in any face-to-face meetings. Similarly, though there are more support groups of various kinds than ever before, Putnam reports that the purpose of such groups appears to be for people to talk about themselves in the presence of the group, not to participate in a community.

A parallel trend of increased wealth, improved transportation and better housing goes hand in hand with the increase in reported loneliness in the United States. Middle-income Americans tend to buy larger houses that are spaced further apart and situated in the suburbs, factors that contribute to the demise of public transport and an ever-increasing dependence on cars to reach distant shopping malls and services situated outside towns. Some claim that cheaper telephone rates and, now, the Internet provide an antidote. But is this likely?

These reports and the Carnegie Mellon study raise disturbing questions about whether and in what ways online communities, and the Internet, will affect society. For a variety of reasons, life is easier and more socially satisfying in a community that has what sociologists call "social capital". "Social capital refers to features of social organization such as networks, norms, and social trust that facilitate coordination and cooperation for mutual benefit" (Putnam, 1995, p. 66). Social networks also foster strong norms of reciprocity, encourage social trust, amplify reputation, and enable social dilemmas to be resolved. Opportunism is reduced and opportunity for collaboration enhanced. "I" centeredness tends to be converted into "we" centeredness.

It is important for online community developers, moderators, managers, and participants to be aware that their activities may be eroding face-to-face social activity. How can this be prevented? Tying online communities more closely to face-to-face social gatherings, as community networks aim to do, may be one way. Raising awareness among participants may be another. It is also important not to overreact. Much more research is needed before making judgments about the positive and negative influences of online communities. For example, there are many reports of people receiving support and empathy from online relationships (Hiltz, 1985; Preece, 1999; Preece & Ghozati, 1998; Sproull & Faraj, 1997; Sproull & Kiesler, 1991). Nevertheless, meeting in an electronic forum is not the equivalent of participating on a bowling team (Putnam, 1995). Still, for people who are unable to attend local functions, meeting in an online community and developing weak ties is better than not meeting at all.

Hate crimes, pornography and other negative interactions

The Internet empowers groups to organize themselves across local, national, and international boundaries. A call to action, a warning message, a cheer of encouragement, the inspiring words of a leader can be distributed to members at lightning speed and at almost no cost, with just the click of a few keys. (*Chapter 3* discusses the power of clearly stating the community's purpose, of forming a homogeneous group of participants, and of establishing meaningful policies for developing an online community.) Political groups of all kinds usually have this clarity and dedication.

Unfortunately, any powerful medium can also be a powerful weapon in the hands of extremists, criminals, and those living at the edges of the law. The Internet is no exception. Along with the millions of online communities that pursue noble goals of support, discussion, and innocent games are the communities whose activities can destroy or injure others. The first hate site was created in 1995, and since then others have been added weekly. The Intelligence Project reported that the number of hate sites increased from 163 at the end of 1997 to 254 by the end of 1998 (Report, 1998). In 1998, the number of neo-Nazi sites climbed from 27 to 63. Pornography is also a problem on the Internet, as exemplified by the Alt UseNet group, alt.sex.abuse.recovery (Mehta & Plaza, 1997).

In the United States, the First Amendment endorses the laudable right of free speech. Unfortunately when this right is invoked by the likes of hate groups, it is very hard to take action to stop them. Add to this the difficulty and controversy associated with policing the Internet and it is easy to see why this medium is so dangerous in the wrong hands.

Introducing Sociability and Usability

Developing successful online communities is not trivial. Successful online communities satisfy their members' needs and contribute to the well-being of society. Everyday, thousands of new online communities are launched, but many falter or disappear without trace. Some survive with a transient population—people come and people go. Anecdotes reveal a wide spectrum of experiences. Some report their lives changing in remarkable ways as a result of participating in online communities. Others describe empty chat rooms, unanswered messages, shallow comments, excessive advertising and junk mail. Some tell stories of receiving empathy and support from total strangers, while others report being victimized by unwarranted verbal attacks.

Most definitions treat community only as an entity; in fact, community is a *process* (Fernback, 1999). Communities develop and continuously evolve. Only the software that supports them is designed. Thus, the role of a community developer is analogous to that of the mayor of a new town, who works with town planners to set up suitable housing, roads, public buildings, and parks, and with governors and lawyers to determine local policies. Community developers work with community members to plan and guide the community's social evolution. Putting basic policies in place helps members know how to behave, what to expect from each other, and provides a framework for social growth. As the community develops and forms its own character, its social policies and structure also evolve. Communities are more likely to succeed when early social planning constrains the community just enough to discourage inappropriate behavior while facilitating the community's evolution. Achieving this balance requires skill, sensitivity, and acknowledgment that the community's purpose and needs may change over time. Sociability is concerned with planning and developing social policies which are understandable and acceptable to members, to support the community's purpose.

Community developers also have to design software with good usability so that people can interact and perform their tasks intuitively and easily. Software with good usability supports rapid learning, high skill retention, low error rates and high productivity. It is consistent, controllable, and predictable, making it pleasant and effective to use. Many community developers will have to select and buy software or obtain it free. They will have to identify software with suitable usability, then tailor it to more closely meet the community's needs. Some developers may design and code their own software, to have more control over its usability.

Sociability focuses on social interaction; usability focuses on human-computer inter-action. Understanding a community's needs is essential for developing communities with good sociability and usability (Figure 1.1).

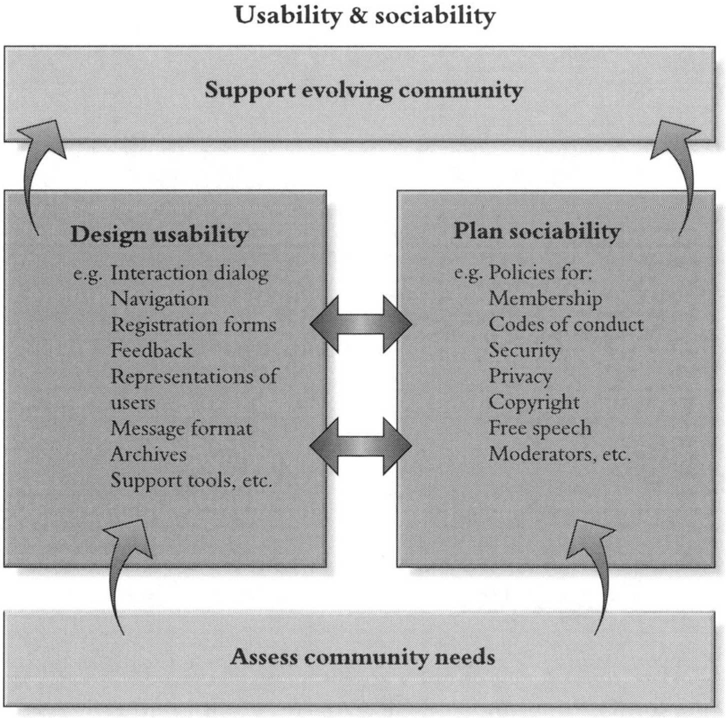

Usability & sociability

Figure 1.1   Usability and sociability

Usability and sociability are closely related, but separating the two encourages developers to focus on each issue with more clarity. Consider for example, *registering* to belong to a community. The decision to enforce a registration policy is a sociability decision. It strongly impacts who comes into the community and, thus, the social interactions in the community. The *mechanics* of registering are determined by software design, which involves usability decisions. The design of the registration form, how it is displayed, the nature of prompts and help messages associated with completing the form are usability issues.

Summary

Communicating via the Internet is no substitute for actual human interaction. A virtual hug, shown in the form of two parentheses—( ), is certainly not as warm, comfortable, and satisfying as a real hug. And sharing a nourishing, tasty meal is impossible in cyberspace. But online communities do enable meaningful communication among people separated by distance, time, and, to some extent, culture.

While enthusiasts argue *ad infinitum* that online communities are important for the twenty-first century, we have to recognize that no one community is exactly like the next. Furthermore, just as in "real life", not all online communities are admirable (Jones, 1999b). Many critics tend to compare online communities to ideal real communities, while failing to acknowledge that cities are often very lonely places (Kollock & Smith, 1999).

Developers and users have responsibility to plan, guide, and mold communities to support the people in them. Like twentieth-century town planners and architects, community developers can profoundly shape the online community landscape. Attention to sociability and usability will be a big step along the way to ensuring development of successful online communities.

Further Reading

HomeNet: A Field Trial of Residential Internet Services (Kraut et al., 1996), and "Internet Paradox: A Social Technology that Reduces Social Involvement and Psychological Well-being?" (Kraut et al., 1998)

Research findings from the HomeNet study, carried out by researchers from Carnegie Mellon University, hit national headlines in America. A small amount of evidence suggested that people who use computers are more prone to depression than nonusers. The issues raised in the second report are worthy of consideration by anyone interested in online communities.

"Bowling Alone: America's Declining Social Capital" (Putnam, 1995)

This highly acclaimed but disturbing article tells of decline in community involvement in America during the past thirty years. It is alarming, but important to read. The combination of clearly presented facts, supported by real data, and the thoughtful articulation of possible explanations make this article a "must read" for anyone considering the role of online communities, their relationship to physical communities, and desirable values of society.

The Virtual Community: Homesteading on the Electronic Frontier (Rheingold, 1993), and "A Slice of Life in My Virtual Community" (Rheingold, in L. M. Harasim, ed., 1994)

Read either Rheingold's book or his chapter in Harasim's book for a warm, percep-tive, and intriguing introduction to online communities. Both report his experiences in the WELL, one of the first online communities, and both are rich in amusing anecdotes, and reveal a deep, personal understanding of life online. The WELL was, without doubt, a community. Rheingold's writing is lucid, easy to read, and hard to put down. Readers who do not want to read a whole book on the topic can gain a good understanding of the WELL and many key issues from his chapter in the Harasim title.

"Community Networks: Building a New Participatory Medium" (Schuler, 1994), and *New Community Networks: Wired for Change* (Schuler, 1996)

Douglas Schuler's book, *New Community Networks: Wired for Change* is a seminal, socially aware treatise that addresses important issues concerning online communities. Specifically, it discusses the philosophy, goals, and processes involved in developing the Seattle Community Network. Readers who prefer a shorter account will enjoy Schuler's article, which documents the state of community networks in 1994, and discusses many of the same issues as the book. Both strongly address the social and political needs of communities. Schuler looks for ways that technology, and specifically community networks, can help support democracy, education, heath, equality, information exchange, communication, and so on. Schuler's enthusiasm to harness technology to improve community life and to address big issues is inspiring.

"Connections: New Ways of Working in the Networked Organization" (Sproull & Kiesler, 1991)

This seminal work provides an excellent foundation for anyone interested in the empowerment and implications of working online. Much future research is based on the insights reported here.

"An Electronic Group is Virtually a Social Network" (Wellman, 1997), and "Virtual Communities as Communities: Net Surfers don't Ride Alone" (Wellman & Gulia, 1998)

Social networks comprise a set of people, organizations, and other social entities connected by socially meaningful relationships. These articles provide a good introduction to the way sociologists think about community. Lay readers interested in online communities are strongly encouraged to familiarize themselves with related work from sociology.

"Widening the Net. Workshop Report on the Theory and Practice of Physical and Network Communities" (Whittaker et al., 1997)

This report lists the main attributes associated with community. It is a useful starting point for thinking about online communities.

2 Community Tours

What amazed me wasn't just the speed with which we obtained precisely the information we needed to know, right when we needed to know it. It was also the immense inner sense of security that comes with discovering that real people are available, around the clock, if you need them.

—Howard Rheingold, *The Virtual Community* (1993, p. 17)

This tour introduces readers to online communities for health, education, and e-commerce. It explores sociability, by observing how developers describe the community's purpose, and the type of social policies in use. The software that supports the communities is also examined, noting how its design supports user tasks. Experienced readers may want to skip through this introductory chapter and move on to the next.

Contents

The World According to Mark
Mark Kostabi 1992 © Kostabi World

People join communities to satisfy needs: to develop new friendships, discuss a new interest, debate about politics, get information, share their knowledge, receive empathy from like-minded people, get support to deal with a problem. There are many reasons for joining online communities, and strong relationships may develop over many months, as occurs in some health support groups. Other relationships are short-lived, shallow, or almost nonexistent, as in online auction interactions.

Initially, people are attracted to a community by what it projects outwardly about itself. Its name, description on a Web site [Box 0], or a statement of purpose help potential participants judge whether it is likely to meet their needs and is worth joining. The policies that direct behavior in the community influence its character by guiding how people communicate. By clearly indicating a community's purpose, developers can establish a focus that will influence who joins the community. Subsequently, guided by what people do and what attracts them to return to the community, developers can help to develop the community to continue to meet the needs of its participants. Community development, then, is a continuous process of evolution.

People are the key to a thriving online community. Obvious as this may sound, the importance of drawing people into the community and encouraging them to participate and keep coming back can not be overemphasized. Without people, there is no community. The ebb and flow of messages expressing new ideas, comments, reactions, jokes, reflections, suggestions keeps the community engaged and draws new people, as well as encouraging others to return. Compare Web pages, which are a useful community resource; but the information may not change or change infrequently, and is not personal. Once read, people look for new information.

Box 0 World Wide Web

The World Wide Web, known simply as the Web, is a vast network of information, presented on millions of sites located on computers throughout the world. The Web offers academic articles, journals, free software products, personal biographies, newspapers, online communities, education, extensive retail opportunities, and endless advertisements. Like a big department store, it contains many things you want and many things you don't want. Having access to so much information at the click of a few keys can be wonderful, but there are two big problems: the first is finding what you want; the second is judging the quality of the information you find.

Search engines and Web browsers such, as Yahoo!, AltaVista, Hotbot, Excite, and Lycos enable users to search the Web. By specifying the Uniform Resource Locator, URL, users can go directly to a particular page or site. Alternatively, users can search by topic. For example, typing `support` will produce a long list of items with support in their title. Typing the words `support + group` will narrow the search to only those items that contain both words. Typing `support` or `group` will enlarge the search to include items that contain either support or group.

Communities offer new information, often accompanied by personal anecdotes that make compelling reading. Characters emerge, and relationships form to shape the community. Special roles may also develop, such as an expert, a provocateur, the social conscience, a moderator or mediator, along with various characters.

Developers cannot and should not attempt to control social interaction; but they can and should support desirable social interaction. For example, policies that call for civility will help reduce aggression. By setting up policies from the outset, developers can influence how a community evolves. Some communities have a manifesto outlining expected behavior of members; others are much more casual. Just as in face-to-face communities, being confronted with a list of do's and don'ts can deter people from joining. Conversely, a community with no rules can be a wild and unpleasant place. Achieving a balance is important, particularly for a new community (see *Chapter 3*). As the community evolves, it can take over its own governance.

Just as the architecture of a house is intimately related to how its inhabitants live (cooking, serving meals, or supervising children can be pleasure or a nightmare depending on the facilities available), the functionality provided by software and the ease with which users can make the software do what they want—its usability—strongly impact user activities. Variations between different kinds of software may be significant, making the selection of appropriate software important. Interactions on a bulletin board are different from those in a MOO or chat room. Online communities serve many purposes, but the support of information exchange and communication are particularly important. Software must be designed so that users can do their tasks rapidly and accurately. They must be able to learn to use the software quickly and to retain the skills they acquire. Some communities will be more concerned with empathic communication, others with rapid chat, still others with detailed technical descriptions. Developers can make a major contribution to online communities by recognizing the characteristics of different tasks and ensuring that software is designed to support them (see *Chapter 4*).

The remainder of this chapter takes readers on a tour of online communities from three domains: health, education and entertainment, and e-commerce. It identifies examples of sociability (e.g., indications of the community's purpose, the people who participate, and policies that guide social interaction) and usability (e.g., software features that support users' tasks). This tour will introduce sociability support and usability design in a variety of online communities. Readers with limited experience of online communities, in particular, will benefit from this material. Later chapters (particularly *Chapters 3* and *4*) build systematically on the concepts identified in this tour.

Health communities

In the mid- and late 1990s, the general public started to realize that via the Internet they could get information about health issues. Dramatic headlines touting this capability began to appear in *USA Today*, the *New York Times*, the British newspaper *The Times* and other national and local newspapers. On Wednesday, July 14, 1999, for example, *USA Today* published a special report entitled "The Internet Changes Medicine", that contained articles with titles such as: "Net Empowering Patients," "Millions Scour the Web to Find Medical Information," and "A Network of Support." *USA Today* claimed that "In ever growing numbers, patients clutching Internet printouts and a list of smart questions are marching into doctors' offices nationwide" (Davis & Miller, 1999). It is anticipated in the year 2000, that more than 33 million Americans will have researched a medical problem on the Web. "The Internet is going to irrevocably affect how patients and doctors interact. This is not going to go away" (Davis & Miller, 1999, p. 1A).

Patients who go online for health-related information want several things: to understand their problems better; to find information about diseases and treatments, to get support from others; to help fellow sufferers; to feel less afraid and so on. Web sites offer some information, but online communities are more personal resources. Patients can interact with each other and with professionals (getting enough face-to-face interaction with doctors is a well-known problem everywhere in the world). *The Guardian*, a well respected British newspaper reported "[R]esearch has shown patients enjoy on average 16 seconds to explain their view of their medical problem to doctors" (*The Guardian*, May 14, 1997, p. 9). Many patients are therefore turning to the Internet for information and support.

Sharing with other patients can also be comforting and reassuring in ways that talking to even the most skillful and communicative physician may not be. Face-to-face support groups are available in some locations and for some health problems, but they may be scheduled at inconvenient times or in hard-to-get-to locations. In contrast, online communities enable patients to share experiences and relate to each other's problems whenever they want and no matter where they are. Other patients can empathize, and they may know of solutions to problems that doctors don't know about, because they haven't experienced being a patient (Preece, 1998). Experiences involving either emotional or physical pain often lead to very strong empathic ties between people (Ickes, 1997), which in turn can become a basis for strong relationships. People are therefore coming to online health communities in great numbers. The following quote is typical of the kind of messages that appear in online support communities.

[I]t is finally time to take the plunge and have the . . . procedure performed. I have referenced this site quite frequently since my decision about a month ago. I just wanted to say that I appreciate all the input. Keep me in your prayers and I hope to get back to you with a great story of recovery.

Unfortunately, online health communities also have a dark side. Physicians are rightly concerned about patients getting incorrect information. Some also find it disconcerting that patients may know more than they do about their illness. An increasing number of online communities now support question-and-answer sessions with real doctors, but some doctors do not like this practice either, arguing that online doctors do not "see" their patients or know their backgrounds. These are real dangers and patients need to learn to become discerning consumers of medical information.

Online communities and Web sites developed by organizations such as the National Institutes of Health (NIH) can be identified as reputable sources by their names, logos, and other branding information. The National Cancer Institute (NCI), for one, provides different resources for its three main user populations: authoritative, up-to-date information for physicians; research news and articles for researchers; and careful, in-depth explanations for patients. Links to online communities enable users to communicate with others who have similar concerns.

The upcoming tours point out interesting features from two different kinds of communities. The first is of a not-for-profit community developed by a patient to help other patients. The second examines the drkoop.com Web site, which illustrates how online communities are integrated into a site. It also raises interesting questions about terminology. Is the whole site a community? Communities support relationships among people, however fleeting they may be. Web pages do not directly encourage relationships, but they do influence who comes to the chat and bulletin board discussions.

Bob's bulletin board: a personally owned community

Millions of small communities are being developed by patients to help fellow sufferers. They are usually supported by bulletin board [Box 1] or listserver [Box 2] software, though sometimes they are embedded in a personal Web site such as in the case of Bob's ACL bulletin board community. Members of this community have torn an anterior cruciate ligament (ACL) or severely injured their knees in some other way. The anterior cruciate ligament is one of four major ligaments in each knee. Sports enthusiasts, especially women athletes, are particularly prone to this injury. Tearing an ACL is often devastating because though this is a common nonlife-threatening injury, athletes dread it because it prevents them taking part in sports activities for many months and sometimes years. Thus it can bring dramatic changes in lifestyle that are frustrating and depressing.

There are two main ways of treating a torn ACL. The ligament can be reconstructed by surgery, or the patient can follow an intense program of physical therapy to strengthen surrounding muscles to compensate for the missing ligament, thereby avoiding surgery. Surgery tends to be the favored option by athletes because, for most, it brings nearly full recovery and return to sporting activities. However, recovery from surgery often takes a year or more, and can be painful.

Box 1 Bulletin Board

Electronic message boards, also known as bulletin boards, are metaphors for traditional message boards. The messages on most of these boards are available for everyone to see. Unlike on listservers, users have to go to a bulletin board to get messages. Many are embedded within Web sites, which help to give them context and to define the purpose of the community. An increasing number of bulletin board discussions are being moderated.

Bulletin boards present messages in chronological order of receipt, unless they are replies to earlier messages. Some also provide threading capabilities (e.g., Bob's bulletin board in Figure 2.1) in which replies are positioned—threaded—with the message to which they relate. Often, replies are indented beneath the original, with replies to replies further indented. The abbreviation ''Re'' also indicates a reply. The first message in a thread contains a subject line in which the sender indicates what the message is about. The user's ID and date of posting is also contained in the header. Messages are often several lines long. In this asynchronous mode of communication, participants have time to think as they compose their messages. Archives of old messages are generally kept for several months. Many bulletin board systems now offer good search and filter tools, and icons for signalling the content of messages and emotional intentions of the sender.

Box 2 Email and Listservers

Email is the pulse of the Internet. The first people to use email were scientists and university academics; today it is widely used by businesses, families, government agencies, and schoolchildren alike. Millions of people send innumerable email messages every day (Anderson, Bikson, Law, & Mitchell, 1995). Like the Internet itself, email was developed as a military research project in the early 1970s and was then expanded for civilian scientific research endeavors. Large companies such as IBM and Texas Instruments quickly began using it, but messages were sent as files to a target machine, not to individual recipients. It was not until the early 1980s that messages could be sent to individuals and the Internet as the public knows it today came into being.

Mail programs vary from system to system. Until ten years ago users had to learn cryptic commands. Now most systems have a graphical user interface (GUI). The basic components include: an *inbox* to receive new messages; *files* for storing messages; and *commands* for replying, creating, forwarding, and sending messages to individuals or groups of individuals. Most mail systems also provide searching and sorting facilities and filters that can be set to collect mail from particular sources. Users can also append files to messages; develop an address book for storing frequently used addresses; create aliases for individuals and groups. For example, I have a list of thirty addresses of friends stored under an alias, *friends*. When I type `friends` in the address slot of a new message template, the message will be sent to everyone on my friends list.

A listserver, often simply referred to as a listserv after that product, makes it even easier to create a mailing list that could contain hundreds or thousands of names. With listserver software, participants add their own addresses using a simple `subscribe` command. A listserver is one of the most widely used, basic forms of communication for online communities. However, while there are few technical hurdles, sociability and usability are still issues for consideration (*Chapters 8* and *9*).

The choice of treatment is, however, not as straightforward as it might seem. If surgery is chosen, patients must select from among different versions of the reconstruction. Furthermore, patients must understand that everyone responds differently to treatments; they have different pain tolerance and experience varying recovery times, so what works for one person may not work for another. Age, gender, body weight, lifestyle, and attitude are other factors that influence the success of the surgery. Of course, the skill of the physician is an important variable, too. Having made a choice, the patient then has to work through the recovery phases, which may, as noted, be tedious and painful. In addition there may be stresses associated with lifestyle changes after surgery and the uncertainty of whether full recovery will be achieved.

Orthopedic surgeons can answer medical questions, and may be able to draw on observations of hundreds of patients, but most patients want to know what it was like for other patients. They want to hear first-hand accounts of others' experiences. How much did it hurt? How does what I am experiencing compare with what you experienced? If I do this, what should I expect? One way of getting answers to

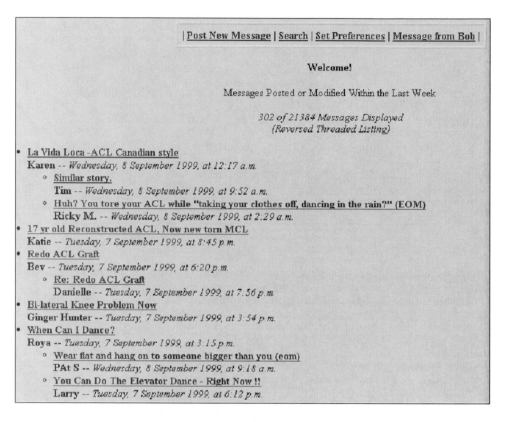

Figure 2.1   Bob's ACL bulletin board

Reproduced by permission of Bob Willmot [bobwillmot@yahoo.com]

such questions is to seek out other patients on Web bulletin boards such as Bob's (Figure 2.1).

Notice that Bob's bulletin board has a name, and that messages are *threaded*, which means they are positioned to indicate how they are related. In this example, replies to a message are positioned beneath the original message and are indented. A reply to a reply is indented further. Messages with no replies are listed below the thread in the order in which they arrive. Each message has a subject line; "Re:" indicates a reply. The login name of its sender and the date it was posted are also shown. Bulletin boards with this structure have been in use for many years; but there are other styles [see Box 1]. These features help to make the bulletin board user-friendly.

Members of this community ask medical questions, circulate helpful information, make jokes, offer and ask for support. An analysis of 500 messages sampled from the board during a period of ten months in 1997–1998 showed that in addition to serving as an exchange of factual information, this was an extraordinarily empathic community; 45 percent of messages were empathic compared with 17 percent that focused on factual information (Preece, 1999). Comments like the following were common:

> We're all in this together, which helps!

> Thanks for this list—it is nice to know you're not alone.

> Dr. X and Dr. Z said they were amazed at how well I was recovering, and give credit to "my good attitude and emotional preparation for surgery" ☺ I thank you all for much of that, thank you for your positive support.

> My feeling is that nobody knows what we are going through. A lot of my friends have had this, and though they know it is a terrible time, they can look back on it (we will be able to do this too, one day) but for now . . . I kind of feel alone. For me, I just want to sleep three hours straight, just once. I guess what I am saying is that I know what you are saying. We just have to hang in there. Good luck.

This community was strongly focused; digressing from the community's purpose was rare. Likewise, hostility and sarcasm were almost totally absent even though discussions were not overseen by a moderator. In fact, no obvious policies were in use at that time, though at the top of the bulletin board there was a short statement of purpose. The associated Web site provided additional information and a place where anecdotes about injuries could be posted. In this example, little sociability support was needed, probably because the community had a narrow focus. Everyone in the community either had the same problem or was posting on behalf of a friend or relative who was suffering.

Whether this is an online community, a discussion group, or a special interest group is debatable. Certainly, there was evidence of relationships developing among participants: people supported each other; patients returned after recovering to help others; several members appeared to be self-proclaimed experts and answered questions for newcomers. Bob himself had torn ACLs in both knees, and his Web site told the tale, complete with amusing photographs and videos. Bob frequently directed participants to information in archives and on his Web site. At the time of my study, between 8–30 messages were posted on most days. Now that number is much higher. But as in other studies (Carroll & Rosson, 1996), many participants posted only once (Preece, 1999); however, we do not know how much private communication occurred by email and phone.

drkoop.com: A large web site with embedded communities

In July 1999, drkoop.com was listed as the most popular online medical site, with a population of almost one and half million visitors per day. Since then, despite competition from other health sites such as webmed.com, medlineplus.com, and others, people still flock to drkoop.com. In contrast to Bob's ACL community, this large, professionally developed site deals with every conceivable medical problem. It has hundreds of screens of information, search tools, facilities for recording personal medical histories, and numerous bulletin boards and chats supporting online communities.

Typing `drkoop.com` in a Web browser brings you to drkoop's home page which looks similar to Figure 2.2. (Note: Like most busy Web sites, this one is constantly changing, so it may now look a little different.) Categorized menus indicate the kind of information and facilities on offer. Such things as `Home`, `Search`, `Help`, `Join`, `Site Map`, `About Us`, `International` and `Ad Info` were included at the time of this writing (but have changed several times since then). Clicking on `About Us` leads to a list of Dr. Koop's medical credentials, the site's privacy policy, information about job openings, advertising, and more. A picture of the well-known Dr. Koop, retired U.S. Surgeon General, his credentials, and the American Medical Association's logo all convey the impression that this site is reliable; the explicit information about the site's privacy policy adds to this impression. Some people might find the advertising disconcerting, but as at many sites, advertising provides sponsorship. Finally, the About Us page offers tours and previews to help newcomers get oriented.

Clicking on `Alzheimer's`, for example, brings a screen similar to Figure 2.3. Notice that this page contains many resources, including recent articles, which are changed frequently. It also lists community activities for the day and other hot news and communities.

In particular, notice how the communities are handled. They are integrated with the other information on the site. It is possible to move around the site, from one feature or community to another without encountering changes in the interface. News

Figure 2.2   Part of home page for drkoop.com

reports and communities seem to belong to the same site. They look the same—use the same fonts and color scheme and have the same general design. More important, the menus, commands, and terminology across the site are consistent, so you learn

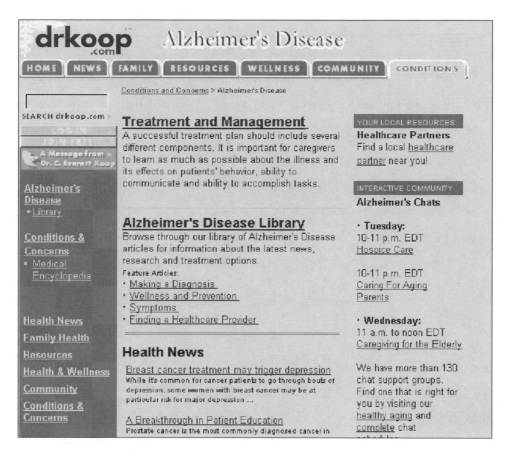

Figure 2.3   Alzheimer's page at drkoop.com

what to expect as you become familiar with the site. There are no disruptive surprises. The interface is seamless, a valuable usability feature.

Two types of communities are available. The chats [Box 3] are interactive, real-time, textual environments, in which participants have to be present at the same time, communicating via short typed comments and responses (Figure 2.4). There are

Box 3 Chats

Online chats are similar to telephone conversations, except they use text. Users type messages that appear letter by letter, word by word on the screen. Millions of chat groups exist, and can be found using a general Web browser such as Yahoo! Many require participants to register. The Internet Relay Chat (IRC) network, one of the oldest networks, serves many countries. Some chats are "hosted" and are analogous to telephone call-in discussions. Busy chats have several channels or *chat rooms* for dealing with different conversations. In very hectic chats, attended by many people, conversations move rapidly from topic to topic, and getting heard can be a problem, particularly for slow typists.

Joining instructions at chats explain how to select a name or nickname, and list commands and details of expected etiquette. A help command offers information about a particular chat feature—for example, /HELP ETIQUETTE. Some chats are moderated, and some have a host to direct questions. During the Gulf War, chats served an important information dissemination role.

also communities supported by bulletin boards, known as message boards at this site. These are similar to Bob's bulletin board. They contain asynchronous messages that people leave for others. Asynchronous means that communication can occur over a longer period. Hours, days or weeks may pass between messages, depending on replies. In this format, messages tend to be longer, usually several lines or more. In contrast, chats typically have a steady flow of short comments.

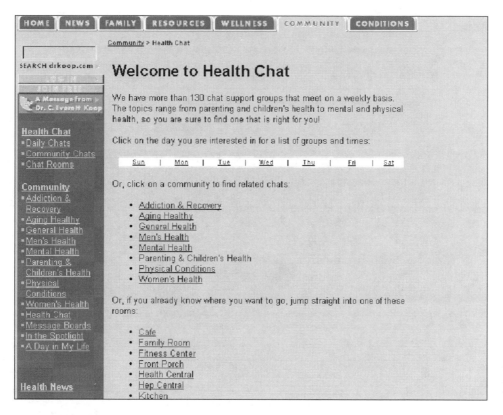

Figure 2.4   Page of chats at drkoop.com

The drkoop.com site has two types of chats. *Scheduled chats* are hosted by experts who are available to answer questions on a specified topic. *General chats*, known as cafés, enable patients to chat any time. Often, patients organize meeting times among themselves or know when to find each other. The site has over 130 general chats, some ongoing day and night by people seeking advice, support, and company.

Search facilities enable users to learn about special scheduled chats, identify chats by topics, or obtain a complete list. This design supports newcomers as well as those who are familiar with the site. In café chats, as the metaphor suggests, any topic can be discussed, whereas named chats have a specific purpose. To participate in a chat, visitors have to register, which typically requires supplying a login name and password. This information is protected, as confirmed by the following message: ''You have requested a secure document. The document and any information you send back are encrypted for privacy while in transit. For more information on security, choose Document Information from the View menu.'' Joining a café produces a screen similar to the one in Figure 2.5.

Tips about online behavior are included for newcomers and a set of small icons (Figure 2.6), known as *emotes* or *emoticons* enable participants to connote emotions. Expressing emotions is a well-known problem in textual environments where

Figure 2.5   The café chat at drkoop.com

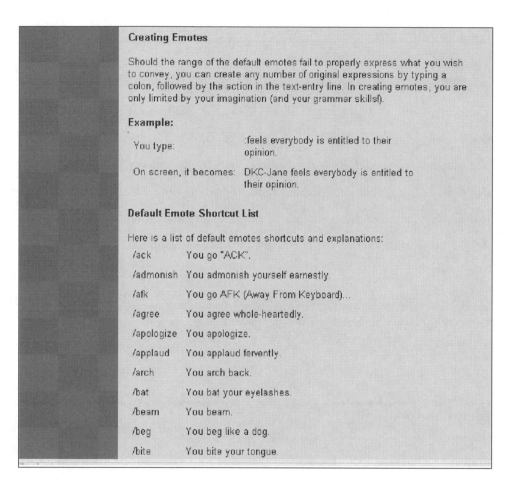

Creating Emotes

Should the range of the default emotes fail to properly express what you wish to convey, you can create any number of original expressions by typing a colon, followed by the action in the text-entry line. In creating emotes, you are only limited by your imagination (and your grammar skills!).

Example:

| You type: | :feels everybody is entitled to their opinion. |
| On screen, it becomes: | DKC-Jane feels everybody is entitled to their opinion. |

Default Emote Shortcut List

Here is a list of default emotes shortcuts and explanations:

/ack	You go "ACK".
/admonish	You admonish yourself earnestly.
/afk	You go AFK (Away From Keyboard)...
/agree	You agree whole-heartedly.
/apologize	You apologize.
/applaud	You applaud fervently.
/arch	You arch back.
/bat	You bat your eyelashes.
/beam	You beam.
/beg	You beg like a dog.
/bite	You bite your tongue.

Figure 2.6   Sample of emotes from drkoop.com

body language and tone of voice are not available. For example, inclusion of a smiley face indicates that the comment is intended to be amusing or that the sender is amused. In addition, instructions tell users how to create their own emote symbols. The chats and the message boards are overseen by an administrator in case of problems.

This large Web site is typical of many commercial sites. Whether the entire site is a community or just the chats and message boards is debatable. Information provided on Web pages, the tone, and the overall interface influence who comes to the chats and boards and what happens in them. Thus, the Web and the communities are closely interrelated. To satisfy academics who take a more sociological view of community, we would have to examine the activity among people, to answer questions such as: Is there a stable "resident" population? Do people depend on each other? What are the benefits? What kinds of relationships have developed? And so on. But to Internet entrepreneurs, these are communities.

This section discussed two health examples, communities distinguished by their clear purpose, their participants, their policies and social processes.

Education Communities

Online communities offer new opportunities for students. They can work together, exchange information, comment on each other's work, share resources, meet people from across the world, search the Web for information without leaving their homes. The days of learning constrained to specific times and confined to particular places are rapidly disappearing. *Distance education* is spreading so rapidly that most universities will soon offer some distance education classes. Before the widespread use of the Internet and the World Wide Web, distance education was offered only by a few specialist institutions, such as the British Open University, other open universities that developed later, and various correspondence schools. Computers supported educational administration, but played only a small part in delivering education. Printed texts were the main instructional media, supported by video, television, audio cassette, computer simulations and the like.

Today, the Internet supports the concept of learning anytime, anywhere. In addition to courses developed by professors, people have greater access to terabytes of information just waiting to be accessed. Some students do not even come to class, preferring to get their lessons online, turn in assignments online, and talk to their friends online. Online communities can have a major role for supporting student-to-student interaction and professor-to-student interactions. This way of learning is particularly welcomed by students with full-time jobs, because they can update their skills without taking time away from work. Naturally, this is also appealing to their employers. The downside is that these students may never meet their classmates in person, which is a concern because learning is—or should be—an intrinsically social process (Vygotsky, 1978, 1986).

Educators, too, are going online to deliver their lecture notes. Unfortunately some instructors see online education as a forum for the dissemination of knowledge, precluding the classroom in favor of the computer. Sadly, this uninspiring method of teaching is even welcomed by some, who see it as a fast way to get a degree or training qualification without leaving the comfort of their armchair. Educators (Winner, 1995) caution against this approach, which has been disparagingly called a "digital diploma mill" (Noble, 1998). Online communities, however, can add inspiration and community to education. Students can learn together, and benefit from sharing ideas and resources. This change is coming, and hopefully, putting texts on the Web will give way to learning in a community guided by skillful moderators and mentors (Salmon, 2000).

In the meantime, even in the classroom, students' and professors' roles are changing because of the Web. Students can work in ways and tackle projects that would not have been so easy before its advent. For example, students can develop their own encyclopedias of knowledge, containing links to sources on other Web sites. Their work can then be made available around the world to others for comment. Internet technology has also increased the possibility that students may know things that their professors do not. This can add an exciting new dimension to learning, though it may also be threatening for professors. More and more, professors are having to accept that their role is to guide students to meaningful learning activities, rather than to provide knowledge.

The big question for educators is how to best use the Internet and the Web to promote education. What is worth doing? How can we ensure that information is correct and useful? What types of communities support students well? Who should teach what and to whom?

The next part of the tour briefly examines three different types of learning communities: a support community for a class that meets in person weekly, a distance education community, and a MOO environment [Box 4] for teaching programming.

An in-person and online class community

Many teachers support teaching and learning with online communication. For example, I teach a graduate class on online communities each fall, which meets

Box 4 MUDs and MOOs

MUDs (multiuser dungeons) are a hybrid of an adventure game and a chat. In the 1970s, adventure games became very popular. Typically, these games involved single players wandering through a labyrinth of mazes, making decisions about which routes to take on the basis of clues found along the way. The next step in this evolution was to make a game that a group could play by talking with each other, as in chats. In modern versions of MUDs, players assume a character represented by an *avatar*. Disguised as this character, the player moves through rooms and passages slaying dragons, purchasing goods, and engaging in adventures.

MOOs are objected-oriented MUDs, text-based virtual worlds that use physical metaphors such as houses with rooms and cities. Everything in the MOO, including the characters, is an object that is created and owned by someone. The variety of objects is often huge, and may include pets, notes, documents, rooms, and much more. Players move from place to place communicating with people along the way. Some of the best known MOO environments are briefly described below.

MUDs and MOOs are managed by systems administrators, known as wizards, who have special privileges. They grant passwords and manage activity on the MUD, including arbitrating disputes (i.e., moderating). Dictionaries of commands enable players to correspond with each other. These include commands for expressing emotions, such as smiling, laughing, crying, and so on. Learning these commands can be quite time-consuming, so participating in MUDs and MOOs requires commitment.

LambdaMOO, the largest, and one of the earliest, MOOs was created by Pavel Curtis (Curtis, 1997) and his colleagues at Xerox PARC. It was envisioned as a large house, with grounds; it has been expanded to include a Japanese garden, beaches, underground caverns, passages, and many fantasy worlds. LambdaMOO has over 9,000 players, and often as many as 200 play at once.

MediaMOO is a professional MOO created to enable media professionals to meet and discuss research. For example, each week those interested in using computers to teach composition meet at the Tuesday Night Café.

TinyMUD is a small MUD developed in 1979 that did not require much computing power and so became very popular on the Internet. In its more recent, object-oriented version, TinyMOO has over 3,000 players and 14,000 rooms (Lehnert, 1998). TinyMOO is mostly a social organization.

weekly. The class uses email extensively for one-to-one communication, class discussion, broadcasting messages about class events, sharing interesting online communities or articles, and so on. This discussion list is supported by a listserver [see Box 1].

Semester-long group projects are an important part of this class. Students work in threes to develop an online community. There are three important requirements for these project assignments. First, students must work together, not alone. Typically, teams consist of technically trained students from information systems and from social sciences. Second, the project has to fulfill a real need; that is, be a contribution to society that lives on after the class has finished. (*Chapter 11* describes some of these projects.) Third, the online communities must follow the iterative community-centered development process (described in *Chapter 7*). These projects are exciting, challenging, and rewarding. In addition to working in their groups, project members review each other's projects, share software, and in general help each other. Without the Internet, they could not work as productively.

The following snippet shows the kind of feedback that students provide to their peers:

> Your team has done a great job on this site. Here is my feedback. Most of it you already have from Wednesday night's class. All the links appear to work well. I did not exercise every single one of them though. Consider this feedback a gift – do with it what you think is necessary.
>
> 1. The opening paragraph is pretty long. How about dividing it into two paragraphs for easier reading?
> 2. Bold the statement "What is an online community?"
> 3. Add a title just above the picture row, e.g. "Read the Reviews and Send Us Feedback."

Researchers question whether this is a community. If the listserver were used only for broadcasting information, this would not be a community. However, along with meeting in class and outside of class, visits to other team members, phone calls, and other forms of Internet communication such as instant messaging [Box 5], the list-

Box 5 Instant Messaging

Instant messaging is like a chat except that users develop their own membership list containing the addresses of people they want in the group. Communication is in real time. This form of messaging has existed for many years but modern graphical systems like ICQ ("I seek you") have recently made it popular, particularly among high school and college students. In 1999, the membership of ICQ was said to exceed 30 million. It is a particularly appealing alternative to the phone in countries that charge for local phone calls, because it is free to those with Internet access.

ICQ runs "in the background" while users attend to other tasks. It has a continually expanding set of features; for example, users can send themselves reminders; or can be anonymous so that others cannot detect them; or request to be informed when someone joins or leaves a session. ICQ supports communities scattered across the globe.

server contributes to strong relationships developing among students. Used in this way, the listserver contributes to networking the physical community.

A distance education community

Numerous software products are available for distance education. Much commercial software, such as WebCT and Blackboard, provide entire educational environments comprising communications software for discussions, Web pages for presenting information, and support tools to make it easy for instructors to keep class records and prepare quizzes. Researchers have also developed their own environments. For example, the British Open University (Eisenstadt & Vincent, 1998) and New Jersey Institute of Technology (Hiltz, 1994) have successful virtual universities that have been developed over a period of years and are used by thousands of students.

Because everyone wants to learn the secrets of e-commerce, there is considerable demand for courses on this topic. Dr. Ross Malaga, a professor at University of Maryland, Baltimore County, teaches his classes using the Blackboard distance education environment. This environment provides Web authoring facilities, quizzes, and student recording-keeping facilities for instructors, as well as email, chats and bulletin boards, and Web page templates that support student learning communities. Dr. Malaga incorporates these facilities in an exciting approach that he refers to by the acronym RED, which stands for read, explore and discuss.

Using Blackboard, Malaga provides class notes, suggested readings, and a detailed class schedule for his students. These resources support both those students learning independently and in groups. A key aim of his approach is to encourage students to develop a learning community in which they support each other. This helps to keep students connected and involved, and is an excellent source of feedback, thereby solving the well-known problems of distance education.

How does such a community develop? A variety of techniques are used. Students meet a couple of times so that they can recognize each other and to meet Dr. Malaga. They are also encouraged to design their own home pages and group pages to introduce themselves, talk about their work, and express themselves. Simple-to-use templates make this easy, even for those without much skill with HTML, Perl scripts, and Java. The templates guide students as to the kind of information to include. Photos are also encouraged to help to create a sense of personal presence (*Chapter 5*), to remind fellow students that these are real people.

A simple but creative chat environment supports real-time communication and enables students to draw and show slides of their work as they chat. A traditional, threaded discussion board provides scope for deeper, more reflective discussion of ideas. Being asynchronous, the students can leave messages at any time of day or night, which is very useful for students with professional or personal commitments. Of course, students also use email and the telephone for private conversations. In addition, Malaga is available at specified times for meetings in his office.

By creatively using the online facilities provided by Blackboard and combining them with conventional communication techniques, Malaga's classes become thriving learning communities of 20 to 40 students, who are thrilled to be guided through the fast-moving world of e-commerce and to experience being part of an online learning community.

In order to stimulate feedback on distance education Malaga started a provocative discussion thread called "Distance Ed Stinks," and invited comments. One student responded that the online discussion was just as rich as that in a traditional classroom setting. Another said she was an introvert who rarely spoke in her regular classes, but in the online learning community was one of the most outspoken students. She liked the asynchronous discussion board because it gave her time to formulate her ideas before posting them. A student whose native language is Chinese enjoyed the online discussion because he could interact more than in class. Interacting online allowed him time to compose thoughts in English and to overcome the cultural barrier against interaction in class.

The students in the class were also interested to hear what it is like for a professor to teach online. Malaga acknowledged that as an extrovert he preferred the traditional classroom setting for interaction, but that an online learning community has other advantages. He reported that students tend to help each other more in an online class. After the class ends, a review of the online discussion is used to determine which topics the students found most interesting and beneficial. This information is then used to facilitate improved discussions in future classes.

Clearly, used this way, online education can provide an exciting and valuable alternative; certainly, it cannot be considered a diploma mill (Noble, 1998). Should all classes be held online? Absolutely not, students need face-to-face interaction, too.

A MOO community for teaching programming

Professors and their students are also venturing into MOOs [see Box 4]. Dick Seabrook regularly invites his students to meet him online in his room at Diversity University (DU), one of the most well-established MOOs on the Internet. The MOO classes help to supplement Seabrook's traditional classes and offer additional opportunity for students to seek help with their programming problems. Students appreciate being able to reach Seabrook and their peers after regular class hours, and a strong sense of community develops as they share their expertise and support each other.

Seabrook prefers to use Diversity University rather than a chat because he can build the features that support the community. However, in order to avoid burdening students with having to learn many commands or MOO programming, Seabrook generally uses only half a dozen basic commands, although, some students extend this repertoire.

Using basic MOO communication, Seabrook's comments such as "hello every-one" go only to characters in the same room. However, if he types: page harry "Are you still logged in?" only Harry, who can be in any room in the MOO, gets the message. The page command allows messages to be sent privately to characters in the same room or anywhere in the MOO. MOOs also have a complete internal MOOmail service with an editor, multiple addressing, and so on, enabling users to email any other MOO characters or groups. Characters receive MOOmail notices immediately or the next time they log in; and invoke the @mail command to read their messages. MOOmail enables Seabrook and his students to communicate asynchronously, meaning they don't have to be logged in at the same time, as is necessary for synchronous MOO chatting.

DU also has a very long list of forums, where users can read and post messages via MOOmail, plus a number of communications channels to which users can subscribe. These operate like CB radio; whatever is said on a channel goes immediately to all others presently subscribed and logged in to that channel, in any room. Users can also create a $note object, type text on it, and "drop" it in a room for others to pick up and read.

In fact, there are many techniques that MOO room designers can use, including: rigging a room so that whenever someone enters a message is automatically sent to him or her; creating a MOO robot that "hears" all the speeches in the room and responds to particular words and phrases; and creating a slide show—an automatically sequenced and presented set of canned speeches that everyone in the room "hears".

Emotes enable users to express emotion. Seabrook often uses these to amuse his students. For example, if he types: `:jumps on a chair`, everyone in the room gets the message `Seabrook jumps on a chair`. Using emotes he can punctuate speeches in interesting ways with acts of various kinds.

Within any MOO is a hierarchy of MOO users. Different privileges are available to members depending on their levels in the hierarchy. Seabrook has been a member of DU for many years, so he has privileges that are not available to his students. As users advance up the hierarchy, more modes are available to them. For example, wizards can "`@shout`" a message to everyone on the MOO at once. There are also international wizard channels that allow wizards from most major MOOs to communicate with each other instantaneously, as long as they're logged in to any MOO in the world. MOO wizards have the most power and authority, but it is MOO programmers who create all the tools and services, and maintain them when they break.

Unlike a simple chat room with temporary inhabitants, a MOO represents an extended community with diverse interests, backgrounds, motivations, and more. Managing such diversity takes considerable expertise and time and requires detailed policies, so that misunderstandings and disputes are kept to a minimum. The excerpt that follows from the balloting system at LambdaMOO (July 23, 1999) hints at the kind of issues that have to be addressed. It also serves to demonstrate that petitions and ballots are not trivial requests for wizards to fix a bug in the system; they are intended to democratically determine governance policies within the community.

On LambdaMOO, the wizards are intended to work purely as technicians, maintaining the MOO, fixing bugs, and implementing new core features requested by the users. Some kinds of implementation requests, though, are very controversial because they involve attempted technical solutions for social problems. The petitions and ballots mechanism is for making such requests in a form that fairly clearly represents a MOO-wide consensus, thus compelling the wizards to act.

Petitions and ballots, therefore, are for proposals that the wizards perform some set of purely technical actions that only wizards can perform, where those actions are intended to address some social goal. For example, the actions might be intended to:

- directly achieve some social goal (such as banishing some individual from the MOO or removing some person from the list of wizards),
- grant some piece of wizardly power to the general MOO in some form that's intended to be used to address social problems in the future (such as creating a truly escape-proof jail or giving players a way to temporarily banish each other from the MOO),
- restrict some or all players in some way that is believed will help to achieve some social goal (such as keeping guests from logging in anonymously or making it impossible for players to print out messages containing certain words), or

- modify the petitions and ballots mechanism itself in some qualitative way (such as changing it to require fewer signatures on petitions or only a simple majority on ballots).

As you can see, participating in a MOO community requires a commitment to learn commands and gain acceptance from other players. And working to overcome problems can engender a strong sense of community (Feenberg, 1989, 1993). Naturally, governance issues can become emotionally charged in MOOs when participants become intensely involved (Bruckman, 1994). Virtual environment enthusiasts argue that such online relationships are indicative of a real community (Bruckman, 1993; Turkle, 1995). *Chapters 5* and *6* discuss other aspects of behavior in virtual environments.

The three online communities discussed in this section are all concerned with education, but they have quite different purposes. The need for policies to guide social interaction varies strongly, as does the software that supports them. The distance education environment is the most formal. Software facilitates a variety of different educational tasks, and clear policies guide behavior. Because MOO environments can become intense, policies are carefully devised to resolve issues and settle disputes. In this example, the MOO, like the class listserver, supports a class that meets in person, but many MOO communities are online-only entities.

Other E-commerce Communities

The Internet gold rush is on. Just as thousands of prospectors flocked to the icy mountains of Canada and Alaska at the turn of the twentieth century, the new millennium is marked by a rush to invest in the Internet. There is now a huge range of e-commerce companies, many of which see online communities as a way of enticing customers to their sites, to draw them back again and again, as they become enthralled by conversations with fellow shoppers. Some, like Amazon.com, exist solely online; others maintain an offline presence as well. Some sell products, others sell services; some do both.

People who do business with Web-based companies want to be sure they get value for money, that their personal data is kept confidential, and that they receive their goods or services in a timely manner. Trust and privacy are important issues for e-commerce customers, so being able to talk with other customers in online communities can be reassuring and helpful. Of course, customers may also make critical comments about e-commerce companies, so ensuring that online communities support a company's purpose of drawing customers to the site, improving customer satisfaction, and ultimately increasing sales can be difficult.

The large number and wide variety of e-commerce companies make it difficult to select a single online community that represents the category as a whole. But rei.com has some interesting features, and will be used to provide a basis for discussion.

rei.com: A reputable retailer goes online

REI is a chain of stores that sell outdoor gear. It is a respected cooperative with outlets across America, recognized for its high-quality products. Before launching rei.com, REI already had a large, but clearly defined, customer population of outdoor enthusiasts. Like drkoop.com, rei.com has embedded online communities in its Web site. Figure 2.7 shows a version of the REI home page. A menu supports browsing. Part

Figure 2.7 Part of the home page for rei.com

Figures 2.7–2.9 are reproduced by permission of REI

way down the list of categories is `Learn & Share` which contains communities and discussion forums that provide expert advice. There is also a search facility; and on the right side of the screen are news items and advertisements for products.

Clicking on `Community` brings up a screen similar to Figure 2.8. Notice that before joining a discussion participants are told its purpose and are invited to read conduct guidelines describing how they are expected to behave. Both are written in a low-key but authoritative tone. Clicking on `Conduct Guidelines` produces the policies, plus a disclaimer that the opinions expressed are those of participants, not REI. Selecting

Figure 2.8   Community screen from rei.com

the `Camping/Hiking` category takes the user to an active message board, on which people discuss their experiences, not REI products as you might expect.

Returning to the main community menu, you can follow the sequence of choices: `REI Adventures`, `North America`, `Alaska` brings up information about trips and other items of interest (see Figure 2.9). In a separate part of the menu is the `Contacting Us` option, which enables users to send messages directly to REI

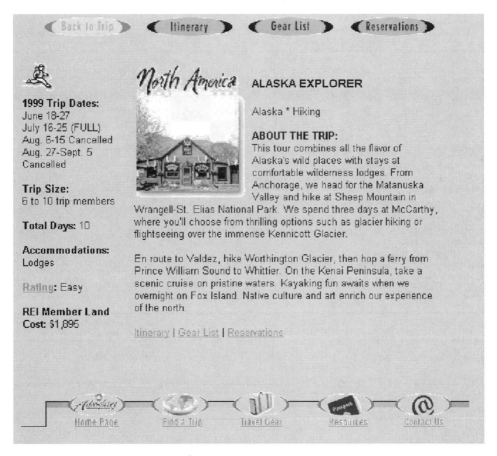

Figure 2.9 An example from REI Adventures

personnel (Figure 2.9). The menu also contains other topics of interest to people involved in outdoor activities.

The rei.com site demonstrates how sales details and topics that interest community-oriented customers can be skillfully and tightly crafted to entice customers to browse the site. And note that the communities are open; visitors do not have to register, and there appears to be no moderation. These sociability decisions are marks of a confident company with a trusted clientele.

A variety of different techniques for encouraging communities can be seen on other sites. For example, ragingbull.com is a site about buying stock. It contains the latest market news, advertisements, message boards, and a Bull Pub at which users are invited to leave messages. Many of these messages are associated with stocks, but others are on unrelated topics, such as food and wine—for example, about wine best buys. The pub metaphor is intended to evoke community, relaxation, and enjoyment. Silicon Investor, techstocks.com, boasts that more than 10.5 million messages make it the largest financial discussion site. There, some boards focus on the stock of particular companies, while others address the market as a whole; still others are on off-beat topics, such as a coffee shop, where herbal teas are discussed.

The co-op model is becoming common for online auction sites, such as eBay. Vendors pay to advertise their goods, and buyers are invited to place their bids. The role of eBay is to facilitate interpersonal interactions between vendors and purchasers. To that end, it has a reputation manager, which is an ingenious method for supporting trust online. It works by having purchasers rate the service provided by the seller. A questionnaire asks them to judge such things as value for money and speed of delivery. Ratings based on buyers' responses are then made available to the public.

The variety of techniques used to engage potential customers in community again raises the question how to define community. For e-commerce, this issue is unimportant compared with the need to stay ahead in the marketplace. It is no greater concern to academics studying community. Are the sites discussed in this chapter examples of community? The online book seller amazon.com invites readers to send reviews of books and to rate them on a five-star scale. Authors have the right to reply but cannot change a review. This does not fit with any of the definitions of community given in *Chapter 1*, but it can be argued that it connects groups of people. (In this book, "community" is used loosely, but with respect for relationships, responsibility, and trust, the hallmarks of community.) Amazon also hosts chats in which an author is available at a scheduled time to host questions from readers. Other sites offer hosted chats. Another interesting example is provided by the large clothing store, Lands End, Landsend.com, where customers can shop online with a friend. Two people, who may be situated many miles apart, can see the same item and discuss it.

Summary

This chapter introduced a variety of online communities in the health, education, and e-commerce arenas. The tour was a casual introduction to some sociability and usability features that are discussed in *Chapters 3* and *4* and later chapters. It also introduced most of the main genres of software used in online communities (except

Box 6 Immersive Virtual Environments

Immersive environments attempt to mimic natural communication by enabling users to see, hear, and feel each other and objects that are part of the 3D world. Stereoscopic vision, stereo sound, touch and pressure feedback are provided to create a sense of being present as in the tele-immersion project (*www.advanced.org/tele-immersion/*). In this project, *telecubicles* link different sites across the United States. "A telecubicle has a stereo-immersive desk surface, as well as at least two stereo-immersive walls. These three display surfaces meet, in the formation of a desk against a corner. When a telecubicle is linked to others on the net, the walls appear to be transparent passages to the other cubicles" (*www.advanced.org/tele-immersion/cubenet.html*).

Immersive virtual environments hold promise for communities with specialist tasks, such as manipulating scientific and architectural models, gaming, and for training surgeons and pilots.

two, immersive virtual environments [Box 6] and UseNet News [Box 7]). *Chapter 8* examines this software in more detail. Though a small sample, the sites discussed in this chapter make it clear that sociability (purposes, people, and policies) and usability (tasks, users, and software environments) can vary considerably across communities.

Some communities exist only online, while many, like rei.com, start offline and later develop an online presence (Lazar & Preece, 1998). Wherever a community falls in

Box 7 UseNet News

UseNet, also known as UseNet News, started in 1979. It supports thousands of UseNet discussion groups on hundreds of topics. Newsgroups and their content are organized hierarchically in communities of related messages. For example, the `biz` hierarchy contains communities about business topics. The `comp` hierarchy has communities about computing and computer technology. Topics that do not fit within the hierarchical classification system are placed in the `misc`, for miscellaneous, hierarchy.

Typing `DejaNews` in a Web browser produces a list of newsgroups that can be visited by clicking on their headings. Messages are like email except that users must go to the UseNet News community. Generally, past messages are archived for short periods, or not at all. Most discussions are open to anyone and are not moderated. Unfortunately, this can result in aggressive and obscene comments, and junk mail is common. Cross-posting, posts between groups, also occurs in UseNet communities.

this spectrum, its success will be strongly influenced by its purpose and how well that purpose is communicated, in addition to the people in the community and the policies by which it governs itself. How the purpose and policies are portrayed to potential participants determines who joins and what expectations they have. Software influences how well people can achieve basic tasks such as reading, sending messages, and searching archives and doing specialized tasks. The population of computer users has become highly diverse. Some online communities have to cater to this diversity;

others, designed for specialist audiences, may have a less diverse user population. It is the developers' job to understand the needs of the user population and make sure that software is tailored to support them. Developing online communities with appropriate sociability and usability is challenging, but can be satisfying and, possibly, financially rewarding.

Further Reading

If online communities are a new concept to you, you will learn more from visiting a broad variety of communities yourself, and exploring the examples given in the text and on the web site.

Recommended texts that provide a general introduction to online communities include the following.

Hosting Web Communities (Figallo, 1998)
This book was written for those who develop communities for e-commerce and other commercial reasons. It provides thought-provoking discussion from a business perspective.

The Network Nation: Human Communication via Computer (Hiltz & Turoff, 1993)
The Network Nation was considered a visionary book when it was first published in the late 1970s. It is now available in a revised edition. It focuses on computer-mediated communication, and is written with the deep understanding that is the benefit of long-term knowledge of the field. It provides excellent discussion of many important issues.

The Virtual Classroom: Learning without Limits via Computer Networks (Hiltz, 1994), and "Community Support for Constructionist Learning. Computer-supported Collaborative Work" (Bruckman, 1998)

These publications both insightfully discuss how online communities can be used to enhance and support learning.

Culture of the Internet (Kiesler, 1997)

Edited by Sara Kiesler, this collection focuses on social issues that affect online communities. It contains nineteen chapters covering a broad range of topics.

Internet 101: A Beginners Guide to the Internet and the World Wide Web (Lehnert, 1998)

Many books provide a simple introduction to software. Wendy Lehnert's book is clearly presented, easy to read and is used in hundreds of introductory classes about the Internet

3 Sociability: Purpose, People, and Policies

We have been long expecting that you would tell us about the . . . life of your citizens. . . . What is the nature of this community? . . . For we are of the opinion that the right or wrong management of such matters will have a great or paramount influence on the state for good or for evil.

—Plato, *Republic* (360 BC)

This chapter builds on the previous one by expanding on the concept of sociability. It examines the relationship between a community's purpose and online behavior. Then it discusses how different people's interactions and roles, and the policies that guide them, influence an online community. The aim of this chapter, then, is to lay out components of sociability so that developers can operationalize them.

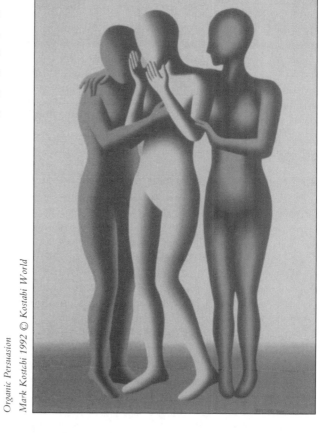

Organic Persuasion
Mark Kostabi 1992 © Kostabi World

Contents

The purpose of an online community, its participants, and governing structure all influence how individuals interact and determine the character of the community contribute to the community's sociability. Determining the balance between freedom and laws, and how those laws are justly enforced, is complicated for any community, and varies from society to society. America, for example, relies on its Constitution as the foundation for developing government and legal systems. How these affect local communities depends on where the community is located, its size, and to some extent how local lawmakers interpret, extend, or embellish the principles laid out in the document. Online communities have to develop their own policies. In addition, they are subject to broader Internet policies, determined by national and international lawmakers. For example, national policies on privacy, security, and copyright all apply to online communities.

This chapter looks in more depth at the three components of sociability—purpose, people and policy—and builds on ideas raised in the tour in *Chapter 2*.

Purpose

What draws people to a community? The reasons vary. Some want information or support, to interact with others, have fun, meet new people, or voice their own ideas. Even casual participants come for some reason (Nonnecke & Preece, 1999). Understanding what motivates people to join and return informs technical and social development decisions.

Communities that have clearly stated goals appear to attract people with similar goals and who are often like each other; this creates a stable community in which there is less hostility. Broadly based communities tend to experience more interpersonal confrontations because participants have different expectations and may become frustrated when these expectations are not met. Interestingly, however, some evidence suggests that off-topic ideas introduced by cross-posting from outside the community can have positive impact on discussion (Whittaker, Terveen, Hill, & Cherny, 1998; *Chapter 6*).

A community's purpose is one of several factors that influence people's interactions in online communities (Wallace, 1999, p. 9), as well as the character of a community. In a study of one hundred listserver and bulletin board communities, empathy among participants was strongest in patient and emotional support communities, and hostility was low (Preece & Ghozati, 1998a,b). Aggressive comments were voiced most frequently in religious, political, and cultural communities; little empathy was expressed in these communities. Professional communities of practice also tend to have their own characters. Heated discussion and disagreement about ideas is integral to these cultures and is to be expected. In contrast, similar behavior in a patient support (Preece, 1999) or commercial community can devastate trust between members.

For newcomers, knowing the purpose of a community and stating it clearly (as in rei.com, discussed in *Chapter 2*) also helps to deter casual visitors who lack commitment, along with those who will become frustrated because they are not getting what they expected from the community. But statement of purpose is not enough;

sociability is complex, and many factors interact to influence people's behavior. For example, the purpose of a community, together with a registration policy requirement, gives individuals a strong sense of focus, letting them know what to expect of future meetings; this in turn reduces aggression (Walther, 1994). People with similar attitudes and ideas are attracted to each other, and meeting in online communities has the advantage of eliminating prejudging based on someone's appearance (Wallace, 1999, p. 141).

People

People are the pulse of any community. Without them, there is no community. Vibrant discussion, new ideas, and continually changing content distinguish online communities from Web pages. Personalities come and go; some are not missed, while others leave large dents in the community's character. For example, Gerard Phillips became a well-known character and provocateur in a scholarly discussion group (Berge, 1992). He hotly debated topics, always had an interesting, though often controversial, comment, and was very active. Thus, his presence contributed greatly to the community's character. People loved him or loved to hate him for his feisty rhetoric. When Gerard died, so did the group.

The broader a community's purpose, the wider the range of people that may be attracted to it, which can be challenging for online community developers. Knowledge of cognitive and social psychology is important for understanding people's online behavior (Wallace, 1999). This is discussed in *Chapters 5* and *6*.

Awareness of the special roles that people fill, like Gerard Phillips's provocateur role, is also helpful, because such roles can have strong positive or negative impact on a community. Some roles that have been identified include: moderators and mediators, who guide discussions and serve as arbiters in disputes; professional commentators, who give opinions and guide discussion; provocateurs, who provoke; general participants, who contribute to discussions; and lurkers, who silently observe. Let's examine each in turn.

Moderators and mediators

Moderators and mediators help to govern communities. Moderators' roles vary according to the moderation policy of the community, but they generally try to ensure that people behave reasonably and help to direct activity in the community. Mediators, called in to settle disputes, generally take a less active role than moderators; they may even be on call to several groups at once.

People marvel at the unusually open, honest, and sometimes intimate nature of much online communication (Harasim, Hiltz, Teles, & Turoff, 1995; Hiltz, 1994; Hiltz & Turoff, 1993; Sproull & Kiesler, 1991). The dark side is that people can be just as aggressive and unpleasant online as in face-to-face situations. In fact, not having to face people, and knowing that you may never encounter them again online seems to encourage participants to vent negative feelings, often for no apparent reason. Such *ad hominem* attacks are known as *flames*. A key role for moderators and mediators is to prevent flames, particularly in health and support communities where they can be devastating (Preece, 1998, 1999).

Another problem for many groups is dealing with unsolicited junk mail known as *spam* (Cranor & LaMacchia, 1998), a term coined from the British television comedy show *Monty Python*, in which people kept saying spam, spam, spam, spam, spam in a nonsensical manner. Uncontrolled spam can jam email accounts and bring down servers. By the spring of 1996, spam made up a considerable portion of the email received by customers of major Internet service providers. At times, as much as 50 percent of the email on the Internet was spam. This figure dropped to 30 percent in 1997, but since then it has started to rise again despite attempts to use filters and other techniques to reduce it (Cranor & LaMacchia, 1998). Unfortunately, spam is cheap and easy to send. You can do it yourself or pay as little as $200 to a commercial company to send 100,000 messages (Cranor & LaMacchia, 1998). As William Baldwin wrote in *Forbes* magazine, "Junk email courses through the Internet, clogging our computers, and diverting attention from mail we really want. America Online estimates it is the unwilling bearer of at least a million pieces of spam per day" (Baldwin, 1998, p. 254).

The moderator role is not confined to just preventing flaming and spam, however. Moderators of electronic discussion groups perform many different tasks (Berge, 1992; Collins & Berge, 1997; Salmon, 2000), including:

- Facilitating, to keep the group focused and "on-topic."
- Managing the list—archiving, deleting and adding subscribers.
- Filtering messages and deciding which ones to post. Typically, this involves removing flames, libelous posts, spam, and inappropriate or distracting jokes, and generally keeping the ratio of relevant messages high, often described as the *signal/noise ratio*.

- Being the expert, answering frequently asked questions (FAQs) or directing people to online FAQs, and understanding the topics of discussion.

- Editing text or digests, or formatting messages.

- Opening questions, to generate discussion.

- Marketing the list to others, which generally involves providing information about it.

- Helping people with general needs.

- Ensuring that flaming and *ad hominem* attacks are done offline.

Levels of activity, too, vary among moderators, from reading, making judgments, taking action on every single message, and updating FAQs regularly to stepping in only occasionally to deter a future transgression. Most moderators are self-taught or have learned by observing others on the job (Feenberg, 1989). As in face-to-face meetings, keeping discussions focused can be difficult, especially as each thread of conversation represents a participant's personal entry to the discussion. Repeatedly calling the discussion to order is likely to produce perplexed withdrawal, whereas by extracting key parts of themes, moderators can "weave" the discussion together.

Being a good moderator requires skill and experience (Collins & Berge, 1997). Moderation can be very time-consuming, if done diligently; it is essentially a labor of love that may take many hours every day. Consequently, it can be difficult to find people willing to moderate, in which case, mediation may have to be used in which a member of the community calls in a mediator only if a problem occurs.

Of course, there are those who believe that the Internet should be a place for free speech and that everyone should be able to talk about anything, regardless of the community's "purpose." The following quote illustrates the ambivalence of one listserver moderator:

> Hmmm. How inviolable should the original purpose be? I manage a list that now only rarely touches on the topic it was originally supposed to talk about. So? The conversation is shaped by the community's current and compelling interests. The original topic reemerges when someone needs to talk about it, when it has some kind of immediate relevance to someone's life. Fine with me (Berge, 1992).

This comment is an interesting one, which raises an important sociability issue: How much can we set social policies, and how much should we let them evolve with the community? After all, some of the most enlightening conversations are "off topic." Conversely, it can be extremely frustrating when facilitators allow discussions to wander too far off course. Rules and roles are needed, certainly, but at the same time it must be remembered that people are not machines. They should not be regulated by rules all the time. To protect moderators from criticism, most online communities make their moderation rules public. *Chapter 9* discusses how community developers can help moderators to be skillful facilitators.

Professionals

Some communities, like the hosted chats in drkoop.com (*Chapter 2*) and Amazon.com invite experts to lead discussions and answer questions. These sessions typically are scheduled and take place on chats. For example, many medical communities have allocated times during which physicians are present. At other times members of the community talk among themselves, and information exchanged during these conversations may not be correct. Similarly, literature groups often invite authors to lead discussions or discuss their latest book.

Many communities seem to develop unwritten rules about professionals declaring themselves as such to the community. Nurses, doctors, and others with medical expertise often are expected to say who they are to the group. The presence of professionals in a community changes the knowledge hierarchy, which can have both positive and negative impacts on interactions within the community.

Lurkers

Lurker is the term used to describe someone who does not participate; he observes what is going on but remains silent. Some people spend many hours lurking, and know the topics of conversation and key players in the community well (Nonnecke, 2000). Others become so familiar with the community that they feel they belong to it in spite of their bystander behavior (Nonnecke & Preece, 1999). Little research has been done on lurking, but it is known to be a common phenomenon; estimates of the ratio of lurkers to posters are unreliable, but 100:1 is commonly quoted. In the WELL, a community network known for high interaction, about 80 percent of its 6,600 members did not post during a one-month period (Sproull & Faraj, 1997). In a study that compared 77 health support groups with 21 technical support groups, the average percentage of lurkers in the health support groups was 46 percent, whereas in the technical support groups, it was 82 percent (Nonneckc & Preece, 2000a).

In the vernacular, the term lurker has pejorative connotations. Many think of a lurker as someone who hangs around, often with sinister or, at best, annoying (to us) motives, or as a free-loader, someone who wants something for nothing. Since the goal of most online communities is discussion and interaction, there may be some justification for this less than flattering view of lurkers. After all, the success of the community depends on active participation and ongoing contributions that will entice current members back and encourage new ones to join. Lurkers get the benefits of belonging to the group without giving anything back. A sense of shame in this regard is evident in a comment from a participant in a recent study.

> Maybe it's a sign of my own mild discomfort around being a lurker, but I found it reassuring to recognize myself and my behavior within the continuum you describe, and to see lurking treated seriously, with both acceptance and respect. As a lurker, I'm so used to observing from the sidelines and participating vicariously that it's strangely gratifying to read an article that speaks directly to that experience. It's almost like suddenly feeling part of an (until-now) invisible community of lurkers (Nonnecke & Preece, 1999).

For some people, the notion of lurking is sufficiently threatening to the well-being of the community that they question how communities can organize and govern themselves to prevent lurking, which is seen as a lack of commitment to the community (Ostrom, 1990). However, a strong sense of attachment to the group on the part of lurkers may generate a desire for reciprocity as occurs with participants (Wellman & Gulia, 1998; Kollock & Smith, 1996).

In an ethnographic study, ten lurkers were interviewed at length to find out the extent of their lurking, and why they did not post (Nonnecke & Preece, 1999). Collectively, they described 41 communities, of which 25 were listservs, 7 were bulletin boards, 5 were newsgroups, 3 were chat rooms, and 1 was a MOO. All in this study belonged to or had belonged to communities in which they never posted, or posted rarely. Even from this small sample, it is clear that lurking involves a complex set of behaviors, rationales, and activities, in a space rich with possibilities. Reasons given by lurkers for not posting include:

- They didn't understand the community (e.g., they didn't know the audience, comfort level, topic area, individuals)

- Personal factors (e.g., culture of origin, motivation)

- Posting takes time

- No personal or practical need (e.g., able to gather without posting, just reading, no reason to respond)

- No community requirement (e.g., no expectation or requirement)

- Structure of community (e.g., posting not possible, part of community is non-posting: FAQ, moderation)

- Information seeking (e.g., more interested in information than interaction, reading with a specific goal in mind)

- Privacy (e.g., sensitivity of employer, fear of archiving, fear of spamming)

- Safety (e.g., can't offend if don't post, curiosity without exposure)

- Involvement (e.g., maintain emotional detachment, makes leaving easier, shy)

- Community responsiveness (e.g., delay between posting and response, non-response to posts)

- Value of posting (e.g., no response required, nothing to offer, unable to add value)

- Interaction mechanisms (e.g., volume of posting, user interface, anonymity)

- Efficiency (e.g., not posting takes less time, others will respond, value without cost)

One of the most interesting findings from this study was that lurkers can become so immersed in the community's discussions that they feel they know the participants and that they belong to the community even though they have never posted a message. Undoubtedly, individual psychological profiles influence online behavior just as in other aspects of life. There are impetuous, impulsive, A-personality types; cautious participants who watch and size up the community before venturing in; those who don't feel a need to make themselves heard if others represent their opinions; wallflowers who get what they need without intruding or who are too timid to make themselves known.

Participants

In any medium, certain people learn to dominate and groups tend to move in directions driven by dominant personalities (Wallace, 1999). Communities change when certain people join and/or leave them. Dominant characters, those that set themselves up as "stars" in the community, can have a particularly strong impact there. For example, lurking is more strongly associated with some communities than others and can be influenced by stars. In a study in which community participants were interviewed, several said that fear of reactions from others, shyness, or fear that their words would be misunderstood or misquoted inhibited them from posting (Nonnecke & Preece, 1999).

People's "real life" roles also change when they go online. For example, teachers report they change when they go online. Those who are strong and confident in a classroom can find themselves floundering and nervous online (Feenberg, 1989). Lack of familiarity with the medium, and the equalizing effect of the Internet are contributing factors (Wallace, 1999), which are discussed further in *Chapter 5*.

Once online, similar people can strongly influence the character of an online community. In a community that has a strongly stated purpose (e.g., Bob's bulletin board in *Chapter 2*), there is less potential for dramatic change than in those with a broad or poorly defined purpose. In MUDs, for example, it has been observed that players tend to fall into distinct behavioral groups (Bartle, 1996). There are socializers, explorers, collectors, achievers (who focus on developing skills), even some killers. Tensions between groups, depending on population size, can greatly alter the character of the MUD. If one group tends to predominate, it will skew the overall character of the community. For example, when there are many socializers killers get fed up and leave, and the MUD becomes more like a social chat group. Conversely, too many killers will cause other players to leave, and the MUD will die—as in nature, the environment can only sustain a limited number of predatory killers (Wallace, 1999). As in real life, online, reciprocity between people is needed for the group to survive (Rheingold, 1994).

Community size

The size of a community can strongly influence its activities. Too few people will generate too little communication, making the community unattractive to newcomers. Too many people will create a sense of being overwhelmed, of not knowing anyone. Critical mass, the number of people needed to make a communication system or a community useful, varies from community to community (Markus, 1987, 1990; Morris & Ogan, 1996; Rice, 1994).

Critical mass is a meaningful concept, but hard to quantify and somewhat nebulous for practical purposes (*Chapter 6*). As the Internet continues to grow in popularity, the concept of critical mass is likely to develop to include not just a lower bound but also upper bounds. The concern for some systems will be having too many people. Already, some communities, such as Ultima, the fantasy world, and Active Worlds virtual chat environments, have millions of members. Deciding on the optimum number of people in any discussion may not be easy. Furthermore, knowing how and at what point to break groups into subgroups to encourage greater interpersonal communication will also be difficult. As noted, communities have different purposes, so their intrinsic characteristics vary. What works for one may not work for another. Finding better ways to represent participants and their activities on-screen is a challenge for designers (Erickson, Smith, Kellog, Laff, Richards, & Bradner, 1999; Viegas & Donath, 1999). Appropriate representations may also increase the user's sense of social presence (Rice, 1993; Short, Williams, & Christie, 1976; *Chapter 5*) and support better communication in online conversations.

Chat Circles is an example of an abstract graphical environment for synchronous conversations (Viegas & Donath, 1999). The *presence* of participants (*Chapter 5*) and their *activity* are made apparent by changes in color and form. Proximity-based filtering intuitively breaks large groups into conversational clusters, and archives of a conversation are made available. On logging in, each person selects a color, displayed as a circle, with a small label next to it—the user's chosen name. Discriminating between colors may be a problem for large groups, though color ranges can be discerned. Furthermore, in chat conversations colors do not appear to have intrinsic meaning; for example, not all users assume that red means angry. Changes in a person's activity are represented by changes in the size of the circle (Figure 3.1). User messages are displayed for a few seconds and then gradually fade. In

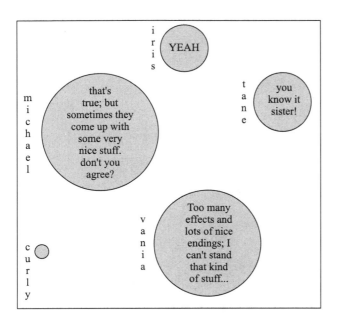

Figure 3.1   The conversational interface in Chat Circles

Viegas & Donath, 1999. Reproduced by permission of MIT Media Laboratory

a separate window, timelines with horizontal bars indicate the length of each message and show the conversational history (Figure 3.2). Individual messages can be read by dragging the cursor over the line. This system provides information about lurkers' nonposting activity, which may concern them.

Babble (Erickson et al., 1999) has some similarities to Chat Circles . It also represents a participant's presence graphically, using small circles. The designers' goal was to encourage greater informality and sense of community and social connection among people in workplace discussions. One member of the group is a teleworker situated many miles away from the others, so an online community offered the potential for drawing the group together. Both Chat Circles and Babble are early

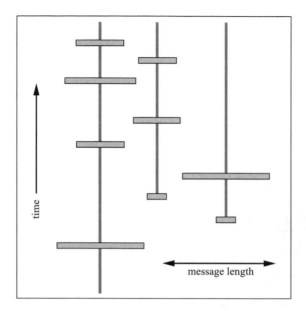

Figure 3.2   Conversational threads represent each user's activity history during a chat session

Viegas & Donath, 1999. Reproduced by permission of MIT Media Laboratory

research efforts to make activity in chat environments more transparent. How well such representations will scale for large groups has yet to be investigated.

Policies

Communities need policies to direct online behavior. Specifically, policies are needed to determine: requirements for joining a community, the style of communication among participants, accepted conduct, and repercussions for nonconformance. Some policy statements are strongly worded, skillfully crafted documents. Others take the form of suggested rules, and as such are much less formal. Unwritten codes of conduct may also exist. The type of policies and how they are presented can strongly influence who joins the community and its character.

Online communities are also subject to national and international laws passed to protect people against copyright infringement, libel, pornography, terrorism, racism, and other offenses, and to protect free speech and democracy. Currently, a number of these policies are being devised specifically for the Internet. Others already in existence are being applied to the Internet. Many online communities explicitly state that antisocial behavior involving obscene language, aggression, unlawful acts, and racism will not be tolerated. Until recently, there have been relatively few reported incidents of extremist behavior in online communities, but as more people come online these will increase, especially as those at the margins of society, such as members of hate groups, dissidents, and the like gain Internet access.

Community governance

Community *governance* directs what people can or should do and what they should not or cannot do. It is intended to help prevent problems. Just as in a physical community, governance can make or break the community. Too little, and the community may crumble under the weight of flames and spam; too much, and the community may begin to feel like a correction center with do's and don'ts posted everywhere.

Governance can span many different topics including:

- Joining and leaving requirements
- By-laws

- Codes of practice for communication

- Rules for moderation

- Issues of privacy and trust

- Practices for distinguishing professionally contributed information that can be relied upon from other information

- Rules for copyright

- Democracy and free speech in the community and on the Net more widely

Governance procedures can have a major impact on the interactions in a community, and hence, on its character, which is well illustrated by this story from the WELL. In 1990, Brian Newman effected "electronic death" in the WELL by removing from the files all the correspondence he had contributed (Branscomb, 1994). Several participants who believed that his contributions were the public property of the group responded angrily. They said he had no right to delete the files from the community's memory. They claimed that by doing so he altered the integrity of the recorded discussions. Note, however, he had not broken any rules. The incident highlights the fine line that separates public and private property in a community.

Joining and leaving policies

Communities that are completely open enable anyone to drop in and out as they please. This may be convenient, but it is sometimes abused, as in many UseNet communities. Open communities encourage unscrupulous people to cross-post spam and flaming messages between communities. Scams can also be distributed rapidly. For example, it was amazing to see the speed at which a message offering a homeopathic cure for cancer surged through open UseNet medical lists. Fortunately, a warning message followed soon afterward, but sadly, not before some victims had parted with their money. For these reasons, many communities have joining requirements. Though still open to everyone, having to register, provide a login name and password, and then wait several hours or days for acceptance does deter less-serious or unscrupulous people from casually dropping into the community.

Joining a listserver requires this information to receive messages, and an increasing number of other communities now also require participants to join. Of course, by requiring registration, it also makes it easier for community owners to keep track of their membership, which is also useful for advertising purposes. Web-based communities generally require users to fill in a form; MUDs and MOOs also ask new members to decide on an alias—a name that identifies them online. In very large MUD communities, this may be more difficult to do than it sounds because many of the preferred names, such as *sexy_sue* or *elvis*, may already be in use. Some communities also require newcomers, known as *newbies*, to develop their own characters, either in the form of a textual description or by selecting an avatar, as in palace.com.

Many systems now grant newcomers visitor status so that they can experience the community for a limited period of time to help them decide whether they want to join. Visitors' activities are generally restricted. Another solution is to allow unregistered people reading rights only, thus preventing them from posting until they are registered.

Leaving a community may involve an active process of deregistration; or, in rare cases, a person may be removed after prolonged inactivity.

By-laws

Codes of behavior in a community may be imposed by a developer or owner or be agreed on by the community democratically. The ideal situation for many online communities is to have developers to institute unimposing by-laws that provide just enough guidance to start the community, but that are sufficiently flexible to allow it to evolve. Such cases indicate an excellent understanding of sociability. During the first four years of the WELL, for example, there was only one rule: "You own your own words" (Figallo, 1998, p. 95). The aim there was to assign responsibility to participants for their own words and to protect the WELL's developers from legal liability. A later by-law was a tersely worded rule prohibiting flame attacks on individuals. These simple rules are clear examples of two key reasons for by-laws: first, to provide legal protection, particularly for community owners; second, to reduce antisocial behavior. From his considerable experience as a Web community host, Figallo specifies the following fundamental, simply stated rules (Figallo, 1998, p. 96–97):

- Words posted are the responsibility of the poster.
- Posting illegally obtained information, such as stolen credit card numbers or personal information, is illegal.
- Posting information to which someone else owns the copyright is not allowed.
- Posting pornography or other unlawful information is not allowed.
- Harassment of others is not allowed.

The Seattle Community Network (SCN) clearly displays a similar set of rules for users entering the community (Schuler, 1996). And a conclusionary item in the SCN code states: "I have read and understand the SCN policy statement and agree to abide by it as the governing policy of the SCN" (Schuler, 1996, p. 268). Contravening these rules can have consequences that vary in severity. Posting confidential personal information that is obtained illegally, or pornography, or sexually harassing or threatening others could be punishable by law. Severe breach of copyright is also a legal offense, though as yet few cases have been tried in a court of law. The usual way of dealing with such transgressions is to remove the person committing the offense from the community.

The style in which by-laws are presented varies considerably. Some are written concisely, others are terse, still others ramble, and some go into formidable detail. A group of graduate students and members of the Down Syndrome Online Advocacy Group[1] agreed on the following two principles for their site:

1. Do not communicate to someone else that which you would not want communicated to you.
2. Our focus is Down Syndrome research and its funding, so please stay on that topic.

Later, even these rules were removed, as they seemed unnecessary in this community.

Codes of practice for communication: netiquette

Ways of expressing oneself online are developing as codes of practice among users and to enhance communication, particularly by adding information about posters' emotional intentions.

---

[1] The correct term is Down Syndrome. It used to be Down's but since around 1985, Down Syndrome has been the term widely used.

When sitting comfortably at your computer in the tranquility of your own home, it is easy to forget that messages posted to mailing lists, bulletin boards and chat rooms are going to hundreds or thousands of people, many of whom have different values and background. What may seem reasonable, understandable, or humorous to you may not be received in that way. This is why newcomers to a community often opt to lurk for a while. They want to assess the community's ambience and get a feel for the style of interaction.

There are also recommended codes of Internet practice, known as netiquette, a contraction of Net etiquette. Well-known examples of netiquette include the following (Lehnert, 1998):

- Avoid replying to the whole list if what you have to say is really only relevant to the person who sent the last message.

- Do not reply with a yes, no, or other cryptic comment, which will be totally meaningless in a few hours or days, when the conversation has moved on. Make sure you include the mail to which you are replying or write a full sentence that will indicate the context of your comment.

- If your topic isn't relevant to the list, think twice about whether to send it.

- Avoid auto-replies if you are active on mailing lists.

- Avoid humor that may be misunderstood or offend.

- Do not use all capital letters; people will think you are shouting.

Netspeak acronyms are also used to clarify meaning and reduce typing. Some commonly used ones are (Lehnert, 1998):

LOL—laughing out loud

BTW—by the way

FYI—for your information

IRL—in real life

IMO—in my opinion

IMHO—in my humble opinion

TIA—thanks in advance.

Widespread use of this shorthand is common among people belonging to a community. In fact, over time, some communities develop their own netspeak. For example, this is from a women's medical support community: HIROTFLOL, which stands for "holding incision rolling on the floor laughing out loud!" Whole dictionaries of emoticons are starting to appear on new bulletin boards and other systems to help people indicate their emotional intentions in text, avoid ambiguity, and prevent misunderstandings. Symbols, such as parentheses for hugs, are becoming universally known. A number of emoticons, such as the basic smiley, are so well established that word processors, such as Microsoft's Word for Office '97, automatically converts the symbols :) into a more recognizable face (☺), whether you want it to or not! Other emoticons include ;-) for winking; :-(for feeling sad; :-D for a big smile, and so on.

Rules for moderation

Earlier, the special role of moderators was identified. Research on electronic conferencing in education indicates that moderating online is significantly different from moderating face-to-face discussions (Kerr, 1986). That said, moderation techniques vary from community to community, and are particularly influenced by what the community sees as its purpose. For example, a moderator in a scholarly discussion community (Berge, 1992; Collins & Berge, 1997) will be concerned with ensuring that discussions stay on target. Moderators in a distance education community will encourage learning, support, and scholarly discussion (Salmon, 2000); they will also be eager to direct discussions so that they meet learning goals. In contrast, moderators of communities discussing controversial political and religious issues will probably have to arbitrate in heated debates. And in support communities, which tend to be less aggressive, moderators are likely to have very little to do (Preece, 1999), which is not to say they have to be less diligent, because if an aggressive message is sent in a support group, it may destroy group morale and trust.

Whatever the level of moderation needed, it is advisable to have a clearly stated moderation policy, to which both moderator and participants can refer as necessary. This helps avoid confusion and prevents people from claiming that they have been treated unfairly. *Chapter 9* continues this discussion and provides examples to help moderators.

Policies for privacy, security, and copyright protection

Privacy, security, and copyright are essential for e-commerce, e-health, and e-education. In fact, most Internet activities depend upon adequate protection of individuals' privacy. To some extent, security and copyright protection are important to everyone, too, and are essential for some communities. For instance, financial transactions and medical information must be private and secure. Professional communities of writers, scientists, computer programmers, and so on, who discuss new ideas, will also be concerned about copyright protection.

The general public also wants email to be private. A survey carried out by Georgia Tech in 1998 showed that 53 percent of the 1,482 participants were very concerned about privacy and security on the Internet. Another 27 percent were somewhat concerned, and 31 percent admitted that they should be concerned (Tech, 1998). Unfortunately, because messages persist on the Internet even after they have been deleted from an individual's personal "mailbox," privacy is not guaranteed (Erickson et al., 1999). Those with sufficient skill and determination can retrieve these supposedly deleted messages; online community developers and managers need to make participants aware of this. This knowledge could have saved Bill Clinton and Monica Lewinsky considerable embarrassment. On the other hand, this knowledge may also inhibit discussion.

Note: The issues of privacy, security, and copyright protection have generated considerable interest, research effort, and a large literature. This discussion can only scratch the surface; interested readers will need to refer to other sources for more detail. Everyone interested in online communities and the Internet should have at least a basic awareness of the importance of policies to protect participants.

Privacy policies

Privacy and security are closely related, but not synonymous. Privacy can be defined as the ability of individuals to control the terms under which their personal information is acquired and used (Culnan & Milberg, 1999). Participants in e-commerce online communities may find that their interests conflict with those of the company (Culnan & Milberg, 1999). When companies have access to private information, it is very tempting to sell that information to third parties. For example, people participating in a discussion about diabetes or BMW cars are prime targets for new products targeted at those markets. Companies producing those products are often willing to pay large sums of money for contact information of potential new customers.

Participants in online communities want reassurance that personal information, such as their name, address, email address, topics that interest them, and so on will not be given to others without their permission. They are justifiably disturbed and angry when they discover that information they provided for one reason is being used for something else. At the very least, it is annoying to have your email inbox cluttered with unwanted advertisements. Explicit policies to ensure privacy are important, particularly in online communities associated with e-commerce and health.

Security policies

Cryptographic protocols that guarantee security are essential. These protocols use classical security requirements such as mutual authentication of communication between trading partners, confidentiality of the transaction, and confirmation of authenticity and integrity of goods (Brown, 1999a,b). Integration of adequate payment protocols is also essential to satisfy the needs and ensure the future of e-commerce (Bhimani, 1996).

Already, considerable work is underway on security and related issues on the Internet. A crucial area concerns the conflict between identification versus privacy through anonymity. Financial transactions and medical records in sites such as drkoop.com must be secure. Those involved in distance education also realize that student grades and histories must be kept securely (*Chapter 12*). It will be important for online communities associated with financial transactions and medical records to convince participants that their personal information is kept secure and private. Clear, prominently placed policy statements will help to achieve this.

Copyright protection policies

As content that is contributed to commercial and noncommercial Web sites and online communities continues to grow at a tremendous rate, the question of *intellectual property* protection becomes more critical. Improved copyright protection is needed (see *Chapter 12*).

Although most of the valuable content lies on Web sites, outside of communications environments usually thought of as online communities, it is conceivable that discussions in such communities might be valuable and thus should be protected— for example, ideas generated in scientific and software communities, which might generate valuable new products. Quite apart from content deemed to be financially valuable, discussion in many online communities is often personal, and members of these communities do not want to see their words appear in newspaper articles or in books without their permission. Information disclosed about health or marriage problems, for example, could severely impact a person's ability to get health insurance, to change employment, or to repair a damaged relationship. Consequently, some communities now carry a warning that anyone found doing academic research or disclosing information found there, will be immediately dismissed from the community. Participants in professional communities that discuss published material will need to be made aware that they cannot put documents on the Web without copyright clearance from originators.

Summary

This chapter introduced a range of social issues that developers must be familiar with in order to support sociability in new online communities. Strategies for doing this are addressed in *Chapter 9*, and research findings are discussed in *Chapters 5* and *6*. Developers have much less control over social interaction than over usability, but planning good sociability support for the early life of an online community can have a strong, positive impact on how it develops.

Terms like *social design* conjure Orwellian images of social control, so sociability support is used instead. It is unrealistic to assume that communities will always be able to sort out their own social policies. Yes, some do, but many others fail because developers assumed that their job ended when the software was implemented. Carefully developed, minimalist social policies can encourage the evolution of good sociability. A clear statement of a community's purpose, the people who belong to it, and its social policies are the basic ingredients for good sociability and a thriving, active online community.

Further Reading

Virtual Culture: Identity & Communication in Cybersociety (Jones, 1998), *Understanding Community in the Information Age* (Jones, 1995), *Culture of the Internet* (Kiesler, 1997a), *Network and Netplay: Virtual Groups on the Internet* (Sudaweeks, McLaughlin, & Rafaeli, 1998), and *Communities in Cyberspace* (Smith & Kollock, 1999)

These five edited volumes contain compelling accounts of social interactions in cyberspace. Several chapters are written by key researchers in the field.

"Consumer Privacy" (Culnan & Milberg, 1999)

This chapter in *Information Privacy: Looking Forward, Looking Back* discusses issues, policies, and the history of consumer privacy in the United States. It contains an extensive reference list.

NetGain: Expanding Markets through Virtual Communities (Hagel & Armstrong, 1997)

This book will be of particular interest to those interested in online communities and e-commerce. It contains useful discussion about privacy and security.

Interface Culture. How New Technology Transforms the Way We Create and Communicate (Johnson, 1997)

This broadly scoped book provides a fascinating discussion of how new technology is changing the way we live and communicate.

The Virtual Community: Homesteading on the Electronic Frontier (Rheingold, 1993)

The WELL is where online communities were born. This well-known, seminal work is a must for everyone interested in online community for any reason. It is full of rich anecdotes, and reveals a deep and impressive understanding of life online. The WELL was a community, in any sense of the definition. The discussion about the community's desire for open self-governance and how it dealt with troubling issues is particularly interesting.

New Community Networks: Wired for Change (Schuler, 1996)

This book has already been strongly recommended as a must-read for those interested in community networks and online communities. The chapters "Strong Democracy" and "Social Architecture" are particularly relevant to this chapter.

www.epic.org

This Web site has information and links to many resources and organizations that provide information about ethics and Internet policy. Privacy, security, and copyright are well covered.

4 Usability: Tasks, Users, and Software

The major changes coming will be in the way people communicate with each other. ... [The] information highway will be as far-reaching as electricity ... everyone will be touched by it.

—Bill Gates, *The Road Ahead* (1995, p. xi)

Developing online communities with good usability requires understanding user tasks, capabilities, and preferences, as well as software that is available. The aim of this chapter is to introduce the three basic building blocks of usability—tasks, users and software—and to discuss how usability impacts participation in online communities.

Contents

Amateurs Imitate, Professionals Steal,
Mark Kostabi 1985 © Kostabi World

The Internet has two particularly important roles: to enable millions of people to access vast quantities of information and to enable them to communicate with each other. Both are essential to the success of online communities. Access to information and people is achieved via Web browsers, search engines, communications networks, conferencing and online community software. Software supports everything that people do online, so it must be designed to support user tasks.

The architecture of a house is intimately related to the way its inhabitants live. Cooking, serving meals to a family, or supervising children can be pleasurable or difficult, depending on the facilities available. Similarly, the functionality provided by software and its ease of use—that is, its usability, as we've previously said, strongly affects users' lives online.

Software with good usability enables users to perform their tasks intuitively and easily. It supports rapid learning and high skill retention. When users make fewer mistakes error rates are low and productivity is high. A well-designed interface is consistent, meaning that actions performed in the same way produce similar outcomes. For example, if a user searches a message archive in one way and then goes to another message archive, the same routine works. Interfaces that are consistent also give users a sense of control; they know that a command once mastered will perform predictably later. Interfaces with these characteristics are typically comfortable and effective to use (Shneiderman, 1998a).

Community developers often have to select and buy ready-made software or obtain it via free downloads. Their task is to identify software that has features that users need and that offers good usability. This means that they need to know who the users are and what they want to be able to do. In addition to community members, developers must consider people with special roles, such as moderators, who need special tools. Knowing who the users are and what their tasks are is the key for designing and evaluating usability.

The previous chapter on sociability focused on the community's purpose, the people who participate in the community, and the policies that help guide social behavior in the community. Usability focuses on similar issues but from a different perspective. Instead of considering the community's purpose *per se*, usability refers to what users actually do via the software interface. Thus, this chapter presents a finer-grained analysis of sociability with a different goal: to describe the importance of being able to perform tasks effectively, which contributes to the community's purpose.

Usability also focuses on users (the people) from a different perspective. Users' cognitive and physical capabilities and needs provide the focus for usability, as opposed to their social activities, which are the focus for sociability. Individual differences, such as gender, age, educational training, and experience with computers and online communities affect how users perform tasks at the interface.

Software provides the space and place where online communities develop, so the functionality and structure of this software obviously can have a strong impact on community activity. To start, the overall functionality of the software determines what people can do. For example, synchronous chat would be possible—albeit to a limited extent—on a bulletin board, if several participants decided to log on at the same time. But it would be much better to use chat software designed expressly for that purpose. Usability, after all, involves how dialogs, commands, menus, links, and so on are presented to the user, as well as how well those elements support the user's task.

The remainder of this chapter discusses tasks, users and software environments from a usability perspective. Many books are available that address usability of software in general (e.g., Dumas & Redish, 1999; Nielsen, 1993; Preece et al., 1994, 2001; Shneiderman, 1998a). This chapter draws on these sources, but focuses on online communities.

Tasks

Online tasks and activities are typically structured around a goal, an agenda, or a timeline (Harasim, 1994). The purpose may be informal and loosely defined, such as a chat with friends; it may be formal, tightly scheduled, and controlled, as in a corporate board meeting; it may be informal and unscheduled, as in a professional community of practice. It may be completed within a set, preagreed time period or it may go on indefinitely.

Before deciding which software to use, or prior to developing new software, a thorough understanding of how users will use the software is needed, both at the community level and at the individual level. Developers sometimes *assume* they know what users want to do, that because they themselves are users others will behave as they do. Designing based on assumptions has resulted in poor, unusable systems that waste hours of users' time. Developers tend to forget how much technical expertise they have, and without realizing it they often take shortcuts that less experienced users would never consider. Developers also know what to do in all kinds of circumstances; not so the new users. A poorly named command, a hidden menu item, a confusing message, absence of feedback, or an unintuitive sequence of keypresses might not cause developers problems—in fact, they probably wouldn't even notice such failings. Inexperienced users, however, might suffer hours of frustration and maybe never succeed at a given task. The result? Feelings of inadequacy and frustration, often leading to abandonment of the software. It is therefore essential to find out what users want from an online community, and to check during development to see that these needs are being met. With so many products on the market, there is a lot of choice, and ease of use and cost influence what people use. Moreover, news travels fast over the Internet, so it is worth paying attention to usability.

Task hierarchies

Tasks can be evaluated at many different levels. For example, sending a message to a bulletin board is a task, as is deleting a word from that note. Between these two is a hierarchy of actions that have to be followed in order to accomplish the overall task-goal of getting the contents of the message to the community. Some tasks have a predictable hierarchy of subtasks, which dictate the only way that task can be accomplished; for instance, there may be only one way to send a message to a chat. Other tasks may have alternative paths for achieving the same task-goal; for example, Active Worlds allows participants to send a message that may or may not be associated with an avatar, depending on the user's preference. Still other task-goals are influenced by the behavior of role players in the environment; for example, a moderator may delay a message being sent to the group, or request that the message be edited.

The purpose of a community can involve any or all of the following high-level tasks:

- *Exchange information.* The primary goal is to get answers to questions or to send out information. This can be unidirectional or multidirectional. Most communities broadcast information to members at various times to announce meetings or to call attention to a particular event or piece of information. Information exchange can also occur in discussion. Someone in a community of doctors, for example, may ask if anyone knows about a disease with a particular set of symptoms.

- *Provide support.* Different from information exchange (Preece & Ghozati, 1998b), this task involves conveying empathy, which involves expressing emotion verbally or nonverbally.

- *Enable people to chat and socialize informally.* Generally requires synchronous communication, whereas information exchange and providing support can be achieved asynchronously. Socializing is likely to involve lighthearted, short comments among several people.

- *Discuss ideas.* May involve writing several paragraphs, so those responding may need time to reflect and compose responses. The pace therefore will be slower than socializing. Discussion may become heated or go off-topic, requiring guidance from a moderator.

Any of these tasks could be influenced by the particular purpose and concerns of the community: Discussions in a health community may require privacy; discussions in a learning community may require access to students' work for show and tell; and community discussions may benefit from being able to check local and state laws. Furthermore, these high-level tasks can involve other components. There may be occasions when a vote is needed at the end of a discussion; or a community organizer might want to broadcast the time of the next meeting; or a small group might wish to discuss something in private. Some of these issues are discussed in the next section.

Operationally, each of these tasks can be broken down into subtasks, some of which require extensive cognitive input. Others are sequences of low-level activities in which users operate the software without much thought to get the task done; for example, pressing Return is a fairly automatic response for frequent users of computer systems. Exchanging information, for example, may involve a scenario similar to the following:

Participant A writes and sends a message to the community, asking for information about developing an online community for a patient support group.

Members of the community read the message.

Participant B sends comments about her experience in a support group, saying what she liked and didn't like.

Participant C sends her opinions, too.

Participant D comments on the notes from the other two participants, and sends the URLs for a discussion group.

Participant E sends a note about a new book by Jennifer Preece, and mentions that there was a similar question two months ago and suggests checking the community archives to find the discussion.

Participant A responds to all the messages with comments and thanks. She also checks the suggested Web sites and archives, finds out about the recommended book from Amazon.com, and contacts the author privately with a follow-up question.

All these exchanges were needed for Participant A to get the information that she wanted. Viewed like this, the task seems highly distributed, involving knowledge held by other participants in other locations and on other parts of the Internet. Viewing tasks at a high level, in terms of distributed cognition, is generally more appropriate for activities in networked environments (Rogers & Ellis, 1994) than as linear sequences of events carried out by an individual (Hutchins, 1995). Though predicting the exact path of such tasks is not possible, from analyzing the needs of other community members (*Chapter 7*), a general task description for the community can be drawn up. From the high-level task description just given, for example, it is possible to identify the following medium-level subtasks:

- Compose messages.
- Edit messages.
- Send messages to the whole community.
- Read messages.
- Send replies to individuals, the discussion group (i.e., a subgroup), and the whole community.
- Access the Web to research the URLs and to go to Amazon.com.
- Find and search the community archives.
- Possibly make personal notes of information found.

Breaking down each of these subtasks further provides a detailed description of the actions that users must take to make information exchange happen. For example, in order to compose a message, the user must be able to log in to an appropriate communications system. Then he or she has to find the command or menu item to create a message, which produces some form of template. Then he or she has to write the text, which probably will involve using the editing facilities of a word processor program. When complete the user has to mail the message to the community, appropriate subgroup, or individual. Similarly, reading a message requires the user to receive the message, open, and read it. And to find information in the archives, he or she must first get to the archives, find those referenced, or search part of the whole archive using keywords or some other form of search. Likewise, finding information on the Web means accessing the Web, preferably without having to leave the community.

At various steps along the way, in all of these activities, new users will need feedback to reassure them that the most recent command or menu selection they made really has done what they intended. If it didn't, they want to be able to undo the incorrect action. In contrast, experienced users will be annoyed by too much feedback, which slows their progress toward their goal.

There can be a wide range of tasks in online communities, depending on the type of community, its size, and the variety of specialist activities that take place there. For example, different tasks are associated with different privileges in MOO communities (*Chapter 2*). In other communities, it is common to find an administrator and moderator, each with a different role and set of tasks. Moderators often review messages or a subset of messages posted to the community. They may edit, then collect them into a bundle to send out as a *digest* in a listserver community (*Chapter 8*). Moderators may also have to take disciplinary action that could involve dismissing someone from the community. (*Chapter 3* discusses moderator roles, and *Chapter 8* contains an example of special features for moderators in bulletin board software.) Each task has a set of subtasks like those just described, which have to be followed in order to achieve the desired result.

Identifying tasks and their subtasks helps to ensure that software will be designed with appropriate usability. Stepping through the sequence of steps needed to perform a task and comparing these with the steps that have to be followed using ready-made software is useful for verifying good software. This process is also useful for identifying typical tasks for user testing (*Chapter 10*). Remember, it doesn't matter how impressive the graphics, or how numerous the functions; if users can't make the software do what they want it to, they won't use it. Developers of early systems failed to recognize this, and many floundered. Amazing as it may now seem, such obvious actions as cutting and pasting messages could not be done easily, causing wasted time and much frustration. Excellent implementations of a poor design still result in poor software.

Specialist techniques have been developed for doing task analysis (Preece et al., 1994). They are primarily designed for single-user systems, but could be broadly adapted for multiuser interaction in online communities.

Tasks and Special-Purpose Communities

There is a wide range of online communities on many different topics, some of which have special needs that influence whether users will use them and how they carry out their tasks. While some issues are not directly involved in operational tasks, they influence whether users will even invoke the community software. The remainder of this section raises some special requirements for health, education, and e-commerce communities.

Health

Health communities have grown in popularity, and many Web sites, like drkoop.com (*Chapter 2*), have a variety of patient communities. Additional features that members of health communities would like, to make finding information and discussing health issues with other patients more secure and comfortable, include:

- *Citation of the source and verification of the accuracy of medical information*. Does it come from physicians and other professionals or from patients?

- *Guarantees of privacy*. Medical problems are very personal, so such guarantees are important.

- *Protection from exploitation and scams offering miracle cures*. Patients are vulnerable.

- *Protection from flaming*, which should be stopped immediately if it occurs. Patients are in a sensitive state of mind.

- *Awareness of need variations*. Patients' knowledge differs, so developers need to take this into account.

- *Facilitation of various forms of communication*. Patients want information *and* empathy from other patients, so community software must facilitate both types of communication.

- *Contact information*. Patients often want to meet others who are similar, so a mediator who helps to put people in contact may be useful. This person will need software that supports facilitation activities. For example, the software could be designed to maintain confidential records of those who are willing to talk with others, to enable matching people, making anonymous introductions, and so on.

Education

Educators are turning to online communities and Web resources to support student learning. It is common today to find professors putting their syllabuses on the Web and distributing information via listservers. Many do much more. For example, I have a Web site devoted to my online communities class, which contains resources for students. I also have a very active listserver community for class discussion. *Chapter 2* contains a description of using the Diversity University MOO to teach programming. Similarly, Amy Bruckman, at Georgia Tech, has developed a MOO community to teach programming concepts to young students (Bruckman, 1998). Being part of a community can stimulate learning because students encourage each other, and can share ideas with peers, even in different countries. For example, a professor at Tel Aviv University conducts an exercise in which students studying English contact students in Florida via the Internet. In addition to gaining English writing skills, the students learn about the others' culture; and many explore sensitive political issues that would be difficult to broach in other circumstances.

The Internet has inspired an avalanche of distance education courses using a variety of software, such as the FirstClass conferencing system. And a type of educational online community has been designed to simulate physical campuses, called *virtual universities* (e.g., Hiltz, 1994; Zimmer & Alexander, 1996). Most educators promote *constructivist learning* (Vygotsky, 1978, 1986), which advocates learning through social interaction and by exploring and building things in meaningful, authentic, real-world contexts (see the educational communities discussed in *Chapter 2*). This notion is further encapsulated in the catchphrase *relate-create-donate* (Shneiderman, 1998b). Students collaborate with other students to create something ambitious and new that is useful to people outside the classroom (Lazar & Preece, 1999a).

For learning communities to be successful, they must support these specialist needs of students:

- *Resources*. To communicate with the class, within small groups, one-on-one, with the instructor; to access resources on the Web, to search the Web, to do collaborative writing projects, to share work, to get feedback, to check grades, and more.

- *Guidance*. Professors have to guide students effectively, to challenge them to use the Internet creatively and to ensure they are rewarded for their efforts.

- *Feedback*. Feedback can take several forms at various points in the learning process. It could be ongoing reassurance from a professor or peers, or acknowledgment of a job well done, or assignment of a grade. Or it could be help that puts a wayward student back on the right track. Some online environments provide special facilities for professors, to support record-keeping, grading, and feedback.

- *Enjoyment*. When learning is fun it is generally more meaningful. Features that encourage sharing, empathy, trust, support, and collaboration, as well as discourage aggression, self- and ego-centered behavior help to make learning enjoyable.

E-commerce and local community needs

There is phenomenal interest in online communities associated with e-commerce sites. Entrepreneurs believe that online communities draw visitors to a site and encourage them to "stick" there (Figallo, 1998)—the concept known as "stickiness". Online communities also enable international reach—that is, help companies gain access to potential customers all over the world. However, to be effective, e-commerce companies have some special functional requirements (Hagel & Armstrong, 1997) that must be met in software usability.

- *Management control.* Managers must be able to control what happens in the community. A community stops being attractive when customers complain about products and services too much. Tools for moderating and monitoring are therefore needed.

- *Trust.* Several issues concern trust in e-commerce. Clients have to be able to trust vendors, and they have to trust that their transactions are kept private. *Reputation management* is proving to be a useful, low-cost technique for supporting trust (Kollock, 1999), whereby sequences of unambiguous, easily understandable actions and good feedback encourage trust in the interface.

- *Privacy and security.* Users have to be confident that personal information (e.g. contact information, financial, and health details) is kept private; that is, that it cannot be accessed by unauthorized people or sold to third-party organizations. Financial transactions and other personal information (e.g., health records) not only must *be* secure, they must be *perceived* as secure.

- *Image.* Just as in a brick-and-mortar business, corporate image online is important. "Look and feel," company name and brand, URL, logo, and so on must convey quality. All online communities have to be appealing to attract people initially, but aesthetic design and fresh content are particularly important for drawing people *back* to e-commerce communities.

- *General ease of use.* All online communities need to be easy to learn to use, but this quality is particularly important in e-commerce communities, because competition on the Web is so intense. There are many options for customers to chose from, and they won't hesitate to switch loyalty to a site that is easier to use.

Though good usability is an asset for any online community, the importance of different aspects of usability varies between application areas. For health communities, privacy, support, and confidence in the source and accuracy of content is particularly important. Education communities need features that support learning and enable professors to guide and inspire pupils. E-commerce communities rely on pleasing design and fresh content to draw in customers. All require ease of use but e-commerce participants are likely to be the least tolerant of user-unfriendly interfaces. Trust, too, is important in all online communities, but with differing implications. Likewise, tools for managing and administering communities are important for all three areas, though needs are different.

Synchronous and asynchronous tasks

Several classification schemes attempt to clarify the nature of communication tasks (e.g., McGrath, 1984). One of the most useful is the *time space matrix* (Ellis, Gibbs, & Rein, 1991), which defines tasks and the systems that support them, along two dimensions: time and space. A major distinction is whether tasks and systems support *synchronous communication*, whereby all participants must be available at a particular time, and *asynchronous communication*, which does not have this requirement. The space dimension describes whether communicating participants are colocated or in different places.

The cells of the matrix in Table 4.1 summarize the differences between four different types of communication tasks. This delineation is particularly insightful, as it maps directly onto communication tools to provide a meaningful description of their potential scope. The table indicates that most computer-mediated communication

Table 4.1   Time Space Matrix*

	Same time	Different time
Same place	Synchronous, colocated interaction (e.g., face-to-face meeting)	Asynchronous colocated interaction (e.g., message left by one person for another to collect later)
Different places	Synchronous distributed interaction (e.g., chats, instant messaging, MUDs and MOOs, virtual worlds, video conferencing)	Asynchronous distributed interaction (e.g., email, listsever, UseNet news group, bulletin board)

*Adapted from Ellis et al., 1991, p. 41.

tools have been developed to support distributed communication, with a range of examples for both synchronous and asynchronous communication.

But before continuing to discuss the mapping between task needs and software features, it is necessary to address the other part of the usability jigsaw, that is, to understand users' needs.

Users

It goes without saying that users come in all shapes and sizes, with different personalities, abilities, experiences, resources, and needs. They also have many things in common, just by virtue of being human. For example, our hearing is limited to a certain frequency range; we share common emotional, psychological, and physiological characteristics. Yet within these general categories, individual differences strongly impact how well we perform as individuals when using computer systems.

Considerable well-documented work has been done by psychologists and physiologists and in human-computer interaction in an effort to understand human characteristics (see *Further Reading* at the end of this chapter).

Human diversity

Dimensions for discussing human diversity include: physical, cognitive and perceptual, personality, cultural, experience, gender, age, and capability (Shneiderman, 1998a).

Physical differences

The fact that people differ from each other physically is important for some types of computer system design; consider systems that use consoles or standalone kiosk systems. While online community developers hope that hardware developers remain cognizant of human physical differences, currently, these differences are not taken into account in online community design.

Cognitive and perceptual differences

These differences are relevant for online community developers, particularly when online communities are closely interrelated with Web page content. A few golden rules based on well-founded psychological research may help in this regard. For example, in 1956, psychologist George Miller demonstrated that human short-term memory is limited to seven, plus or minus two, items (Miller, 1956). Remembering unrelated items creates an added burden.

Identifying items, as opposed to remembering them, is much easier. Consequently, Web developers are advised to create broad, shallow menus rather than narrow, deep ones (Larson & Czerwinski, 1998). In a study of three menu hierarchies of 8×8 (i.e., eight items on the surface and levels of menu depth), 16×32 and 32×16 items, broader and shallower menus were optimal; and overall, 32×16 won the day.

Personality differences

The terms *extroversion* and *introversion*, *assertive* and *passive*, among others are well known for describing personality. The Myers–Briggs Type Indicator uses a number of paired dichotomies for rating personality differences. While it seems possible that personality type may influence reactions to user interfaces and behavior in online communities, there is no evidence to support such a hypothesis.

Gender

Some evidence does link gender and personality. Men, and especially young men, often rank higher on aggressiveness, competitiveness, dominance, and task orientation. Women tend to be orientated more toward connectedness and relationships, showing greater empathy and sensitivity to the emotions and feelings of others (Wallace, 1999). This evidence has led to some superficial assumptions that women are particularly attracted to online communities that focus on support, connection, and discussion, such as those offered by iVillage.com. However, there is no solid evidence to support this assumption, and there are counterexamples.

Gender differences in conversational style (Tannen, 1990) have been observed to transfer to online textual communication (Herring, 1992). Women use more "fillers" (relatively meaningless words), hedging (reluctance), intensifiers (e.g., so, really, awfully, etc.), and questions; and they apologize more than men (Wallace, 1999). While such observations speak more to sociability (*Chapter 3*) than usability, they remind developers that gender differences do exist and could affect how the wording of feedback and instructions is interpreted.

Cultural diversity

Prior to the popularity of the Internet the impact of cultural differences on the way computers are used was acknowledged but largely ignored by developers. Now that the marketplace is truly global, however, more attention is being paid to cultural diversity. Apart from obvious usability challenges—for example, designing screen displays for languages that read from right to left as in Hebrew, rather than from left to right as in English and most European languages—there are many other potential affects of cultural diversity. Colors, for example, have different meanings in different cultures. White signifies purity, and is associated with weddings and birth in western countries; in Japan, white is associated with death. Such cultural differences could also affect the workings of online communities. For example, it is well known that Japanese business delegations generally involve a group of men who work together collaboratively. How might such a custom translate to the conduct of business over the Internet?

Experience

Experts and novices obviously have different requirements for software design. Typically, experts want shortcuts, often provided by programming function keys. Novices, on the other hand, want clear, logical sequences of actions supported by explanatory feedback, particularly when errors occur (Mayer, 1997). There are also many differences between expert and novice problem-solving strategies; clearly, experts can rely on tacit knowledge that is deeply internalized. How such differences play out in online community design is unclear, but they are important factors for user interface design.

Age

Users of different ages have different needs, look for different types of content, and prefer different interaction styles. For example, ICQ and chats tend to be popular with teens and students. But should age be taken into account in usability design of online communities, which exist for all age groups? There is a growing body of knowledge about the general usability needs of users of different ages, and for the purposes of this discussion, we will address the needs of seniors in online communities as the example, because they have been overlooked by many computer vendors until recently.

It is becoming more widely recognized and publicized that seniors have much to offer due to their life experiences. They have much to gain, too (Ellis & Bruckman, 1999; Mynatt, Adler, Ito, Linde, & O'Day, 1999). Human-computer interaction studies indicate that the physical and psychological affects of aging do create special interface needs for this age group of users, in the form of larger fonts, higher-contrast displays, easier-to-use pointing devices, amplified audio, and simpler command sequences (Shneiderman, 1998a). However, researchers admit that there are still too many questions to be answered before design guidelines can be developed to accommodate the needs of older adults (Czaja, 1997).

One of the great benefits of online communities for seniors is that they offer new, easier, and cheaper ways to connect with family, friends, and other seniors. A year-long ethnographic study of SeniorNet demonstrated how uniquely supportive and cohesive such communities can be (Mynatt et al., 1999). SeniorNet is a robust organization founded over twelve years ago to help seniors gain access to computing technology. Anyone over age 50 is eligible to join, and there are over 25,000 members whose ages span a range of over 40 years. Consequently, the study noted that treating SeniorNet participants as a single group was not feasible. The study also noted the high level of civility in this community and that many participants were surprisingly adept and eager to learn, thereby challenging researchers to reconsider their stereo-types of seniors.

Interestingly, projects that bring together people of different ages are also starting to emerge, such as the writing history project at Georgia Tech for young people and seniors (Ellis & Bruckman, 1999). Working collaboratively in this format would seem to make the need for special age-related usability design less imperative. Still, more specific and abundant information about the usability needs of people of different ages would be helpful to online community developers.

Disabilities

User interface designers face special challenges when attempting to serve the user population with physical and mental disabilities (Newell & Gregor, 1997). Both Braille and speech interfaces enable blind and partially sighted users to interact with computers, but other generic interface designs for more wide-ranging physical disabilities have been more difficult to identify. Fortunately such high-profile cases as that of physicist Stephen Hawking, from Cambridge, UK, author of a *A Brief History of Time* (Hawking, 1998), help to draw attention to the needs of disabled people. What may also promote this area of development is the recognition that interfaces that are well designed for people with disabilities often help able-bodied people, too (Newell & Gregor, 1997). Furthermore, the benefits of online community may be even greater for this group of users.

Social and economic

User access obviously is an important consideration for online community developers. Interface designers cannot rely on everyone having access to state-of-the-art equipment, particularly high-speed connections and fast machines with extensive memory, as that would preclude the participation of great numbers of people. Although there is a continued drive toward more bandwidth, which is being reflected in designs, developers are realizing that often they must provide two versions of software (*Chapter 8*). A recent U.S. government report draws attention to the fact that the gap between the number of male and female users on the Internet has declined dramatically but that the gap between rich and poor, well-educated and less educated is increasing (National Telecommunications and Information Administration & U.S. Dept. of Commerce, 1999).

In conclusion, much is known about human diversity that is relevant to online community design, and a few salient issues are particularly important. First, the international reach of online communities means that the potential impact of cultural differences may be greater. While many cultural groups will continue to prefer to maintain communities that uphold their cultural norms, e-commerce entrepreneurs will undoubtedly be striving to extend their markets across cultures. Whether the result will be good for cultural groups and intercultural relations remains to be seen.

An associated issue, though not strictly a usability issue, is the question access to what? In *Chapter 1*, the problems of perpetrating hate-based content and pornography across the Internet were raised. Design of filtering software to prevent access to such sites does raise usability issues, especially as many parents are less adept at using computers than their children.

Many users or few: Collective characteristics

Knowledge of human diversity is important for designing the interfaces with which users will interact, and to date, too little attention has been given to this (Gaines, Chen, & Shaw, 1997). That said, major usability issues emerge when considering the collective activity of participants in online community spaces, and this topic is just starting to be addressed (e.g., Erickson et al., 1999; Viegas & Donath, 1999; and see *Chapter 12*). Many of these usability problems concern representation. For one, many systems provide little or no indication of the number of people in the environment at any time. Users don't know whether they are one of 10, 100, or 1,000. Message trails, the speed at which messages scroll on the screen of a chat system, the number of active avatars, and other indicators may give some clues, but this information is inadequate to answer questions such as: Who else is there? What are they doing? How long have they been there? This kind of feedback is largely unavailable.

Visual representations, like those discussed in *Chapter 3* will help. Developing such graphical representations, however, will require trade-offs involving screen "real estate." For example, avatars may improve an individual's sense of being present in a community (*Chapter 5*), but there are limits to the number of avatars that can be shown on a screen at any time, especially when messages are also placed alongside the avatars, as in Active Worlds (*Chapter 2*). Moving these messages to a separate text chat screen is one way of alleviating the overcrowding, but it is still unsatisfactory. Scaling online community software so that it supports very large numbers of participants presents an interesting research challenge (*Chapter 12*). Likewise, the usability of tools to help moderators and administrators will become increasingly important.

Traditionally, usability has addressed users, tasks, and the constraints of the physical environments in which users operated the software, so much is known about the impact of physical environments (Dumas & Redish, 1999) on usability. In contrast, there is still a lot to learn about the impact of social changes on online environments.

Software

The tours in *Chapter 2* informally introduced the main software genre that supports online communities. This section raises some basic usability issues, to be discussed in relation to synchronous and asynchronous software.

Usability

Good usability supports people's creativity, improves their productivity, and, simply, makes them feel good. Poor usability leads to frustration, and wastes time, energy, and money. Again, the concise definition of usability as given in *Chapter 1* and at the beginning of this chapter states that software with good usability supports rapid learning, high skill retention, low error rates, and high productivity. It is consistent, controllable, and predictable, making it pleasant and effective to use.

The link between understanding user task needs and user characteristics becomes apparent when this knowledge is mapped to interface design. Using any tool, whether it is a hammer or a computer, requires users to translate their goals into a sequence of actions, which can be achieved using the tool. When the tool is a computer, the sequence of actions involves entering instructions or selecting items. The computer responds with a message, the next screen, or perhaps it is unresponsive. Whatever happens the user has to evaluate the response, determine his or her next move, then issue further instructions to make the process continue.

Norman describes the transactions between humans and computers in terms of crossing two gulfs: the *gulf of execution* and the *gulf of evaluation* (Norman, 1986).

Meaningful commands, menus and icons, a well-designed navigation system, and comprehensible feedback messages help to reduce the cognitive and physical effort required to bridge these gulfs. Graphical user interfaces (GUIs), based on visual metaphors such as the desktop or town hall, support users' inferences about how the computer system works. Upholding the following three general principles (Shneiderman, 1998a) helps to ensure good usability, which in turn helps users to bridge the gulfs of execution and evaluation.

- *Consistent.* Software should use the same terms and procedures for achieving the same functionality throughout. For example, if Exit is used to leave part of a community, such as a bulletin board, then Exit should be used consistently throughout all software to take leave of the current state. Sequences of actions also need to follow the same format. Color and typographic layout, too, should be consistent, meaning that font and size, capitalization conventions, justification, and title positions should be the same throughout.

- *Controlable.* Users want to be in control; they want software that supports, not takes over. They want to be able to do what they want, when they want, and not be constrained by the software.

- *Predictable.* Software that is consistent and controllable is predictable too. It enables users to continually build on their experiences, and to develop more sophisticated and accurate mental models in their heads about how the software works (Norman, 1986). Users want to be sure that if a particular set of commands worked in one situation, it will work in a similar situation. Their confidence and skills increase with this type of predictable experience.

One annoying usability problem that occurs in communities is caused by using different software to form parts of a Web site. For example, many community sites consist of discussion boards, chats, and Web pages. Because chats and discussion boards often are downloaded free from the Internet or hosted at a different site, they have different interface features. Consequently, the community site lacks a common look and feel. This not only creates usability problems, it also destroys the sense of community, causing users to become very frustrated. Unfortunately, the amount of "freeware" that can be tailored may be limited; therefore, developers are advised to trade off functionality for improved usability by offering fewer modules. Are two or three different ways of communicating really needed? *Chapter 9* presents heuristics to help online community developers make these decisions about usability.

Synchronous and asynchronous systems

Synchronous software supports communication in real time. Participants have to be present at the same time, though not necessarily in the same place, so that comments can follow one after another as in verbal conversation. Asynchronous software does not require participants to be available at the same time. Responses may occur minutes, days, weeks, or even months later. Table 4.2 summarizes well-known software genres used in online communities, and notes their synchronicity, the tasks for which they are most commonly used and well-known usability issues.

There are a number of basic tasks that users of any kind of software need to do. These include: registering and leaving the community; composing, sending and reading messages; searching for messages, information and people; and expressing themselves naturally. Users also need reassurance that their financial and/or personal information will be kept confidential and secure.

Table 4.2   Software: Synchronicity, Tasks, and Usability

Software Genre	Synchronous or Asynchronous	Common Tasks and Usability Issues
Web site	Basic pages are asynchronous, but synchronous software is frequently embedded.	Provides a location for Web-based online communities. Pages provide information about the community, answers to frequently asked questions (FAQs), and links to other sites. Typical Web usability problems, such as poor navigation, obsolete links, inconsistent typographic design, and others influence Web-based communities whose identity is closely associated with the site. In addition, continuity between the Web pages and imported software modules such as discussion boards and chats can be a major problem.
Email	Asynchronous. Email comes to the user. It is a *"push"* technology.	Supports a one-to-one communication with other individuals and groups via lists and listserver software. Attachments ("enclosures") can be sent in most systems. Textual, command-driven systems are being replaced by GUI interfaces, as in Eudora and Outlook Express. This improves usability, particularly for new and infrequent users. The form of email can appear differently when read by various email readers.

Table 4.2   Continued

Software Genre	Synchronous or Asynchronous	Common Tasks and Usability Issues
Listserver (commonly referred to as a listserv, after the well-known product)	Asynchronous. Arrives like email or as a collection of messages known as a digest.	Supports communication with a group. Everyone must register in order to participate. This is a powerful medium for broadcasting messages to thousands of users, though it can also support intimate, small groups. Like email, usability is determined by the email system used to send and read messages. There is no capability for replying to a single message within a digest, and there is no threading.
UseNet, also known as UseNet News	Asynchronous. Like email except that users go to the UseNet group. It is a *"pull"* technology.	Enables communication with whomever leaves messages in a UseNet community; membership is not controlled. Thousands of communities exist, classified hierarchically, under different topic headings. Messages are ordered chronologically, and users choose when to read.
Bulletin boards, also known as discussion boards	Asynchronous. Users leave messages for others to read.	Based on the metaphor of a physical bulletin board. Messages are usually threaded by topic so their relationship is apparent. Many bulletin boards offer authoring templates, search facilities, private mailing capabilities, and icons for annotating messages.

Table 4.2   Continued

Software Genre	Synchronous or Asynchronous	Common Tasks and Usability Issues
Chats	Synchronous text. Often very fast-moving short messages.	Enable the short rapid exchange of comments. The result is fast-moving conversation, often emphasizing greetings. Begun as textual environments, but an increasing number of 2D and 3D environments with avatars are being developed to give participants a sense of presence (*Chapter 5*). Usability issues involve representing group activity on the screen, controlling the number of participants, and scaling for very large numbers of participants.
Instant messaging	Synchronous text.	Instant messaging systems run in the background. Group members are registered, and each time one of them logs on, other members are notified. Members can send short messages to each other.
MUDs (Multiuser dungeons)	Synchronous text with graphical environment and avatars.	Engage in interactive fantasy games with others. Participants usually adopt a fantasy persona and engage in games that take place in fictional worlds. Some of these systems (like Ultima.com) have millions of paying users, and feature state-of-the-art graphical interfaces.

Table 4.2   **Continued**

Software Genre	Synchronous or Asynchronous	Common Tasks and Usability Issues
MOOs (Object oriented MUDs)	Synchronous textual and graphical object-oriented environments.	Enable interactive discussions with people in a metaphoric community. Most participants contribute programs to build the community. To people who do not participate, the textual environment may look uninteresting but MOOers participants enjoy constructing images in their minds.
Virtual environments	Synchronous 3D graphical environments.	Communicate with others in a 3D virtual environment that requires high bandwidth. These are most useful for simulations and fantasy games. Many usability problems may occur due to state-of-the-art software.

Environments

Online communities certainly can exist based on a single type of software, such as a chat or listserver, but the current trend is to embed community modules into a Web site and create a complete environment. Custom-built software environments also exist, for distance education, conferencing, group support, "shells" for content, and homesteading environments for hosting others (discussed in *Chapter 8*).

The seamless integration of components is a central usability issue for software environments, but is particularly important for online communities that have been developed by incorporating ready-made modules into a Web site. Other issues include those mentioned earlier, plus basic usability of the interface to support operation by individuals, and representations and issues related to group dynamics.

Though online communities are considered a new phenomenon by virtue of their environment—the Internet, much can be learned about them from earlier work done on other kinds of group support systems and conferencing systems, which have been around for twenty years or more. In 1985, Roxanne Hiltz, a professor at New Jersey Institute of Technology, coined the term online community to use as her book title (Hiltz, 1985), which contains an account of her work, with Murray Turoff and their colleagues, on the EIES conferencing system.

EIES was built to enhance communication within geographically dispersed small research communities of scientists consisting of 10 to 50 individuals sharing similar interests (Hiltz, 1985). It enabled members to send private communications to individuals or groups on the system, that is, conferences. Permanent collections of transcripts on topics of discussion were assembled. EIES provided facilities for the joint authoring of papers and for other specialist requirements, such as databases. One group had an electronic journal. EIES also used a voting system that supported group decision-making as well as standard voting.

Hiltz and her colleagues recognized the importance of usability, noting that ease of learning, quality of documentation, and user friendliness were all important determinants of the system's success (Kerr & Hiltz, 1982). Others also recognized the importance of interfaces designed to support user tasks such as learning (Feenberg, 1993; Harasim, 1993; Mason & Kaye, 1989). In contrast group support systems (GSSes) support collaboration between users working on a group task (Ellis et al., 1991). GSS designers recognize that they have to consider sociability problems, which raise usability design issues; for example, how to deal with one person dominating the group; the influence of high-status members and, concomitantly, lack of acknowledgment of ideas of lower-status members; violation of social taboos; rigidity of working practices; threats to existing political power structures; and the influence of group size (see *Chapter 6*).

Social impact of software design

Though obvious that the design of software influences how it is used, less apparent is that the impact of certain software design features may be far greater than is recognized. The structure of software can affect how users go about their tasks, and their social attitudes. For example, having a private discussion is made more difficult if there is no provision for it and users have to leave the community.

Though designed and built variously, American houses have rooms in common, including a bathroom, kitchen, a living room, and one or more bedrooms. Many have much more. In theory, a person could live in any of them, but the way each individual house is designed and built will influence the details of how the person carries out his or her daily activities (Alexander et al., 1977). Likewise, how online community software is developed will influence how its participants communicate and interact with each other. Imagine two scenarios involving two fictitious email users, Mary and John. Mary, an expert user, sets up a filter to collect inappropriate messages from a couple of individuals known for their disruptive remarks in her professional discussion group. Mary never sees these messages. John, less technically savvy, does not know about filters, so he receives all the messages. Consequently, Mary and John have different experiences in the same online community.

The term *adaptive structuration* (DeSanctis & Gallupe, 1987; DeSanctis, Poole, Dickson, & Jackson, 1993; Poole & DeSanctis, 1990; Hiltz & Turoff, 1993) describes how the design of software influences how it is used. More specifically, the theory relates the *effectiveness* of the technology to how the design impacts use and, hence, communication within the group. Interestingly, this influence is felt in two directions. Not only does the design of the system influence how it is used, the converse also occurs, because software use can influence future versions of the software (Hiltz & Turoff, 1993).

A similar idea that comes from human-computer interaction research is the *task-artifact cycle* (Carroll, Kellog, & Rosson, 1991). "A task implicitly sets requirements for the development of artifacts, and the use of an artifact often defines the task for which the artifact was originally developed. For example, typewriting altered office tasks, word processors altered them again, desktop publishing systems altered them still more. In each case, changed tasks themselves suggested new needs and opportunities for further change" (Carroll, 1990). Now that online communities composed of hundreds and thousands of people are forming, users will begin to adapt familiar software for new tasks. For example, when chatting with their friends, teenagers are known to switch between chats, instant messaging, email, and the phone as though they are a single system. People find creative ways to leverage designs and solve problems if the benefits are significant, just as they learn to work around the absence of social cues in text-only systems (Parks & Floyd, 1996; Walther, 1992; Walther, Anderson, & Park, 1994).

Summary

This chapter identified the factors that contribute to the usability of online community software. These include: the nature of user tasks; individual user characteristics and, particularly, human diversity; and software environments. Two broad types of usability issues were identified. The first concerns the way software is designed for use by individuals sitting in their homes, schools, colleges, offices, and other environments. Can individuals access the online community, use it, and leave, having satisfactorily achieved their aims in a pleasant way? Internet software designers must account for the fact that user populations can be distributed across the nation, and around the globe. A second concern is how can feedback be provided to give users a sense of who else is active in the community and what they are doing?

Chapters 5 and *6* discuss research studies conducted to help to explain social behavior online and to inform sociability and usability. These final two chapters of *Part One* contribute to laying a firm foundation for *Part Two*.

Further Reading

Hosting Web Communities (Figallo, 1998)
This book, an excellent practitioners' guide, contains useful advice about features to

look for when selecting software for online communities. Usability is not discussed as a separate topic, but much of the material has a strong user orientation.

Note: The following general sources are not specifically geared for online communities or even distributed systems, but may be of value in understanding this material more comprehensively.

"The Role of Task Analysis in the Design of Software" (Jefferies, 1997)

This chapter in the *Handbook of Human-Computer Interaction* (Helander, Landauer, & Prabhu, 1997) provides a practical introduction to task analysis. It includes information about collecting user needs data and gives an example of a task analysis. The texts by Preece et al. (1994, 2001) describe a range of techniques and offer examples.

"From Novice to Expert" (Mayer, 1997), "Computer Technology and the Older Adult" (Czaja, 1997), and "Human Computer Interfaces for People with Disabilities" (Newell & Gregor, 1997)

These chapters in the book by Helander et al. (1997), provide evidence that individual differences impact success of computer systems. Also of interest is that, contrary to popular belief, so-called normal users can benefit from designs directed to people with disabilities. The first chapter in Ben Shneiderman's book (1998a) has a concise but full account on accommodating human diversity.

Human-Computer Interaction (Preece et al., 1994), *Human-Computer Interaction, Second Edition* (Dix, Finlay, Abowd, & Beale, 1998), and *Designing the User Interface: Strategies for Effective Human-Computer Interaction, Third Edition* (Shneiderman, 1998a)

All three texts feature chapters on tasks, users, systems, and usability. All provide excellent basic material for general computer system design.

Usability Engineering (Nielsen, 1993), *Designing Web Usability: The Practice of Simplicity* (Nielsen, 2000), "The Usability Engineering Framework for Product Design and Evaluation" (Wixon & Wilson, 1997), and *A Practical Guide to Usability Testing, Revised Edition* (Dumas & Redish, 1999).

These books and chapter are written by professional usability specialists, hence are practically oriented. All provide excellent guidance on usability features and testing techniques. The chapter by Wixon and Wilson contains a useful section on setting usability goals, and includes a piece on doing a task analysis. Nielsen's new book, focusing exclusively on the Web, is a "must read"—it is a terrific resource.

5 Research Speaks to Practice: Interpersonal Communication

Everybody gets so much information all day long that they lose their common sense.

—Gertrude Stein (quoted in Sumrall, 1992, p. 13)

Communities are composed of individuals who can be observed individually, in small groups or in toto. The aim of this chapter is to examine communication within and among pairs and small groups of community participants. Common-ground theory is used as a framework for this discussion, to help to inform online community development by explaining why certain types of social interactions tend to be associated with particular media characteristics. Practically oriented developers who are not strongly interested in research are encouraged to skim this chapter and the next.

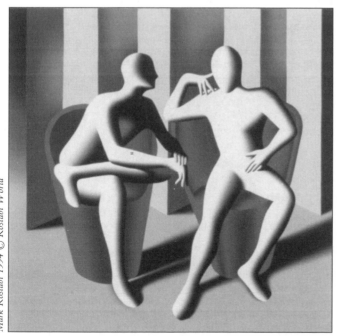

Conversation
Mark Kostabi 1994 © Kostabi World

Contents

Theory helps explain, predict, and guide our understanding of physical and social events. The theories that are relevant to online communities could fill several pages. They come from sociology, anthropology, psychology, human-computer interaction (HCI), communications studies, computer-mediated communication (CMC), computer-supported cooperative work (CSCW), and computer science. Because the topic of online communities is relatively new, researchers have to reach out to established fields for theories to help explain the behavior they observe.

We begin this chapter with a brief review of early work in computer-mediated communication, specifically by discussing social presence and media richness, two closely related theories that describe participants' sense of "being—or not being—there" when communicating via computers. Social presence theory provides the background for examining common-ground theory, which helps to explain how pairs and small groups negotiate shared understanding—that is, common ground. Understanding how common ground develops helps to explain why some media support communication better than other media and why certain types of social interaction may occur.

Early Work in Computer-Supported Cooperative Work

Early research in computer-supported cooperative work (CSCW) examined the effect of different media on groups working remotely on collaborative tasks. Much of this early research was done in controled laboratory environments (Olson & Olson, 1997), and used face-to-face communication as a benchmark for comparison.

Although email, listservers, Internet Relay Chat (IRC), and bulletin boards were common (*Chapter 2*), the spotlight was on video conferencing during the 1980s and early 1990s. However, because of the high demand for bandwidth, video conferencing was expensive. Not only were special computers, cameras, and audio facilities needed, most networks at that time provided insufficient bandwidth for video conferencing to be widely used, except in large companies.

The advantage of broadband video conferencing is that it more closely resembles face-to-face communication, in which voice tone, gestures, body language, and contextual information (where speakers are located) are communicated. Decision making and socially oriented communication are greatly enriched by this array of nonverbal information. Narrow bandwidth (i.e., textual systems), in contrast, is limited, and cannot transmit much nonverbal information. However, for communicating basic factual information, such as a list of names, addresses, and phone numbers, low-bandwidth systems are adequate (Sellen, 1994). Prejudices against low-bandwidth textual communication also tended to over-emphasize reports of negative experiences (Parks & Floyd, 1996). Therefore, knowing which tasks required high bandwidth and which could be done using low bandwidth became important. (See Olson & Olson, 1997, for an excellent review of research in CSCW.)

Researchers working on computer-mediated communication in business reported that consensus building using textual systems is less effective than in face-to-face meetings (e.g., Kiesler, Sproull, & McGuire, 1984; Sproull & Kiesler, 1991). Similar reports came from education (e.g., Hiltz, 1985). This led to an early assumption that textual CMC systems support communication poorly, particularly socioemotional communication. Two closely related theories that help to explain these observations are *social presence theory* (Short, Williams, & Christie, 1976) and *media richness theory* (Daft & Lengel, 1986).

Social Presence

Social presence theory (Short et al., 1976) addresses how successfully media convey a sense of the participants being physically present, using face-to-face communication as the standard for the assessment. Social presence depends not only on the words people speak but also on verbal and nonverbal cues, body language, and context (Rice, 1987a, 1993). Reduced social cues (i.e., gestures, body language, facial expression, appearance and so on) are caused by low bandwidth, which affects communication (Walther, 1993).

Media richness theory is similar to social presence but takes a media perspective (Daft & Lengel, 1986). It describes the media's capacity for immediate feedback—how well it conveys cues, and how many and in which ways the senses are involved (Daft & Lengel, 1986). As an aside, it is interesting to note that social presence theory originated ten years earlier than media richness theory. Why? Because researchers in one field are not always cognizant of related work in other fields. It seems that Daft's contribution, and Lengel's, though extremely useful because it takes a different perspective, was made without knowledge of Short, Williams, & Christie's work (Short et al., 1976; Rice, 1999).

Reduced cues

Social presence fundamentally affects how participants sense emotion, intimacy, and immediacy (Rice, 1993). Early studies reported fewer personal messages with lower socioemotional content (e.g., Hiltz, Johnson, & Turoff, 1986) that lacked cues about social context (Sproull & Keisler, 1986). The "cues-filtered-out hypothesis" was used to explain these observations (Culnan & Markus, 1987). Bandwidth was insufficient to carry all the communication signals needed for communicating social, emotional, and contextual content. In text-only systems, for example, both task information and social information are carried in the same single verbal/linguistic channel, which, though adequate for most task information, cannot transmit nonverbal information such as body language, voice tone, and so on (Walther, 1994, p. 476).

The consequences of filtering out social, emotional, and contextual information vary depending on their importance to the communication task. There are three main ways that this affects communication. First, signals needed to understand conversation may be missing; for example, when face to face, speakers can check frequently with each other to ensure they understand the conversation as it progresses. This is the aforementioned important concept known as common ground, which will be discussed in detail in the next section. Nonverbal signals such as a nod of the head, a quizzical look, or a wave of the hand can say a lot. Second, conversations proceed by speakers taking turns; various signals such as pauses in speech or a gaze are used to cue the next speaker to take his or her turn. Third, seeing and hearing the speaker enables the listener to infer information regarding the context of the conversation and the speaker's feelings. Olson and Olson succinctly argue that differences in "local physical contexts, time zones, culture, and language all persist in spite of the use of distance technologies," and that these differences take a toll on communication. Furthermore speakers do not get evidence of each other's emotional states. They cannot see if the person is having a bad day or is tired, so they do not know whether or how to temper their comments. Consequently, "distance matters" (Olson & Olson, 2000).

In addition, reduced social cues can encourage unusual behavior that would not occur if people could see each other. Some people feel comfortable behaving aggressively online because they are hidden behind a veil of anonymity. The way participants form impressions of each other and how much personal information they are prepared to disclose are also influenced. In addition, with fewer social cues to monitor, some people find it easier, even fun, to assume different persona or even switch gender. These effects are interrelated in complex ways, therefore separating them is not straightforward.

Misunderstandings

Both speakers and listeners develop mental models of each other (Norman, 1986), as well as of the information content of their discussion, but speakers in low-bandwidth environments have to work extra hard to compensate for missing nonverbal information. Not surprisingly, in these environments misunderstandings and frustration occur widely. Furthermore, relationship development is inhibited, which is sometimes indicated by angry comments; in extreme cases, people launch unwarranted attacks, known as flaming, on others they may not know and have never met (Hiltz et al., 1986; Spears & Lea, 1992; Sproull & Keisler, 1986).

People using low-bandwidth systems also tend to send fewer messages during the same time period, over high-bandwidth systems, and this, too, inhibits relationships developing (Hiltz et al., 1986; Walther, 1993). Nevertheless, given sufficient time, people in closed textual discussion groups do form strong relationships (Walther, 1993). In fact, there is evidence that some people develop extremely rich social relationships this way (Spears & Lea, 1992). It just takes longer to send a comparable number of messages, and correspondingly longer for relationships to develop, than in high-bandwidth environments.

Because of the high potential for misunderstandings to occur online, some developers believe that the best way to prevent the problem is to develop systems that enable participants to represent themselves with icons, photographs, or 3D avatars, to increase social presence. An alternative, low-tech, solution is to educate participants about their online writing style (*Chapter 9*). For example, *linguistic softeners*, such as phrasing a comment tentatively, to avoid being thought aggressive, are used by experienced participants to avoid conflict online (Wallace, 1999). When stating an opinion, they commonly preface it with the acronym IMHO, for "in my humble opinion." Emoticons can also be used as softeners; a smiley, for example, may be included to assure the reader that a comment is well meant (see *Chapter 3*).

Impression development and self-disclosure

Filtering out social cues impedes normal impression development. The cartoon of a dog sitting at a keyboard with the caption "Nobody knows you're a dog on the Internet," captures the essence of this well. First impressions are developed in face-to-face conversations primarily from nonverbal signs. Physical appearance—how people dress, their physical attractiveness, their race, age and gender—have an enormous impact on the impressions others develop. Furthermore, although those impressions tend to develop very quickly, they can be remarkably powerful and resilient to change, even when evidence suggests they are incorrect (Wallace, 1999). Age and gender in particular are strong *social markers*.

Psychologically, the more people discover that they are similar to each other, thus, the more they tend to like each other, thus, the more they will disclose about themselves. *Self-disclosure* reciprocity is powerful online—if you tell me something about yourself, I'll tell you something about me (Wallace, 1999). Anonymity often encourages people to disclose more about themselves; they even become *hyper-personal* (Lea, O'Shea, Fung, & Spears, 1992; Spears, Russell, & Lee, 1990; Walther, 1996) as in a support group for those suffering from knee injuries (Preece, 1998). Verbal probes are used to find out about another person and it is particularly easy to do this via text. Consequently, it appears that, rather than eliminate social information or blinding participants to it, the limited bandwidth of CMC may retard normal impression development and relational communication (Walther, Anderson, & Park, 1994). CMC seems to affect the time it takes for relationships to develop though this is also influenced by experience (Walther, 1993; Ogan, 1993). Experienced users, for example, are adept at finding ways to deal with the absence of visual cues (Rice & Barnett, 1986).

Online personas and gender

Revealing one's gender online can have startling consequences. For example, it is well known that in some online environments, responses to men are different from those to women (Bruckman, 1993; Herring, 1992; Turkle, 1995, 1999). One of the first questions a newcomer is asked is what his or her gender is. A person identified as female may receive from men excessive, unwanted, attention and be bombarded by questions and sometimes propositions or harassment. Consequently, women frequently disguise their gender so that they can maintain their freedom in the electronic world.

For less practical purposes, some people like to explore changing their persona to see how people treat them in their new guise. Both men and women are known to switch genders, a practice known as *gender bending*, in order to explore what life is like as the other sex. There are also other reasons for assuming a new persona online. The classic book, *Life on Screen*, by Sherry Turkle tells how people take on new identities to explore their own personalities, particularly aspects of themselves that they find troubling in the real world (Turkle, 1995). Online, there is little risk for the ultra shy person who decides to be outspoken or become a passionate romantic. If the situation starts to feel threatening, poof! the person can log off and vanish, never to be heard from again. There are, however, risks associated with gender bending. People can and do get hurt, for example, when heterosexuals discover that their online relationship is in fact homosexual or vice versa. Gender bending online, however, is not as easy as it sounds. People reveal themselves without realizing it. For example, women tend to hedge their comments, to be more self-deprecating, and apologetic, and to include more adjectives in their speech (Tannen, 1990, 1994). Hence, linguistic style can betray a person's gender. Research on textual communication suggests that emotions are typically transmitted—both semantically and syntactically (Herring, 1992; Reid, 1993). For example, Susan Herring gives an example of how women avoid criticism in email discussions by phrasing their questions in defensive forms, such as "This may be a naïve question, but . . ." (Herring, 1992).

Likewise, online romances of any sort may fail when real-life meetings result in dashed fantasies. For example, online, no one is overweight, but in reality a person's extra 25 pounds can make a difference. And dishonesty works only as long as the relationship remains online only. A ten-year-old photograph will be revealed as misleading in a face-to-face meeting.

What this research says to online community developers is that they need to look for ways of educating participants about how they are perceived by others online. Moderation may help but it is time-consuming and expensive. Examples of possible solutions are given in *Chapters 3* and *9*. Lack of social presence also impacts how well people understand each other in conversation.

Common Ground

Common-ground theory can be used as a framework for determining how two people or a small group validate that they understand each other. It focuses on how communication process and content are coordinated. Much of this coordination depends upon social presence or appropriate ways of compensating for its absence. In the words of Herb Clark and Susan Brennan, developers of the theory:

It takes two people working together to play a duet, shake hands, play chess, waltz, teach, or make love. To succeed, the two of them have to coordinate both the content and the process of what they are doing . . . They cannot even begin to coordinate on content without assuming a vast amount of shared information or common ground—that is, mutual knowledge, mutual beliefs, and mutual assumptions. . . . [T]o coordinate on process, they need to update their common ground moment by moment. All collective actions are built on common ground and its accumulation (Clark & Brennan, 1993, p. 222).

If person A speaks to person B about "my dogs," the two of them must understand that person A is referring to the two dogs sleeping in front of the fire in his or her home, and not dogs that live down the street. Common ground is established by a process called *grounding*. Grounding varies from situation to situation. It takes one form in face-to-face conversation, another in computer-mediated communication, still another when calling, for example, directory assistance, chatting with a friend, or engaging in intellectual debate. Grounding is, therefore, influenced both by the *communication medium* and the *communication task*.

Grounding leads participants to a mutual belief that they share a common under-standing. Several rounds of verifying that the person has heard and understood a comment may be needed. While this may sound cumbersome, most conversations require a series of twists and turns that move the conversation forward only when the speaker is convinced that he or she has been heard and understood. Usually, con-versations have identifiable entry points, "bodies," and exits. Noticing how much attention a partner is paying to his or her comments enables the speaker to judge whether there is shared understanding. Utterances, gazes, nodding, and facial expression are all indicators of attention. Checking, repeating, or rephrasing incomplete or misinterpreted comments encourage common ground.

Generally people try to establish common ground unconsciously, with as little effort as possible. This is where media have an influence. The amount and type of effort changes with the communication medium. Techniques that work in one medium may not in another; and even if available, they may require more effort to achieve grounding. Furthermore, people who are not used to a particular medium will be unfamiliar with good ways of solving problems. For example, a nod may work in a face-to-face conversation, not over the phone, where instead a grunt or other spoken word is needed. Similarly, a word, exclamation mark or some other textual expression is needed in a bulletin board discussion. Establishing common ground has been an issue in video conferencing design, where low bandwidth, poor resolution, and small screens have obscured facial expressions, voice tone and body language, thereby hampering development of common ground and delaying turn-taking.

Different media also offer different opportunities, as the following list of characteristics indicates (Clark & Brennan, 1993, p. 229).

- *Co-presence: A and B share the same physical environment, as in face-to-face conversation.* Compensating for lack of co-presence is an important aim for online community developers. Years of learning the nuances and pleasantries of face-to-face conversational protocol train individuals to expect, if not assume, the same rules apply to other media. Human beings assume face-to-face communication as their standard. Many online community developers strive to find ways of creating a sense of co-presence. Avatars can help to provide partial solutions. (Co-presence can be similar to social presence. (Short, Williams, & Christie, 1976). However, co-presence refers to people having temporal and geographical proximity, which is not always necessary for a social presence.)

- *Visibility: A and B are visible to each other, as in face-to-face communication and video conferencing.* Being able to see one another enables participants to "read" each other's body language, which is important for communicating emotion. Developers provide emoticons and other techniques to compensate for lack of visibility in textual systems.

- *Audibility: A and B communicate by speaking, which can be very effective for conveying factual information.* Voice tone provides clues about emotional state.

- *Cotemporality: B receives at roughly the same time as A presents, so the message is received immediately.*

- *Simultaneity: A and B can send and receive at once and simultaneously.* The communication comprises rapid, short exchanges as in busy chats, MUDs, and MOOs.

- *Sequentiality: A's and B's turns cannot get out of sequence as in asynchronous communication.* In asynchronous communication, periods of several seconds, minutes, hours, or days may pass between a message being sent and a response being generated.

- *Reviewability: B can review A's message.* For example, text messages can be reviewed, whereas spoken messages are lost when the speaker stops talking.

- *Revisability: A can revise messages for B.* If messages persist, they can be revised— providing they can be accessed.

If one of these opportunities is not present, the communication is constrained by its absence, and ways of overcoming or dealing with it have to be found. Overcoming constraints generally takes time and effort (Clark & Brennan, 1993, pp. 230–231). Interestingly, some circumstances that at first might seem to be disadvantageous turn out to be the opposite. For example, the delay between receiving a message via asynchronous textual conferencing and sending a reply can provide valuable time for reflection. In a study of recovering alcoholics, for example, participants of a listserver community said they liked having time to reflect and compose, which they could not get in face-to-face sessions (King, 1994).

Common Ground and Different Media

Table 5.1 summarizes the communication opportunities offered by different types of media/systems, and comments on their advantages and disadvantages.

Examining each of the media in terms of common ground helps to identify features that support or inhibit grounding, and to make explicit comparisons between the various media and face-to-face communication. Keep in mind, originally the theory was developed to explain grounding face-to-face, and has been drawn on in CMC and CSCW research (Isaacs, Morris, Rodrigues, & Tang, 1995). Interestingly, however, face-to-face communication lacks some opportunities offered by other media. For example, it is difficult to review a face-to-face conversation, and there may be little time to reflect, whereas a text-based interchange is a much better medium for reviewing and reflecting. Of course, no one medium is perfectly suited to all tasks, so none can be considered the "best"; different attributes are better for various communication tasks in specific contexts (Rice, 1987a). Consequently, if online community developers focus on the communication task(s) rather than on the media, they are more likely to select media wisely.

Table 5.1   Media and Common Ground★

Medium	Opportunities	Comments
Face-to-face	Co-presence, visibility, audibility, cotemporality, simultaneity, sequentiality	*It may be difficult to delay response to reflect. In addition, people may communicate certain feelings unintentionally via body language. An awkward glance, for example, may reveal lack of agreement despite the words being spoken.*
Telephone	Audibility, cotemporality, simultaneity, seqentiality	*No opportunity to "read" body language thereby limiting socioemotional communication. Voice tone helps. Good for conveying factual information.*
Video teleconference	Visibility, audibility, cotemporality, simultaneity, sequentiality (*in some systems*)	*Response capability of technology can adversely influence synchrony and impede turn-taking. Reception of messages may be slow; delays may cause misunderstandings. Small viewing window makes seeing cues and body language difficult. Helpful as introduction among participants, but video often abandoned thereafter unless discussion is about an object that must be seen, such as an architect's model. High bandwidth required to prevent a frustrating experience.*
Terminal teleconference (*textual*)	Cotemporality, sequentiality, reviewability	*Production takes more time, but there is some macro control over timing. Having time to reflect can be very useful, because understanding message content is often heightened. Emotional understanding, however, may suffer from poor social presence; developers need to seek ways to remedy this problem.*
Answering machines	Audibility, reviewability	*Receiving only. Social presence limited.*

Table 5.1   Continued

Medium	Opportunities	Comments
Electronic mail	Reviewability, revisability	*Production takes more time, though some macro control gives time to reflect. Turn-taking is often delayed, but understanding of verbal messages is often better; however, emotional understanding can suffer from poor social presence. Alternatives are needed to make up for absence of body language transmission for supporting socioemotional and contextual communication.*
Letters	Reviewability revisability	*Very slow turn-taking. Generally the effect is adverse, though understanding may be improved by reflection time.*
Bulletin board messages	*Reviewability, revisability, sequentiality*	*Production takes time, though macro control offers time to reflect. Understanding verbal messages is better. Threading helps delineate among speakers. Socioemotional communication is often supported by use of icons.*
Chats	*Cotemporality, simultaneity*	*Often very fast moving, which prohibits long messages. Turn-taking is often chaotic, as there is no time for delay or fault correction. This format can be difficult for poor or slow typists.*
MOOs—text only	*Cotemporality, simultaneity*	*Learning curve prohibits casual participation. Response time depends on number of participants. Ways of displaying emotion are well developed in some systems.*
MOOs & MUDs— graphical, with avatars	*Cotemporality, simultaneity*	*As above; but sense of social presence is aided by avatar and graphical world of community action.*
Computer virtual environments	*Cotemporality, simultaneity*	*Requires high bandwidth. Strong sense of co-presence provided with intention of improving communication.*

★ Adapted from Clark & Brennan, 1993, p. 230. Material added by author appears in italics.

Despite the limitations of the various media listed in Table 5.1, many fulfill the tasks for which they are commonly used surprisingly well. For example, chats are very restricted. Participants cannot see each other, and often, at best, they can send only short remarks—if they can type fast enough. There is little time for reflection, no time for fault correction, and speaker turn-taking (i.e., change-over) is chaotic here. Despite these limitations, people who use chats regularly love them, particularly students and other young people. Many switch between chats, instant messaging and the phone with ease.

Online community developers play a key role in identifying the best media for their users' communication tasks. But whatever they are given, as users get to know a medium's limitations, they often develop ingenious ways of getting around them (*Chapter 4*) so that it works well for them. For example, chat users speed things up with short acronyms (*Chapter 3*), which are fast to type and easy to remember. Experienced chatters become adept at following the threads from different channels, as though they were in a room listening to several conversations going on at once— they participate in one and eavesdrop on others. Chatters also seem willing to accept lag times of two to three seconds; but at eight or nine seconds, frustration starts to mount (Wallace, 1999).

Only a few attempts have been made to apply common ground theory to mass interaction (Whittaker, Terveen, Hill, & Cherny, 1998); nevertheless, it is useful for identifying constraints in one-to-one and small group communication via different media.

Common Ground and Empathy

Empathy is defined as "knowing what another person is feeling, feeling what another person is feeling, and responding compassionately to another person" (Levenson & Ruef, 1992). Although empathy has value to all forms of communication, its importance is most pronounced among people who share very similar experiences (Eisenberg & Strayer, 1987; Etchegoyen, 1991; Ickes, 1993, 1997). The more similar people are, the less they have to "go outside themselves" to gather cues; hence the more readily they can respond naturally to their circumstances (Hodges & Wegner, 1997, p. 324). A recent comment from an online support community aptly sums this up: "We're all in this together, which helps!" Empathy can be a powerful force online, especially in support communities (Preece, 1998, 1999a).

Many researchers have observed empathy online. As early as 1993, Howard Rheingold reported how the WELL community in San Francisco supported the parent of a dying child (Rheingold, 1993). Other researchers have commented on how fellow workers (Sproull & Kiesler, 1991) and learners (Hiltz, 1994) understand each other's problems and support each other. Still others analyzed messages from listserver communities for people with chronic and acute illnesses and found that empathy was important in both (Schoch & White, 1997).

There is, however, no research on the relationship between common ground and empathy, though it seems likely that when socioemotional content is involved, establishing common ground is aided by empathy, or vice versa. Empathy, like common ground, depends heavily on nonverbal communication, such as gaze and body language (Eisenberg & Strayer, 1987; Etchegoyen, 1991; Lanzetta & Englis,

1989), so it is likely to be influenced by the properties of different media in a similar way to common-ground development. Empathy is such a fundamental component of human communication (Ickes, 1997) that online community developers need to be aware of its impact, particularly when designing for communities in which trust is important (*Chapter 6*).

Summary

Forms of communication—chatting, discussing, debating, asking and answering questions, consoling, advising, empathizing—are the magic ingredients of a community. Indeed, it is the ability to interact and communicate that draws millions of people into online communities everyday. In contrast, Web pages can be fascinating on the first read, maybe even on the second, but unless their content changes readers get bored.

Social presence, or more particularly lack of social presence, can critically influence how people behave online, form impressions of others, and negotiate common ground. Empathy is important in communities in which emotional topics are discussed. Over 80 percent of empathy is conveyed nonverbally (Goleman, 1995). Like common ground, empathy is also affected by how the various media convey social presence. Thus a leading question that online community developers must answer is how to facilitate common ground and empathy online. Emoticons, dictionaries of acronyms, and advice on how to phrase comments are some solutions (*Chapter 9*) Developers familiar with these theories and who work to compensate for shortcomings in media will be the most successful at creating good sociability.

Chapter 6 builds on some of these ideas, and discusses how relationships develop and can be supported at the group and community level, rather than between individuals.

Further Reading

"Grounding in Communication" (Clark & Brennan, 1993)

This seminal paper, which provided a basis for this chapter, explains the theory of common ground, and discusses how it applies to different kinds of computer-mediated communication. It contains a detailed discussion of the constraints and costs of using the different media. It is essential reading for anyone interested in this subject.

Empathic Accuracy (Ickes, 1997)

This collection contains papers by most of the key researchers in this field. It describes the nature of empathy, and addresses many key questions, such as whether empathy is gender-related. But note, all of the studies covered are concerned with face-to-face communication, which limits the book's value for those working in online communication.

"Research on Computer-Supported Cooperative Work" (Olson & Olson, 1997)

This chapter in the book by Martin Helander et al. provides an excellent overview of major research and development contributions in CSCW. Many of the concepts discussed in this chapter, such as social presence, are also addressed in this work.

"Distance Matters" (Olson & Olson, 2000)

This paper is an interesting follow-up to the work cited in the preceding listing. It reviews much of the work by the two authors and others in the field, and provides a compelling justification for the types of communication and situations that are well suited to online transfer. The overall conclusion is that, for many types of interactions, "distance matters."

"Empathic Communities: Reaching out across the Web" (Preece, 1998), and "Empathic Communities: Balancing Emotional and Factual Communication" (Preece, 1999a)

These papers describe studies of empathy in online communities, which is particularly important in health support communities but is also evident in other communities. Online community developers need to seek better ways of supporting empathy, as well as information exchange.

Connections: New Ways of Working in the Networked Organization (Sproull & Kiesler, 1991)

This seminal work describes computer networking within organizations and how it is changing the way people work. It contains many insights about the benefits and problems of electronic discussion groups.

The Psychology of the Internet (Wallace, 1999)

I encourage everyone to read this book. Lucidly written, it provides an excellent and enjoyable account of why people behave as they do on the Internet.

6 Research Speaks to Practice: Groups

The individual is what he is and has the significance that he has not so much by virtue of his individuality, but rather as a member of a great human community, which directs his material and spiritual existence from the cradle to the grave.

—Albert Einstein, *Ideas and Opinions* (as quoted in Murphy, 1978, p. 164)

This chapter focuses on social interactions in large groups, communities, and networks. As in the previous chapter, much of the research discussed is borrowed from other disciplines, particularly sociology and social psychology. Practically oriented developers who are not strongly interested in research should nonetheless skim this chapter to gain insights into sociability and design.

Contents

Studio System
Mark Kostabi 1991 © Kostabi World

Millions of people flock on the Internet every day in search of community, to interact with others, to find out what's happening, and to feel part of things. This chapter expands on the issue of community begun in *Chapter 1*. To start, it considers mass communication and examines the relationship between interactivity and common ground. Next it delves into social networks and network analysis, established sociological concepts for explaining social interaction and for defining community in physical environments. Network analysis is based on the premise that resources and relationships determine human behavior in social networks. Although only a small body of research demonstrates the efficacy of network analysis in online communities, it promises to be useful in this field.[1]

Cooperation and trust help build online communities, just as in physical communities. This chapter examines how such concepts are manifest online. Carefully crafted policies can play a major role in guiding behavior, supporting cooperation, and deterring antisocial behavior that destroys trust. Such policies are key to enabling online community developers to support sociability. This chapter ends by considering how social interaction and design can be related in online communities via the notion of participatory design.

Critical Mass

Common-ground theory (*Chapter 5*) can be used to explain communication in pairs and small groups, but how might it apply to the kinds of mass interactions observed

---

[1] The discussion in this chapter draws heavily on the ideas of sociologist Barry Wellman and his colleagues, Laura Garton, Milena Gulia, and Caroline Haythornthwaite, which help to explain social behavior on the Internet.

in UseNet newsgroups (Smith, 1999), bulletin boards, chats, and listservers? In a study of 2.15 million messages from 659,450 participants, collected from 500 UseNet newsgroups over a six-month period (Whittaker, Terveen, Hill, & Cherny, 1998), *cross-posting*, in which participants posted the same message to several different groups, was common. Interestingly, although cross-posting may introduce irrelevant topics, it appeared to stimulate conversation, according to this study. Although a focused discussion establishes common ground, such conversations may grow stale; thus they benefit from outside comments. This suggests an interesting balance: too many off-topic comments will deter common ground; too little variation causes boredom. To achieve an ideal balance, many factors may be involved, and the problem for developers is knowing which are most important (Rogers, 1986; Rafaeli & LaRose, 1993).

The number of people an online community needs to attract others is known as its *critical mass*. The community will be perceived as worth joining only if there are sufficient people and enough activity to make it interesting and worthwhile (Markus, 1987, 1990; Morris & Ogan, 1996; Rice, 1994). Too few people, and there will not be sufficient discussion to retain people's interest and draw them back; too many participants, and the community may become chaotic, and people will start to leave. Lurking too will not prove worthwhile unless there is a critical mass of people to generate interesting content (Morris & Ogan, 1996).

The concept of critical mass has been used to explain the success or failure of technology adoption, for example, of a BITNET communication network in major universities in the United States (Rice, 1994) and of an electronic messaging system by a small government office (Rice, Grant, Schmitz, & Torobin, 1990). Critical mass has also been used to explain interactions in CMC, CSCW, and groupware systems (Ackerman & Starr, 1995). However, even though it is a useful, easily understood, common-sense concept, its value is limited because it is difficult to quantify. That said, with greater understanding of the dynamics of online communities, it may be possible to suggest the number of participants or messages needed to make a particular community viable and to ensure its growth. Undoubtedly, critical mass will vary from community to community, according to its focus and personalities, and its participants' needs, activities, and policies.

Critical mass is useful for online community developers who are prepared to intervene and stimulate discussion to draw people into the community. Various techniques are used for this. Moderators, for example, may introduce topical issues (Berge, 1992). E-commerce retailers use online communities to draw people to their Web sites. To do this, they also use special news items, and invite celebrities into their chat rooms. When the discussion appears to be progressing without intervention, it can be assumed that critical mass has been reached. A case could also be made for forcing similar communities to unite in order to achieve critical mass. Alternatively, the apparently harsh action of "pulling the plug" on some communities so that their participants migrate and unite to form a viable unit might have overall benefits. Still, more research on how to measure critical mass is needed to operationalize the theory. Research on mass activity in UseNet newsgroups (Smith, 1999; Whittaker, Terveen, Hill, & Cherny, 1998) and listserver communities (Nonnecke & Preece, 2000a) is a step in the right direction.

Networks and Network Analysis

Communities rely on relationships for their growth, but, as *Chapter 1* explained, defining community is not straightforward. Some definitions accept short-term interactions as part of the criteria, as in many UseNet news communities; but others claim that long-term relationships are necessary, questioning whether an exchange of one or two messages constitutes a community. If someone feels he or she belongs to a community, is that a good enough basis for a definition? Not for most sociologists, who look for evidence of longer-term relationships and networks of relationships.

Networks

For over one hundred and twenty years sociologists have been studying the concept of community (Wellman, 1997) in physical environments. More recently, researchers have started to explore whether these well-known concepts are transferable, and hence useful for explaining online communities. This section starts by defining some terms and then delves into some of these concepts.

Basic terms

In both physical and virtual worlds people are connected in social networks by social *relations*, such as friendship, work-related; or information exchange (Garton, Haythornthwaite, & Wellman, 1999, p. 75). *Communities* and *groups* comprise social networks of people or organizations or other social entities (Wellman, 1997; Garton et al., 1999). A *group* is a special type of network whose members are highly inter-connected. Groups may be closely knit and maintain many different kinds of relations. Their members may also be tightly bound and maintain connections more with each other than with others outside of the group.

Network analysts use the term "group" in a rather specialized way. They rely on their data to determine the degree to which a group is a community. Groups that share important resources, provide social support, and show reciprocity are considered communities. Though most online community developers are not interested in this level of detail, they recognize that the term community is reserved for these more meaningful relationships and therefore may be helpful because it makes it possible to distinguish among different levels of human commitment. Even though e-commerce entrepreneurs are not expecting strong commitment like this, nevertheless the knowledge may be relevant for measuring the success of networked neighborhoods, schools, and support groups.

Understanding the strength of the ties that sustain these relationships is also useful. People who have *strong ties*, such as family relations, share many resources and depend on one another. Typically, those with whom we are tightly linked are the ones who offer to help in times of sickness or other difficult times (Granovetter, 1982). They are the people to whom we pour out our hearts in times of distress and from whom we expect to receive or give support. In contrast people who have *weak ties* tend to share fewer resources and depend less on each other, especially emotionally (Granovetter, 1973). The average person may have several hundred weak ties, compared with very few strong ties. That is not to say that relationships based on weak ties are not important. In fact, such ties are important for learning about new ideas, getting information, meeting new people, and many other reasons (Granovetter, 1973, 1982).

Change of focus

Chapter 1 introduced different interpretations of the term community. The concept may seem intuitively obvious (Jones, 2000), but even the *Dictionary of Sociology* (Abercrombie, 1988) admits that "the term community is one of the most elusive and vague in sociology, and is by now largely without specific meaning." So, though debating the concept of community may be fodder for academic study, it contributes little to informing design. Still, understanding why most sociologists view community in terms of social networks of relationships helps to inform online community development because it serves to indicate why some communities survive and others do not.

There are many definitions of community (Hillery, 1955) and each of us probably has a different image of what constitutes a community based on our individual experiences. For many people, the word conjures up pictures of small, picturesque villages in pleasant rural settings. Not surprisingly, many sociologists associate the term with a geographical location, where friends, neighbors, colleagues, and family gather to live, work, and play. Thinking of communities in terms of spaces was more appropriate prior to the Industrial Revolution (Jones, 1997). Prior to the Industrial Revolution people lived in close proximity to one another, and most of their needs were met from others in their local community. The community was tightly bounded and self-sufficient. But with the advent of technologies—better transport, the telephone, and, more recently email and other computer-mediated communication—people spread out to new geographical locations. The result is that family relationships and friendships now have to be supported over long distances. Consequently, people today rely much less on locally based relationships than fifty years ago.

Although defining communities in terms of physical location and boundedness is common, some sociologists focus more strongly on social networks of relationships, which were not necessarily restricted to a particular geographic region (Garton et al., 1999; Wellman, 1997). Identifying which relationships were weak and which were strong also is proving useful (Granovetter, 1973, 1982) because it explains how people get their needs met, how information and other resources flow through the network, and therefore, what shapes social networks.

Networks and online communities

Prior to public acceptance and widespread use of the Net, many people living in north America and Europe may have known large numbers of people, but usually they had active ties with only around twenty (Kochen, 1989). With access to email, lists, bulletin boards, chats, MUDs and MOOs, suddenly people had easy access to hundreds, even thousands of people worldwide. For many, online access has spawned new relationships both in type and quantity, with people down the road, in the next office, or in far-flung corners of the globe. Often, these relationships are interwoven in rich and varied ways with offline relationships. In short, the Net enables people to extend their sphere of relationships and influence across the world.

An article entitled "Virtual Communities as Communities: Net Surfers Don't Ride Alone" (Wellman & Gulia, 1998) provided a useful framework for most of the discussion that follows, though it set out to answer slightly different questions than those raised and addressed here. (Readers are *strongly* encouraged to read the original article; and details are provided in Further Reading.)

Are strong ties possible online?

In contemporary physical communities most members can be said to really know only family, and small clusters of friends. And even these close relationships, those based on strong ties, provide only a few kinds of social support. Instead, most people tend to get their needs met through a larger variety of people with whom they have weaker ties.

More and more people are going online in search of social support and companionship as well as to get information. Wellman and Gulia (1998) report that many online relationships exhibit strong ties similar to offline relationships, namely, they are marked by: frequency, companionable contact, mutual reciprocity, supportiveness, and longevity. In fact, the online format enables some relationships to endure when otherwise they would probably flounder because of geographical distance. As noted earlier (*Chapters 1, 3, 5*), many examples of strong online relationships have been reported. For example, Hiltz and Turoff report that "some participants come to feel that their closest friends were members of their electronic group whom they seldom or never saw" (Hiltz & Turoff, 1993). Indeed, Walther (also discussed in *Chapter 5*) suggests that the longer people stay in contact online, the stronger their tie tends to become (Walther, Anderson, & Park, 1994).

In summary, there can be no doubt that strong ties do form online.

Are weak ties useful? If so, how?

Relationships in some online communities can and do exist primarily for information exchange (Kling, 1996). Listservers and bulletin boards have been used for this express purpose for many years. For example, members of the special-interest group in Computer-Human Interaction (CHI) (*chi-announcements@acm.org*) can broadcast conference and workshop announcements or request information. The ties among members of such communities are weak. For example, even though many participants meet at the annual CHI conference and have offline contact as well, they do not support each other emotionally or financially—at least not within the structure of the listserver community.

However, there are other, richer channels for communication. Relationships develop between small groups or individuals, via email, in-person visits, or collaborative work. Other bonds may be kindled by spouses and entire families getting to know one another. Social networks are rarely, if ever, as tightly bounded as when based on a single communication channel. Many communities now operate partly online and partly offline. For example, may successful e-commerce ventures build on their established reputations as brick-and-mortar vendors.

Interestingly, some sociologists are asking whether weak ties are easier to maintain online. There is evidence, for example, that distance education students do not find maintaining weak ties online any easier than when colocated (Haythornthwaite, 2000). Currently, not enough evidence is available to answer this question definitively. It may depend on the individuals involved and their experiences with technology. Certainly, those who are used to communicating online find that using email and engaging in various forms of online community are good for maintaining weak ties. But those with less exposure to the digital world may still incur overheads in using these systems, making the advantages less clear-cut.

The important point to make about weak ties is that they are relatively easy to maintain, and can be important for obtaining information, making new contacts, raising awareness of new ideas, and so on.

Does reciprocity occur online, and how is it related to group identity?

"It is a general norm of community that whatever is given ought to be repaid, if only to ensure that more is available when needed. Repayment of support and social resources might be in the form of exchanges of the same kind of aid, reciprocating in another way or helping a mutual friend in the network" (Wellman & Gulia, 1998, p. 177).

Sociologists and online community researchers following or engaging in the debate about what constitutes an online community put great store on the concept of reciprocity. The fact that people can be anonymous online (in that they may never see each other, choose to disguise their identity, and can vanish without trace by pressing a few keys), makes it tempting for many to *take* from the community without repaying (*Chapter 5*). Another phenomenon—feeling a strong sense of community without ever contributing, that is, lurking—is also common (Nonnecke & Preece, 1999). As noted earlier, over 80 to 90 per cent of people lurk in some communities (Nonnecke & Preece, 2000a). Some analysts suggest that the greater the physical distance between people, the less likely it is that reciprocity will occur; nevertheless, there is considerable evidence of reciprocity online, both between those linked by weak ties and strong ties.

Other analysts suggest that people who develop a strong social regard and identity with their social system are likely to make return offers of help, if not to the same person then to others in the system (Constant, Sproull, & Kiesler, 1996 in Wellman & Gulia, 1998).

Interestingly, some evidence from social identity theory suggests that people do not need to be co-present, and that social presence (*Chapter 5*) may even distract from a sense of group identity (Lea & Spears, 1991; Whitworth & Turoff, 2000).

Establishing a strong group identity appears to change the way people behave online (Spears, Russell, & Lee, 1990), which bodes well for group identity on the Internet. It also helps to explain the many examples of apparent altruism, where those who have benefited in the past feel a sense of obligation to help others (e.g., Preece, 1998).

Another interesting phenomenon in online communities is how status plays out in group and personal identity and how it affects the common good online. By contributing to the group, a participant can get credit and bolster his or her standing. For example, despite the risks of getting caught, many hackers keep the same alias for long periods so that others will see their clever work. It's like signing a painting or a clever criminal leaving a tell-tale mark. On the more positive side, there are people in online health support communities, who are long recovered, but who come back to share their experience, to help, and to offer support to current sufferers (Preece, 1999b).

Because group size is usually unknown on the Net, this may encourage people to be more generous. As the adage states, there is safety in numbers—unless you are the person in need of help (Wallace, 1999, p. 196). Many horrifying examples exist of people being mugged or murdered in crowded places and no one coming forward to help. The point is, a group identity may discourage altruism to those outside of the group. However, not knowing who is in the group may counter this tendency. As psychologist Patricia Wallace points out, it takes remarkably little to create a sense of group identity; a group T-shirt or cap will often do the trick (Wallace, 1999). A shared interest in an online group, even though not visible, may have the same effect, as found in a study of WMST-L, an unmoderated list for people interested in women's studies (Korenman, 1999), though gender identification may also have played a part in this study as most participants were women.

For various reasons having to do with personal and group psychology, reciprocity can be strong online, even when social ties are weak. This offers great hope for online community developers. As long as people return to the group, which is often achieved by ensuring fresh information, reciprocity is likely to occur, which will benefit both the group and the individuals in it.

How does the concept of boundedness apply to online communities?

Boundedness refers to the ways in which communities are limited. The term is a legacy from the study of villages and towns with distinct boundaries, which also served to determine the majority of social relationships among people. Other bounds are set by requiring people to register or by setting membership conditions. Intranet communities within companies, for example, are bounded. So although the notion of boundedness still exists online, it is not dictated by geography. Being bounded implies that membership and, consequently, the number of weak ties that people may have are limited, which in turn reduces flow of new information into the group. In some circumstances, boundedness may encourage strong ties through group identity. An unfortunate outcome of this is that members of hate groups and others on the margin of society may also develop strong ties that can have broader—and disastrous—social consequences.

How do online communities affect "real-life" communities?

Even as we participate in online experiences, it is important to keep in mind our ties to the physical world. Without question, developing relationships online is a part of living in an increasingly technical world, but doing so takes time. This raises the question. How does time spent online affect how we live our physical lives? Are online relationships taking the place of close "real-life" relationships? Are people opting to seek advice, companionship, support from online buddies rather than spouses, friends next door, or family living down the road? *Chapter 1* cited evidence that America, and probably other parts of the technologically developed world, are relinquishing their social capital (Putnam, 1995), perhaps because technology enables people to get their needs met without leaving their homes. Consequently, it is suggested that as Americans choose to spend more time physically alone, many are becoming lonely, and are becoming less involved in strong relationships. In other words, strong ties may be getting substituted for many weak ties.

On the other hand, and concomitantly, as the Internet accelerates the trend of people moving away from interacting in physical community spaces, it may also help to *integrate* society and to foster social trust and increase social capital (Putnam, 1995), by making it easier for people to stay in contact and build new relationships. For example, the Internet is valuable for disseminating information to a group, to help members organize action and plan future activities. The advantages of weak ties have already been discussed. What remains to be seen is whether the Internet diminishes preexisting strong family and community ties. Further research is needed to answer this question.

Network analysis: philosophy and techniques

Social network analysis provides a philosophy and set of techniques for understanding how people and groups relate to each other. This philosophy and these techniques have been used extensively by sociologists (Wellman, 1982, 1992) and communication researchers (Rice, 1987a, 1988, 1994; Rice et al., 1990), library and information scientists, social informatics researchers, and others. The aim of social network analysis is to describe *why* people communicate individually or in groups. "Social network analysts seek to describe networks of relations as fully as possible, tease out the prominent patterns in such networks, trace the flow of information (and other resources) through them, and discover what effects these relations and networks have on people and organizations" (Garton, Haythornwaite & Wellman, 1999, p. 76). "It makes sense to use social network analysis to understand the patterns of relationships that people have online, in addition to the fine-grained analyses of online dyads" (Wellman, 1997, p. 181).

Social network analysis focuses on relations between people, rather than on characteristics of individuals, such as gender, age, socioeconomic status and so on. Relations comprising the unit of study include family relationships, communications links between people in an organization, support relationships, friendship structure, and others. Analysts look for resources that are exchanged in creating and maintaining social relationships. These relations can be strong or weak, uni- or bidirectional, and occur over long or short periods of time. Social network analysts look for ties that connect people by one or more relations. Pairs who maintain strong ties are likely to share what resources they have, even though for some people, these resources may be severely limited. In contrast, weakly tied people are less likely to share resources, although having many weak ties generally provides access to more diverse types of resources because each person in the relationship operates in different social networks (Garton et al., 1999). This may help to explain why cross-posting online appears to stimulate activity in the UseNet study cited earlier (Whittaker et al., 1998).

When there are many relations among people, they are described as *multiplex*. Typically, multiplex ties are more intimate, supportive, and durable (Wellman, 1992; Haythornthwaite & Wellman, 1998) and are maintained via more forms of media (Haythornthwaite, 1996). A question that developers want online community researchers to answer is how, and in what ways, do multiplex relations develop over time? Online community developers also need to determine what kind of software, and sociability and usability, supports development of weak and strong ties for communities with different needs.

Network analysts study online relationships either of a whole community or of a key group of people in a large population community. In *whole network* analysis, each individual or a sample of individuals is asked to report their connections with the other members of the network. This approach is most suitable for studying formal networks with clearly identifiable boundaries and small populations (such as departments, clubs or societies, or family groups), or an online community in which membership is restricted, as in a company intranet.

Communities composed of large networks with ill-defined boundaries are analyzed by identifying key people in the community, the *egos*, making them the *center* of the network, and attempting to identify those with whom they have ties, the *alter egos*.

The egos are asked to identify the people who form their social network (the alters). This approach reveals the range and variety of connectivity of these key individuals within the community. However, because the number of people involved can be very large this means that information is rarely collected about all these people.

The type of data collected in *whole network* and *ego-centered* analysis is broadly similar. Data is collected using questionnaires, interviews, diaries, observations, computer monitoring, and ethnography. Figure 6.1 shows part of a typical questionnaire (Garton et al., 1999, p. 91). Most researchers agree that a combination of these approaches provides the best results. Various well-known software tools for this purpose are also available, such as NUDIST, for organizing ethnographic data and identifying patterns in the data. Statistical analysis tools (SPSS and SAS) are used to help analyze the data into matrices and network diagrams, known as *sociograms*, like those in Figures 6.2 and 6.3 (Garton et al., 1999, p. 97). Notice how these diagrams help convey changes in the network of people after computer-mediated communication is introduced. Automated tools also help in network analysis, for example, UCINET (Borgatti, Everett, & Freeman, 1999) and krackplot (Krackhardt, Blythe, & McGrath, 1994).

The Internet is especially interesting for network analysts because it offers a variety of community networks. However, it is also challenging to track because it is really a network of networks. Furthermore some networks, such as many UseNet news communities, are very loosely knit; members have considerable autonomy and move between groups freely, making it hard for researchers to track them. In addition, the continual growth of the Internet makes it difficult for researchers to stay on top of group memberships that are constantly changing and growing. Still, network analysis

	1	2	3	4	5	6	7	8	9	10
1. Overall how often did you interact with this person on work-related activities?										
In unscheduled face-to-face meetings?										
In scheduled face-to-face meetings?										
By telephone?										
By electronic mail?										
By paper letters or memos?										
By tele-(audio)conferencing?										
By videoconferencing?										

Figure 6.1 Part of a survey on communications patterns

Garton et al., 1999 p.91. Reproduced by permission of Sage Publications, Inc.

helps to answer questions about who talks to whom, about what, using which media (Haythornthwaite, 2000), as well as how ties are maintained or change over time. Sociologists can also determine whether networks in online communities form a social group or a community, according to their definitions of these terms (Wellman, 1997).

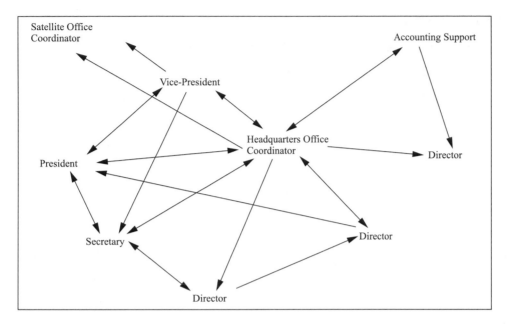

Figure 6.2   One example of a sociogram

Garton et al., 1999. Reproduced by permission of Sage Publications, Inc.

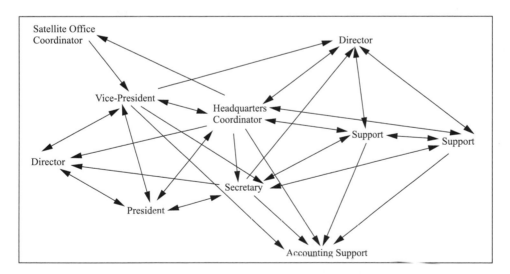

Figure 6.3   A second sociogram example, after CMC was introduced

Garton et al., 1999. Reproduced by permission of Sage Publications, Inc.

There is no denying that network analysis requires expertise and takes time, so it is unlikely that online community developers will do such analysis themselves. However, they can learn from sociologists about the nature of online relationships and how these relationships are affected by sociability and usability, to inform their work in online community development.

Cooperation and Trust

Successful communities are built on cooperation and trust. In practice, however, behavior that seems reasonable to one person, and gets their needs met, may damage the group. As already discussed, reciprocity is a central concern for communities. But given the potential problems caused by the absence of social presence, anonymity and the ability to simply leave a community (*Chapter 5*), how can cooperation and trust develop in online communities?

Cooperation

The tension between what is best for the group and what is best for the individual is known as a *social dilemma* (Kollock, 1998). Social dilemmas are common, and potentially destructive, so they are of central interest to psychologists, sociologists, and anthropologists. In his explanation of trust online, Peter Kollock draws on one of the best-known studies, Axelrod's two-prisoner dilemma (1984), three of whose conditions for cooperation may be relevant to online communities (Kollock, 1998).

The first of these conditions is that the chance of two individuals meeting again in the future must be high, otherwise people may be tempted to take what they want from the community without worrying about the effect of their behavior on others because there are no future implications (Walther, 1994). Thus, the presence of ongoing relationships is important. Communities, such as UseNet News, where people can visit and leave without commitment and consequences discourages cooperation and civil behavior. Though, often, there are no consequences to the individual, the effect of his or her inappropriate behavior on the community can be devastating, especially in support communities (Preece, 1999b). As noted throughout this book, requiring people to register to join a community may help to deter casual hopping from community to community. Reciprocity and trust need to be supported within the context of ephemeral online relations (Rice, 1987b) by registration.

The second condition is that people must be able to identify one another, so that everyone knows who is responsible for a given message or comment. This condition has far-reaching implications for online communities, particularly for text-based environments where it may not be easy to identify a person. On the other hand, as *Chapter 5* pointed out, there can also be advantages from not being able to make quick, superficial judgments based on a person's appearance, as tends to happen in the offline world. Likeminded people like each other more than those from whom they differ (Granovetter, 1982; Walther, 1994), and sharing a passion or a problem in a discussion may foster cooperation more effectively than would happen offline.

The third condition is that there be a record of past behavior and the probability of future interactions, so that those who cooperate and those who do not can be separated out. Anticipation of future meetings is a powerful incentive for encouraging people to behave reasonably (Walther, 1994). But most people communicate with many different people online, and many online communities are large, so it is difficult to keep track of everyone, particularly without physical contact. Keeping archives may help, but search facilities are also needed, because many archives are difficult to search. In any case, searching takes time, so mechanisms for keeping histories of behavior are also useful. The reputation manager in eBay is an example of such a mechanism (Kollock, 1999). Every time a product is sold the purchaser is asked to rate the performance of the vendor for various aspects of the service; these ratings are then added to a reputation profile that is available for view by future customers.

The definition of acceptable behavior in a community will depend on the purpose of the community, the activities and attitudes of the people who belong to it, and the policies by which the community governs itself. Education communities, for example, may be less tolerant of heated remarks than, say, political communities. Medical communities may even be less tolerant because of the sensitivity of participants, many of whom are vulnerable.

It doesn't take much to get people to feel part of a face-to-face group (Wallace, 1999). Online, shared interests may be sufficient, even in the absence of the personal cues. However, those who do feel estranged online may feel freer to respond with even more polarized actions. Lack of physical cues online, anonymity, and the ability to disappear without trace clearly have both pluses and minuses for online communities.

Trust

When there is trust among people, relationships flourish; without it, they wither. Most interactions among people or organizations involve some level of trust. Telling someone your innermost thoughts, empathizing about a medical problem, cooperating on a project, or purchasing a product from an e-commerce company all require trust. The greater the risk associated with the activity, the higher the level of trust is needed. "At the heart of any unsecured transaction is a social dilemma" (Kollock, 1999).

As Howard Rheingold points out, meeting people online is a strange process, one that almost reverses how we do so in person. "[I]n traditional kinds of communities, we are accustomed to meeting people, then getting to know them; in virtual communities, you can get to know people and then choose to meet them" (Rheingold, 1993). Add to this the implications of no physical cues, and the result is the need online for a longer period of time to build trust (*Chapter 5*). Online, trust is somewhat dichotomous: On the one hand, people feel freer to disclose personal details; on the other, lack of actual contact makes trust online fragile.

What exactly is trust? The following definitions provide a basis for understanding the nature of trust in online communities:

> Trust is the expectation that arises within a community of regular, honest, and cooperative behavior, based on commonly shared norms, on the part of the members of the community. (Fukuyama, 1995, p. x)

> Trust is the positive expectation a person has for another person, organization, tool, or process that is based on past performance and truthful future guarantees made by a responsible person or organization. (Shneiderman, 2000)

Trust develops from positive past experiences or is carried by a reputation of responsible, reliable behavior that creates an expectation, a belief, that future interactions with that person, company, or organization will be the same, that "they will live up to expectations." As in the physical world, members of online communities develop trust when promises and expectations are met. "For online communities, specifically, trust is essential because it's the glue that holds together not only your relationship with your members, but the members' relationships with each other. Trust is at the core of any community and any lasting customer relationship. Trust is not granted outright; it must be earned" (Figallo, 1998, p. 83). For certain types of communities, such as many medical and e-commerce communities, obviously trust is extremely important. eBay's reputation manager, noted as a mechanism to support cooperation, is also designed to support trust (Kollock, 1999). Giving customers access to information about vendor reputations provides a basis for trust.

Trust is also important for communities of practice concerned with knowledge exchange and management (Liebowitz, 1999), particularly when sensitive information is involved, such as that which could be detrimental to someone's employment or endanger their ability to get health insurance. Communities in which accepted behavior is defined and monitored are safer places, thus trust in them is easier to develop. For example, a carefully moderated patient support community will encourage more trust than an unmoderated MOO community, where assuming a false persona and role-playing are part of the culture (Turkle, 1995).

When people experience the same response repeatedly, they come to expect it in similar circumstances in the future, and behave accordingly. If their expectations continue to be met, their trust will increase. In the words of Sara Kiesler: "If it walks like a duck and talks like a duck, we are going to treat it like a duck—at least for now. . . . [D]uckliness seems a good clue to its future behavior and how we should respond" (1997 p. 196). Conversely, when people's expectations are not met they are unlikely to continue trusting the person or company that failed them. As in real life, finding ways of supporting and managing trust in online communities is important (Kollock, 1999).

The question is how to encourage trust in online communities, given their diversity and special challenges? Ben Shneiderman suggests a model for facilitating trust (2000), which, though geared toward e-commerce, may be of benefit in other online communities. The model has three components. The first is to clarify the context in which negotiations or interactions are to occur. For example, people or companies can provide evidence of who they are, which could be in the form of competence and past performance in business or a statement of long-term involvement in a community. The second component is to make clear and truthful commitments. In a business or health community, this might include guaranteeing the quality of a product or service; committing to being timely and cooperative; ensuring privacy and security (via an explicit policy with guarantees, for example); or promising to take responsibility for failures and to remedy the problem. The third component is to recognize that trust involves taking a risk, though doing so is based on a good reputation of quality and reliability. Evidence and guarantees are helpful for this component.

Encouraging community members to be responsive and reliable will help to build community trust; but first members must be made aware that trust is valued in the community (Goleman, 1995). To date, recording past behavior and building in expectations of future meetings help to foster trust and group identity online, but more powerful and explicit ways may be needed in the future for this still-new medium, which has specific challenges.

Social Informatics

This section asks the question, if "the medium is the message" as Marshall McLuhan stated in 1960, how can community involvement and social values be encouraged in the design, development, and use of technology that supports online communities?

Social informatics is the term used to characterize research on the *social aspects* of computerization. It is concerned with the interdisciplinary study of the design, uses, and consequences of information technologies within social and cultural contexts (Kling, 1999). The *social context* of information technology development and use plays a significant role in influencing how people work with it, which in turn influences their social relationships. For example, consider two electronic journal systems set up to work with their editorial boards in quite different ways (Kling,

1999). One electronic journal encourages numerous links to other people and infor-mation, thereby forming a thriving community through discussion of articles that includes authors and readers. In the other system, a review panel is organized and controlled by an editor, with no opportunity for discussion of articles. The review process is quick, efficient, and anonymous. Clearly, community involvement in the two systems will be very different.

Historically, the design of artifacts, particularly those involving media, have had strong social and political impact. Johannes Gutenberg's printing press made mass distribution of his bibles possible. Radio broadcasting helped shape events during the Second World War by motivating national support for the cause. Today, we are witnessing the doctor-patient relationship being transformed by the Internet. Empowered by the information they find online, patients approach their doctors on a more equal basis, and force doctors to stay up-to-date with medical advances. Some doctors embrace this change; others are annoyed or feel threatened by patients taking this initiative, feeling that their expertise is being challenged (Kahin & Keller, 1995).

Several questions emerge for online community developers who impart social and moral values (Friedman, 1997, p. 1). For example, how can they collect knowledge about social informatics and translate it into concrete design? They must be sensitive to and aware of the potential social implications of design, especially when used in conjunction with design methods that take account of social and cultural environ-ments, as well as technical issues, as occurs in *sociotechnical systems design* (Eason, 1988). In sociotechnical systems design, system refers to the whole network of users, technology, and environments in which the system will be used. The design process explicitly acknowledges that the design has social and political cachet. Design, therefore, cannot be done independent of the social system in which it will be implemented. Software that will be embedded in a social process should be designed as part of that social process. One way to achieve this is to invite users to participate in online community development through participatory design (Greenbaum & Kyng, 1991; Schuler, 1996; Schuler & Namioka, 1993) and development. *Part Two* discusses how to do this.

Summary

Research that informs the development of online community will take time to complete. Until then, online community developers can borrow from sociology, communications studies, computer-supported cooperative work, and social psychology. This chapter concludes *Part One*. To review, *Chapter 5* focused on individuals and small groups, whereas this chapter looked at the sociological view, in which social network analysis and associated research was used to explain online relationships. This approach drew on some of the same basic psychological knowledge that was discussed in *Chapter 5*, so though the assumptions that can be drawn are different, they are strongly complementary. Some of the same issues were raised, but in a new light. They included lack of physical cues, anonymity, and limited awareness of others. Knowledge of these issues is not, however, the same as knowing how to deal with them. The social context in which interactions occur can be complex, fragile, and highly susceptible to even minor changes.

What, then, are the conclusions that can be drawn from this chapter to inform online community development? One, that people can be remarkably supportive even to strangers with whom they have only very weak ties. In this situation, the absence of physical cues is an advantage because people are less likely to make snap judgments about each other. Furthermore, it seems to make people feel freer to disclose information about themselves and to want to help others. Two, that strong ties can form online, though they often take longer than in offline interactions. Three, that interacting over a period of time with a defined community appears to discourage aggression and flaming. Four, that group identity online seems to be stimulated by common interests and shared experience, in the absence of physical and/or cultural connections that often drive offline relationships. Five, that being anonymous seems to encourage people to more readily reach out to help. The so-called by-standers phenomenon does not seem to happen online as it does in physical environments. Six, that, unfortunately, online people may more easily give in to inappropriate behavior because of the "hit-and-run" atmosphere online.

These conclusions raise the questions, what can online developers do to ensure good outcomes online—the formation of appropriate and strong ties, as well as a rich network of weak ties that generate new information and traffic to the community? To begin, developers can relate these research findings to the community's purpose, to the kind of people in the community, and to the policies that guide the community's development.

To close, it is important to note that the distinction between online and physical communities is becoming increasingly blurred (Lazar & Preece, 1998). Communities that either exist only online or offline will become rarer as greater numbers of people gain Internet access. Whether participating in online communities will supplement or detract from "real-life" relationships remains to be seen. Today, social capital is decreasing in America, and possibly in other Westernized societies (Putnam, 1995), so certainly there is reason for concern but also reason for hope, because the Internet can be used to connect people.

Further Reading

"Studying online social networks" (Garton, Haythornthwaite, & Wellman, 1999)

This chapter in *Doing Internet Research* (edited by Steve Jones) gives a good account of the basic practices of network analysis. In addition to defining terms and describing the processes of network analysis, this chapter gives useful examples of data collection and analysis.

"Work, Friendship, and Media Use for Information Exchange in a Networked Organization" (Haythornthwaite & Wellman, 1998), and "Community Development Among Distance Learners: Temporal and Technological Dimensions" (Haythornthwaite, Guziec, Robins, & Shoemaker, 2000)

The first paper is the report of a study done on work and friendship in an organization. It is a clear example of how to pose and test hypotheses using network analysis, and reports interesting results. The second paper discusses a virtual community study that was much informed by the social network approach.

"What is Social Informatics and Why does it Matter?" (Kling, 1999)

This paper insightfully discusses how technical design impacts social processes as well as individuals. It is a must-read, in that it contains an important message, written in a clear and enjoyable style, for both users and technology designers.

"Internet Paradox: A Social Technology that Reduces Social Involvement and Psychological Well-being?" (Kraut et al., 1998), and "Internet and Society. Preliminary Report." (Nie & Ebring, 2000)

These articles describe studies done to determine the impact of the Internet on social behavior; they raise controversial, disturbing questions, in particular, does intensive Internet usage lead to depression and loneliness?

"Studying Personal Communities" (Wellman, 1982)

This early account of network analysis describes how the technique was used to study physical communities, citing examples of its application to East York, a community outside of Toronto. This chapter in the book *Social Structure and Network Analysis* contains clear definitions and example analyses. Those not familiar with the technique will find value in understanding its original application before considering how it can be used for CMC networks.

"An Electronic Group is Virtually a Social Network" (Wellman, 1997)

This chapter in *Culture of the Internet* edited by Sara Kiesler explains why network analysis is valuable for studying CMC networks. In particular, it clearly positions network analysis as an approach with techniques for examining relationships among larger numbers of people, rather than just dyads, the unit of study for much CMC work done by human–computer interaction researchers.

"Virtual Communities as Communities: Net Surfers Don't Ride Alone" (Wellman & Gulia, 1998b) or this article appears as a chapter "Net Surfers Don't Ride Alone" in *Networks in the Global VIllage* edited by Barry Wellman (Wellman & Gulia, 1999) The *Networks* section of this chapter contains a discussion of social networks and a list of questions based on this source. Readers are strongly encouraged to read the original for a rich background of sociological concepts, illustrated with many examples. It is compelling reading for anyone interested in the sociology of online communities.

Part Two

Developing Online Communities

A building cannot be a human building unless it is a complex of still smaller buildings or smaller parts which manifest its own internal social facts.

Vary the ceiling heights continuously throughout the building . . . in particular, make ceilings high in rooms which are public or meant for large gatherings (10 to 12 feet), lower in rooms for smaller gatherings (7 to 9 feet), and very low in rooms or alcoves for one or two people (6 to 7 feet).

—Alexander, Ishikawa, Silverstein, Jacobson, Fiksdahl-King & Angel, *A Pattern Language* (1977)

Part Two, Developing Online Communities starts with *Chapter 7*, a discussion of community-centered development. After giving an overview of the process, it explains how to learn about user needs and highlights the importance of analyzing user tasks. The chapters that follow examine specific parts of the process in more detail.

Chapter 8 addresses selecting software for online community development. Although products change rapidly and new ones appear every day, usability design, both good and bad, can be judged, to enable wise selections. To that end, this chapter points out features to look for in different types of software. Though written primarily with developers and software enthusiasts in mind, this information avoids too much technical detail, to make it valuable to all interested readers.

Chapter 9 offers guidelines to help online community developers provide good sociability support and design good usability. It draws on knowledge presented in *Part One*, particularly *Chapters 3* through *6*. Examples and a user's perspective make this material more readily understandable and, therefore, usable.

Chapter 10 reviews techniques that can be used to collect information about user needs and then to evaluate how well communities meet these needs at different stages of development.

Chapter 11 comprises example cases of online community development, to practically describe the development process and explain why various sociability and usability decisions were made.

Chapter 12 takes a speculative look toward the future, addressing most of the issues discussed in the book. It then comments on future research needed to solve crucial issues.

Contents

7 Community-Centered Development

Building a community is a fundamentally different activity than [sic] writing computer code . . .

—Peter Kollock and Marc Smith, *Managing the Virtual Commons* (1996)

This chapter provides an overview of the community-centered development (CCD) process, which is a participatory process that involves members of the community. It also explains how to take the first development step in the CCD process—analyzing community needs and tasks. Subsequent steps—obtaining technology, planning social policies, and designing, implementing and testing prototypes; refining and tuning; and welcoming and nurturing the community—are discussed in later chapters.

Day In, Day Out
Mark Kostabi 1991 © Kostabi World

Contents

Online communities, like physical communities, evolve organically, shaped by their members, leaders, and managers. The software supporting the online community and its early social policies also influences how it develops. As people become familiar with each other and/or managers make decisions about how to direct the group, social policies may change. In contrast, there is limited scope for software changes, so it is important to launch with well-designed, carefully selected software.

In some respects, developing online communities is like town planning. Town planners have to map geographical layout and install major services such as electricity, gas, telephone lines, and so on. They must build infrastructures, such as roads, public spaces, shopping facilities, residential housing, and recreational spaces. If a major road is laid through the center of the town, for example, that space becomes unsuitable for a school, town hall, or pedestrian walkway. Or, if shopping is decentralized by developing suburban malls, people will be drawn away from the heart of the town. The point is, one decision may impact upon another, and they all influence social interactions to a greater or lesser extent.

British pubs are prime examples of how a place's physical features and the presence of people impact one another to create a community's social ambience. Visiting a modern pub in the heart of a new town where people leave to go home at 5.30 P.M. feels different from stopping by a 200-year old village pub with small rooms and an open fire, where the locals sip beer and tell stories late into the night.

The relationship between the design of any artifact, the way people use it, and how it both affects and is affected by social norms is complex. (See the discussion of adaptive structuration in *Chapter 4*, p. 142.) Software is no exception. And when the software is intended to support social interaction, understanding this relationship becomes very important. A full investigation of the community's needs and user tasks is required. This is especially important because no two communities are exactly the same, as the community tours showed in *Chapter 2*. In addition, how social processes are planned impacts upon the community, particularly in the early stages of its existence. Ensuring that communities benefit from good usability and sociability is a primary goal for online community developers. In order to achieve this goal, they have to understand the community's needs.

As for any interaction design, developing online communities involves technical considerations. Unlike most other software, for successful online communities, sociability is also essential. Consequently, developing online communities can be challenging because often user populations have not been defined or are not easily reachable. Users may be scattered all over the world, live in vastly different cultures, and use different computer systems. Developers may not even know how many people will use the system; it could be under a hundred, several thousands, or even millions.

This chapter discusses the process of *community-centered development* (CCD). Just as user-centered design (Norman, 1986) puts the user at the center of the design process, the aim of community-centered development is to focus on the community. Community-centered development is participatory. Right from the start, members of the community work with developers to build the community. Community-centered development takes an evolutionary view, in that it recognizes that when software design is complete, the initial social policies are in place, and people start to participate in the online community, an evolutionary process has begun, which will continue over a long period of time. And although most of the developer's role is complete, development continues after the community has been launched, because as community members get to know each other, the community evolves, shaped by their activities and social needs.

Overview of the Community-Centered Development Process

A community's life cycle can be thought of in four stages: prebirth, early life, maturity, and death. Prebirth involves most of the development; during this stage, software is designed or selected, and initial social policies are planned. The activities vary according to whether a new community is being developed or an existing one is being revamped with improved software and new social policies, as in the case studies in *Chapter 11*.

During the early life of the community, the developer's involvement diminishes, but his or her attention and nurturing is still needed to ensure that the community is successfully populated. In maturity, many communities function independently, unless developers see a need for oversight, as in some business communities. Death of a community is brought on when members leave and the discussion slows down or ceases, because it has served its purpose, the number of participants has dropped below the critical mass necessary for it to function (*Chapter 6*), or it has become dysfunctional.

The point at which software design is deemed complete and ready for use marks the start of the community's life. How its members interact and manage the community will determine its evolution. A major reason that communities fail is because their developers assume that once the software is in place their job is done and the community will take care of itself. If they are lucky this may happen, but often more long-term help is needed. An initial *core community* may be created to act as a seed for the community's growth. The core community's activities encourage others to join and, like a seeded crystal, the community grows.

MOOs are the exception. A central theme of MOO communities is that members contribute to the software infrastructure of the community; that is, they build their own software. In some MOOs, contributions include sophisticated graphical metaphors for buildings, such as fantasy homes with tropical gardens, swimming pools, pets, and many others. MOO software development is therefore continuous.

Linux is another interesting exception. Linux, the now-famous operating system, began in 1991 as the private research project of Finnish computer science student Linus Torvalds. This amazing project—described as the "impossible" public good (Kollock, 1998a, p. 230)—has continued to be developed free of charge by the computer science community and is available on the Internet to anyone who wishes to use it. This unusual community and its product are motivated by the compelling technical problem of building a new, more reliable operating system and the political desire for open source code, that provides a strong sense of purpose; thus, both the software and the community continue to develop.

Needless to say, development varies from community to community. For example, a Web-based community that is part of a Web site is different from a non-Web community. Likewise, a community with a strong physical component—such as a networked community—is different from a virtual community. The social needs of the community—that is, its sociability—influences how it develops. For example, as noted, security and trust are particularly important to health and e-commerce communities; and having the capability to comment on articles is important for digital library and academic communities.

Community-centered development

Community-centered development must focus on the community's needs *prior* to making decisions about the technology and social planning. There are two main parts to the process: *software design*, or *selection and tailoring*, and *sociability planning*. Usability is concerned with the appropriateness of the software design for community members' tasks and the community's purpose (*Chapter 4*). Sociability describes the appropriateness of the social policies and plans for guiding social interactions (*Chapter 3*). Both are key components of successful online communities, and as development proceeds they invariably become more closely integrated. As Figure 7.1 indicates, evaluating how well software design and sociability planning meet the community's needs occurs continuously throughout development. Development proceeds iteratively, with many *develop-and-test cycles*, during which community members provide feedback and participate in the development process.

Community-centered development borrows ideas from user-centered design, contextual inquiry, and participatory design. *User-centered design* focuses on users rather than on technology (Norman, 1986). The concept is well understood in interaction design, and a range of techniques are available (see for example, Preece et al., 1994, 2001; Kreitzberg, 1998; Shneiderman, 1998a). User-centered design has been adapted

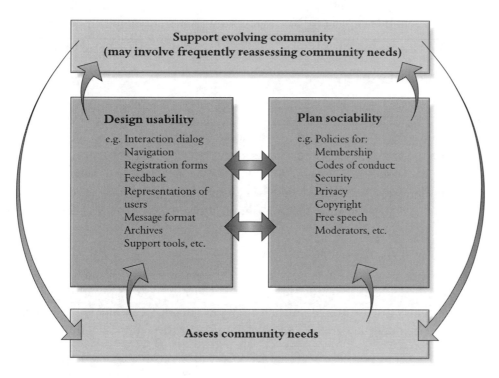

Figure 7.1   Usability and sociability

for a range of systems, including many CSCW (Olson & Olson, 1997). *Contextual inquiry* emphasizes the importance of understanding the user context. "Staying in context enables us to gather ongoing experience rather than summary experience, and concrete data rather than abstract data" (Beyer & Holtzblatt, 1998, p. 47). *Participatory design* (Mumford, 1983; Greenbaum & Kyng, 1991; Muller, 1992; Schuler & Namioka, 1993) advocates strong user and community participation in the design process. Users work with developers throughout the process to explore design ideas and to test and refine the new system. Participatory design has been used successfully to develop community networks (Schuler, 1996) and in the development of a variety of other online communities (Lazar & Preece, 1999a).

To repeat, community-centered development involves continuous iterative develop-and-test cycles. Within this process are five stages, each of which has parallel activities, as shown in Figure 7.2:

- *Assessing community needs and analyzing user tasks.* This stage involves understanding the needs of the community (e.g., what kind of public and private discussion spaces are needed) and examining user tasks (e.g., how does the user actually read or send a message). In order to do both, it is essential to know who will form the community and what they want to do; that is, determine who is the community and what is its purpose? In the language of software deign, this is somewhat akin to requirements analysis, but it focuses on the community's needs.

- *Selecting technology and planning sociability.* During this stage, the community's needs either are broadly mapped to generic technologies or new software is deigned. In this book, this usually means selecting software available via the Internet and tailoring it to provide usability for the intended community. Sociability planning is done in parallel, and policies and social structures are planned.

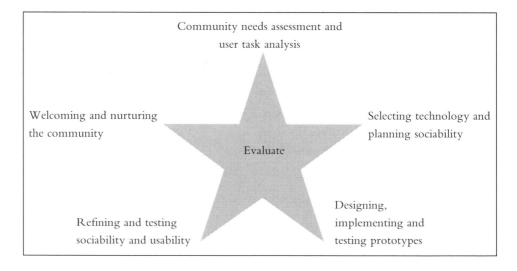

Figure 7.2   Community-centered development

Adapted from Hix and Hartson, 1993

- *Designing, implementing, and testing prototypes.* In this stage, the community's needs are mapped with the features of possible software and the overall conceptual design is determined. For example, having identified a particular bulletin board, it has to be incorporated into the community and linked with Web pages and other software, as appropriate. Interfaces are developed and sociability is planned. This stage can involve many small iterations of design-and-test, with the community in small projects. Large projects with development teams will have a clear schedule with milestones and deliverables.

- *Refining and tuning sociability and usability.* This is the stage in which formal, larger-scale usability and sociability testing is done with the community and problems are resolved. Further testing may be done to refine specific solutions (e.g., perfecting a dialog box, ensuring consistent use of capital letters in a Web site, or clarifying the readability of membership instructions).

- *Welcoming and nurturing the community.* This stage involves "seeding" the community and publicizing it, and, later, welcoming and supporting new members. The community is, ideally, seeded with members who will bring life to it, thereby tempting others to join. A key question developers must answer at this stage is, what will entice people to keep coming back? Also during this stage, community and community leaders (e.g., moderators) learn and define their roles. Community developers also check and monitor hardware and software, typically setting up a help system to deal with misunderstandings and to support participants. Nurturing is important not only early in the community's life, but throughout its existence. Again, communities are dynamic, and change as new people join and others leave, so ongoing support is necessary.

The development team

Multidisciplinary teams work best for community-centered development, meaning they typically comprise social psychologists, sociologists, and others attuned to people's needs. The technical expertise required, for software design and implementation, depends on the size of the project, whether new software is being created or existing software is being tailored, or a community *shell* or template is to be used. And, because usability and sociability are the central issues of community-centered design, the team must have testing skills. Involvement of existent and potential members is also essential.

Team management and goal setting

All project teams, large and small, have to be managed, to ensure that goals are identified, then met. Large corporate project teams will have their own procedures and schedules. Small projects will need to identify a team leader to manage the schedule and ensure that deliverables are ready on time. The following chapters describe the deliverables from each development stage, and can be used as a basis for schedule development.

In addition to identifying major milestones—such as the products from each development stage, or initial, interim, and final project reports and the online community development associated with each stage—it is often useful for the team to set, short-term, interim deadlines. This is particularly helpful for usability and sociability testing, when involvement of community members is particularly important and expert reviewers are needed.

Another important aspect of team management is the splitting up of tasks and the allocation of responsibility to appropriate team members. Apart from participating in brainstorming sessions at the beginning of the project, doing software reviews, and discussing test results, each team member can work on his or her own tasks. Teamwork involves consulting and liaising either face to face or via technology. It is neither productive nor manageable if the team works together all the time. This division of labor clearly requires a mix of complementary skills among the team members.

In a typical three-person development team, the following roles must be filled when developing small online communities, such as those described in *Chapter 11*:

- *A team manager*. Responsible for developing the schedule and ensuring that deliverables including presentations are ready. This person also takes responsibility for the budget and for writing reports.

- *A technical specialist*. Responsible for everything concerning software and hardware. This person guides software selection, obtains necessary products and licenses, builds the online community, and ensures that the server is appropriately managed. This person also hands over the community and software documentation to new community managers at the end of the project and makes sure that the server and community software will be adequately supported.

- *A human-computer interface specialist*. Knowledgeable about sociability and usability. This person is the community advocate. He or she works closely with community members and encourages the team to be sensitive to their needs. This person takes responsibility for community needs and task analysis, plans and runs the user testing and expert reviews (*Chapter 10*), attends to all usability issues, and plans sociability. This specialist also continues to monitor the community after the initial development, to ensure that the community's needs continue to be met. He or she takes action if they are not.

Whenever possible, a team of users is also identified, usually composed of people who have a strong interest in the success of the community. They may have a professional role (e.g., serve as an organization leader) or contribute their time voluntarily (e.g., work as a community activist). Working with the community is more effective when one or two people are identified who will liaise between the community and developers to plan meetings and so on. The more people who can be involved the better, but at least good contacts are needed to help organize the logistics.

Assessing Community Needs and Analyzing User Tasks

The two processes in this stage are the *community needs assessment*, which enables developers to determine the main purpose of the community, and *user task analysis*, which provides information about the actual tasks involved to ensure participation in the community.

Assessing community needs

Presumably, each individual in a community believes he or she will benefit from being part of the community, and so will have preconceived notions about what it can do for them. Thus, the first thing developers must do is to find out who the users will be and what they will expect. For example, will the user population be homogenous, or very mixed in terms of age, gender, culture, knowledge of the topic(s)? But note, it may not be possible to learn the full extent of the user variation at this stage or to reach them if they are widely dispersed. In addition, it is important to determine the user population's level of experience using the Internet and participating in other online communities. The usability requirements of "newbie" Internet users will be different from those of more experienced users or, obviously, technical specialists. Similarly, interfaces for young children and seniors, for example, will have different requirements. *Chapter 4* discussed these issues, and examples of demographic surveys are included in *Chapter 11*.

The next step in assessing community needs is to clearly identify the main purpose(s) of the community that focus its development or redesign. Examples of purposes that communities have been developed to fulfill include:

- A school that wanted to improve communication among its busy faculty and further involve them in the decision-making processes of the administration.

- Anesthesiologists who wanted to share knowledge about new drugs and techniques.

- The Quiz Bowl, a college quiz game community that had several online resources that were scattered, managed by different people, and did not function well. Players wanted to develop a coherent online community free from commercial influences, so that they could discuss ideas and plan tournaments.

- Undergraduate students who wanted to be able to exchange information, find out about courses from those who have taken them, sell used texts, disseminate information about events, and so on.

- A group of researchers and parents of children with Down Syndrome who wanted to develop an advocacy group to report research findings, disseminate information about funding opportunities, and find out about other Down Syndrome communities.

- Parkinson's disease patients who wanted a place to discuss medical treatments and coping strategies, and to find understanding and support.

- An e-commerce business that wanted to develop a community to provide better customer support and entice customers to buy more.

- Distance education students who wanted to make contact with other students studying the same courses.

- A local physical community composed of a number of neighborhoods that wanted a network to discuss local affairs, link the neighborhoods, share resources, and so on.

The developer's role is to gather the information that will lead to a deeper understanding of the community's needs, taking into consideration many factors. For example, each of the purposes listed is much more complex than the one- or two-line description suggests. Social interaction is complex and people's social needs vary according to their age, culture, education, personality, and so on. Groups also take on particular characteristics. There are many ways of finding out about the community's needs. Interviews, whether face to face, over the telephone, or via email, and Web-disseminated or paper-and-pencil questionnaires are two of the most commonly used techniques for obtaining this information (see the examples in *Chapter 11*). Initially, questions focus on the purpose of the community; later, other details are explored.

Often, it is useful to interview the people who suggested starting an online community, as well as others who might want to join it. The answers from the two sources may be quite different. For example, the researchers who wanted to develop the Down Syndrome Online Advocacy Group (DSOAG), were very clear that community members should be able to report and discuss research, whereas parents were more interested in a support community.

If an online community already exists, there will be a population of users who have ideas about how to make it work better, as in the case of the online Quiz Bowl community (see the case study in *Chapter 11*). If a completely new community is being developed, it is important to educate the members about the nature of online communities, so they can participate in its development. Exposing them to other online communities is a good way of achieving this.

If the online community is to support a physical community, and access to members is convenient, it may be worth running a focus group. If part of the community can be reached physically and part via the Internet, as in the Quiz Bowl and DSOAG communities, a combination of methods for eliciting the needs of both populations will probably have to be implemented. This latter is a common situation for online community developers. The developers of Quiz Bowl and DSOAG interviewed available users and passed out paper questionnaires to them, but disseminated online questionnaires to the virtual population.

Understanding the community's needs also involves identifying the main kinds of activities the online community will engage in. Developers must then analyze how the tasks inherent to the various activities will be performed. Do the activities require information dissemination, information exchange, discussion, support, entertainment, social chit-chat, or other?

- *Information dissemination* involves sending messages, announcements, pointers to URLs, articles, and so on to the community. This task may be primarily unidirectional, meaning that posting is supervised by a central person.
- *Information exchange* means that everyone can send and request information, as in most discussion groups. For example, the participants of a usability forum contact each other for information and help with tricky design issues.
- *Discussion* takes place when people discuss and comment on each other's ideas.
- *Support* involves members of the group exchanging information about problems and providing empathy and sympathy for each other.
- *Entertainment* includes participants playing games or circulating jokes.

The developers of the DSOAG worked closely with the group that proposed the community. They also attended meetings of the Down Syndrome community, talked to as many parents and community leaders as possible, and participated in a national walk in Washington, DC. Similarly, the Quiz Bowl team met players at tournaments, where the developers handed out questionnaires, as well as distributing them online.

Analyzing user tasks

This process answers the question what kinds of tasks will community participants undertake? Each of the activities listed in the previous section must be analyzed, as described in *Chapter 4*. For example, what exactly does it mean to disseminate information or to offer and receive support?

Disseminating information involves sending material to a list of other people, so the user has to be able to do so either via an intermediary or by direct access to the list. To do this, he or she has to type in the message and send it or forward an existing message for further circulation.

Offering and receiving support involves reading messages that others have sent and responding. Reading messages requires access to incoming messages; sending messages requires the capability to type in a message and post it to another person, a small group, or the whole community. In addition, it may be useful to be able to distinguish messages with particular types of content.

In summary, then, participation in most online communities involves activities such as:

- Joining and leaving the community, which may entail formal registration and deregistration.
- Receiving and reading messages.
- Composing and sending messages.
- Searching for messages, information, and people in archives.
- Consulting additional sources, such as Web pages and FAQ lists.

All these activities require knowing how to use the computer system to do the task at hand. Logically, making sure that these functions are enabled in an intuitive, easy to master and remember way requires good usability design.

Products resulting from this stage

To better describe typical products resulting from this stage of development, the following example information was collected before developing an online community for bird watchers.

- *The key needs of the community*. The purpose of the community is to inform members of bird sightings, enable them to exchange experiences, and support conservation of wild birds. The needs of the community are:
  To bring together wild bird enthusiasts for discussion.
  To establish a database of sightings.
  To provide a bird identification tool.
  To uphold the purpose of the community, maintain geniality and stimulate social interaction.

- *The tasks that will satisfy these needs (i.e., the information exchange and communication tasks):*
  To establish some kind of discussion forum that will support lengthy comments (e.g., descriptions, explanations, etc.).
  To enable adding records to the database and searching it.
  To enable bird identification using online information.
  To enable discussion with other bird watchers without distractions or the fear of aggressive comments.

- *Demography of population*:
  Members may be all ages, from young children (8 years) to seniors. The majority are age 15–55.
  Most have high school and college educations.
  Two-thirds are male.
  Eighty percent are from North America, 15 percent from Europe.

- *User Internet experience level.* The current population all have Internet experience, but the new community will be advertised through the Sierra Club, the World Wildlife Fund, and leading bird magazines, which will bring new members who may not have Internet experience.

- *Technical constraints* that might influence access (e.g., browser type, Internet connections, processing power). The population will be very diverse, so versions for those with low bandwidth and processing power must be available.

Clearly, the information collected during this stage of development will inform the selection of the technology necessary to support the community. It will also inform the sociability planning that will guide social interaction in the community. Again, *Chapter 11* provides examples of real cases.

Selecting Technology and Planning Sociability

With the community's needs determined, the next steps are to identify software and to support the community and start sociability planning. The first issue to consider is whether communication should be synchronous or asynchronous (*Chapter 4*). Next, the basic software components are selected (*Chapter 8*), which will depend on whether the community will form part of a Web site or be free-standing. Selecting technology involves making initial usability decisions, which will be further refined throughout development. This is also the time to start planning sociability (*Chapter 9*).

Software selection and usability

Once they understand the primary needs of the community, developers move on to deciding how to access the software required to meet those needs. To this end, there are three ways to go. They are described briefly here and in greater detail in *Chapter 8*.

1. *Program it yourself.* For those with technical expertise, enough time, and the appropriate equipment, programming community software gives maximum control over its design and maintenance.

2. *"Glue" it together.* Bulletin boards, Web page templates, chats, and other useful software can be purchased or downloaded from the Web. Building communities by assembling these modules in a Web site is becoming popular, and has much to recommend it.

3. *Be a Web homesteader.* Sites including Xoom.com, geocities.com, theglobe.com, and yahoo.com invite users to create their own community or subcommunity on these sites. But by doing so, you have little control and have to tolerate advertisements.

The method chosen will depend on these factors: costs, technical skills, time, host, technical constraints, and usability. Keep in mind that the user-computer interface must be consistent and intuitive. (*Chapter 8* discusses these issues in relation to different types of software.) If new software is being designed, now is the time to consider whether it will be based on a metaphor which makes inferring which software components support which communication tasks possible (Carroll & Kellog, 1988). For example, software with icons of a town suggests that private chat happens in homes, public discussion in the town hall and so on.

Web site design

If a new Web site is being created, at this juncture, content, navigation, and page design can begin. Also useful at this stage is to conduct reviews with community members to check that user needs are being met and the overall design is conceptually appropriate. Likewise, conducting reviews with Web and community design experts are helpful for identifying early usability problems. (*Chapter 9* provides guidelines for Web site design, and *Chapter 10* discusses evaluation techniques.) Last, and perhaps most important, remember to involve the community, to encourage trust and commitment in the project.

Social planning

The information about social needs that was collected during needs assessment is now translated into a sociability plan. To formulate this plan, the kinds of questions to ask are:

- *Did the needs analysis suggest that a closed community with a registration policy is necessary?* Listserv communities must have such a policy, but bulletin boards, chats, and UseNet groups can be open or closed. The advantage of registration is that the effort required may deter casual visitors, which may reduce the likelihood of flames and spam. The disadvantage is that some people who might be good community members may be discouraged from joining. Exclusivity is also liked by some communities, whose identity relies on boundaries. For example, many professional communities have membership requirements.

- *Should a moderator or mediator or other special roles be assigned?* Moderators can have an enormous influence on the community but moderating is time-consuming, so there has to be people willing to give their time. If there are any special roles, encourage the community to specify what they should be and write a policy or at least guidelines.

- *Will there be an editorial policy?* Many moderators of discussion groups set out a clear editorial policy. This could be done as part of a moderation policy or separate. It's good to start work on it early.

- *Are general by-laws needed? If so, to address what?* If by-laws are deemed necessary, encourage members to start writing them, thus defining them. It is really important that community members do this, not just developers.

- *If the discussion forum is embedded within a Web site, what will its relationship to the host Web site be?* For example, should answers to frequently asked questions be made available on a Web page? What is the status of these? Should they be written by professionals—for example, by a doctor in a medical support community?

- *Should there be disclaimer policies?* These include a statement of copyright, a policy for archiving, and others.

- Even more complex—how should social interaction be supported? What kind of subgroups may form and how will their needs differ? Some of the ingredients needed to answer such questions may be available at this stage of development, others will be revealed as the community develops.

These and other sociability issues are discussed in *Chapter 9*.

Products resulting from this stage

Again using the sample information from our bird-watching community, each of the following products should be available at this stage of development:

- *Identification of software with appropriate functionality and good usability*. For the bird-watching community a Web site will be developed with an embedded commercial bulletin board and a database system for recording sightings.

- *Design of Web site*. Basic material for the bird-watching community will be collected from local and national societies.

- *Identification of main sociability issues*. For this community, a registration policy will be needed. Decisions will have to be made about how to provide 24-hour moderating. Finally, policies for registering, moderating, editing, copyright, and online conduct will have to be written.

Designing, Implementing, and Testing Prototypes

A prototype can mean different things to different people (Preece et al., 1994). In this book, it refers both to paper-based draft policies as well as to partially developed Web sites and software. Prototypes are essentially early representations of ideas to provide a basis for community development.

It is important for the team (community members and developers) to be open to a variety of ideas, so brainstorming is in order at this stage. Brainstorming sessions typically involve several rounds of idea generation and discussion.

Prototypes enable developers to:

- Verify that they understand the community's purpose and needs.
- Explore different design ideas.
- Test their designs and policies by involving users and experts in reviews and through more rigorous usability testing techniques, discussed in *Chapter 10*.

Developing prototypes and scenarios

The Web is a wonderful tool for exploring ideas, which not surprisingly often evolve into the final product. Large sheets of paper, Post-its, and crayons provide alternative ways to depict the community (and Web site). By developing what's called a *scenario of usage* (Carroll, 1995), users can work through the interface design, experiencing the social processes (e.g., the welcome screen, membership regulations, by-laws, etc.), as they go. This process encourages user involvement and provides developers with feedback. It also encourages a stronger relationship between users and developers. If users are local, this can be done on-site; otherwise, email can be used. In the latter case, a short questionnaire may be useful for directing user attention to salient features, with some open-ended questions to solicit general information. (See *Chapter 10* for more on questionnaire design and other testing techniques.)

Testing

A variety of techniques are available for testing usability (Dumas & Redish, 1999; Preece et al., 1994). Some are informal, such as reviews; others are more formal, such as *controled usability testing*, which provides feedback about problems with software and Web site design (*Chapter 9* provides guidelines, and *Chapter 10* discusses testing techniques).

The developers' goal is to produce a straightforward, esthetically pleasing community with good usability and sociability. But when existing software is being used, there is little scope for radically changing its functionality and usability; developers and users alike are at the mercy of the designers. However, users can—and should be—warned about any difficulties. For example, having to log in to join a chat or bulletin board discussion from within a Web site can be frustrating. When this communications software is embedded in a Web site, it creates an impression of a single entity—the community—whereas going through the login procedure reduces this sense of community, especially if the chat and bulletin board have different procedures, which is common. One way of dealing with this problem is to turn the process into a feature. For example, GeoCities.com uses a landscape metaphor with avenues to prepare users for changes (see *Chapter 8*).

Prototyping and testing Web components, particularly the navigation structure, are also important. Many community members will fail to distinguish between Web pages and embedded communities, and poorly designed Web pages will influence their attitude toward the community. Usability testing identifies navigation problems, errors in instructions, inconsistent terminology, annoying graphics, poor aesthetic design, and more. And note, at this stage, the content of medical or other professional sites should be reviewed by appropriate experts.

The general aims of testing, prototyping, and building scenarios are to:

- Evaluate the design by testing its usability and sociability through successive iterations.

- Involve as many typical users from the community as possible.

- Develop scenarios in which users role-play typical activities so that they and the developers understand the community's needs.

At different stages of development the aims will be different. Early, the focus will be on exploring ideas. Later, it will involve testing the basic design, particularly navigation, basic usability, and sociability. As testing proceeds, the focus will gradually home in on details of sociability and usability; encourage community involvement; and build good relationships between users, developers, and managers.

Products resulting from this stage

There should be many iterations of development and testing during this stage. The products from this stage include:

- *Reports and recommendations.* These should be produced after each cycle of testing, and include details of the test findings and recommendations for improvements. Because of the iterative nature of the process, early prototypes may be done on paper or parts of a Web site, or using generic software that still requires tailoring. The final prototype will be the finished community software—that is, a Web site with integrated communications software. For example, the home page and plans for the bird-watcher community were reviewed by community members early in the design phase to ensure that the community's needs were understood.

The working site was reviewed by experts, who commented on usability and sociability design. Close to completion, testing with typical community members was done. Reports were produced of all stages. Informal testing was also carried out to test design ideas.

- *Software with good usability and sociability.* Developers should be confident that the online community will have excellent usability and sociability for supporting the new community and be prepared to make changes if required as it develops.

- *A committed group of community members.* Involving the community in all the development stages encourages commitment, which bodes well for the new community's success.

Refining and Tuning Sociability and Usability

This stage is often indistinguishable from the previous one, except that it focuses on fine-tuning before launching the community. This includes final editing of messages and Web page content. The aims of this stage are to uncover any last-minute problems, such as inconsistencies in instructions or spelling and grammatical errors in editorial content.

Products resulting from this stage

The products from this stage include:

- A list of small usability problems that need fixing.

- A list of spelling mistakes and inconsistencies in content and instructions that need fixing.

Welcoming and Nurturing the Community

In the 1994 movie *Field of Dreams*, the Kevin Costner character spoke the now-famous line: "Build it and they will come." This, unfortunately, is rarely the case for online communities. Rather, online communities die if left to fend for themselves. Therefore, ways of attracting people to a community have to be planned, then actively pursued. Involving the community in its own development is important for encouraging participation as we said.

When the community site is ready for use, developers can send email messages to mailing lists of likely participants. Linking to related sites is another good method to get the new community "on the map." Advertising, too, can be used, in particular to announce e-commerce communities. Professional communities can be advertised through societies, journals, and newsletters. And, as briefly mentioned earlier, seeding the community with people who will give it character, promote discussion, and entice others to join is often a viable approach: If the community is part of an existing Web site, recruiting people will be easier. Web-based communities rely on their sites attracting people. Several of the community Web sites discussed in this book offer a daily news bulletin, or post hot topics that change each day (e.g., drkoop.com, discussed in *Chapter 2*). Supplying new and interesting information both in community discussions and on associated Web pages is essential for attracting people to return.

Developers must also plan to support the community after it is launched, particularly during the first few months. Annoying little problems may emerge that escaped notice during testing; moderators may need advice; policies may turn out to be ambiguous or not needed; conversations may flag. Especially during the first weeks and months, there must be something to draw people into the community and keep them coming back so that they build relationships, trust, and commitment. The Web is full of competing attractions, and people will not hang around a site if the experience there is not satisfying!

Products resulting from this stage

This stage does not signal the end of community development; rather, it marks the beginning of a community's evolution. The products from this stage comprise the plans to support the community in whatever ways are necessary to help it succeed.

- *A plan to seed the community with people who will encourage its development and attract others.* In community-centered development, developers build this group as they work. It is one of the advantages of the process.

- *A plan to carefully observe the community during the first six months of existence and solve problems that occur.* This includes fixing technical glitches (e.g., problems with a server) and solving sociability issues.

- *A long-term support plan.* If the community is moderated, the moderator will complete this role plan. Some communities, such as Diversity University (discussed in *Chapter 2*) have a complex support network that is linked to its governance.

Summary

Community-centered development, as the name implies, focuses on the community rather than technology. Developing online communities involves a blend of technical and social development. As stressed throughout this book, good usability and sociability are essential ingredients for thriving online communities. And careful social planning will get the community off to a good start; ideally, it will guide early social development without stifling the community with do's and don'ts. Thus, any plans implemented should be flexible enough to adapt to the changing needs of the community as it evolves.

To review, community-centered development involves five stages:

1. Assessing community needs and analyzing user tasks, focusing on the purpose, people, and their tasks, interaction and policies.
2. Selecting technology and planning sociability.
3. Designing, implementing, and testing prototypes.
4. Refining and tuning sociability and usability.
5. Welcoming and nurturing the community.

Throughout community-centered development, testing and reviewing the new community site with community members is strongly recommended. *Chapter 8* discusses selecting software; *Chapter 9* provides sociability and usability guidelines; *Chapter 10* discusses evaluation techniques; and *Chapter 11* contains development case studies. Though the chapters in this part of the book describe community-centered development, they do not provide details of mappings between the stages nor deal with technical issues in depth. For more on those topics, readers are referred to the sources given in the *Further Reading* section.

Further Reading

Contextual Design: Defining Customer-Centered Systems (Beyer & Holtzblatt, 1998); *Scenario-Based Design: Envisioning Work and Technology in System Development* (Carroll, 1995), and *Design at Work: Cooperative Design of Computer Systems* (Greenbaum & Kyng, 1991)

These books discuss contextual inquiry and scenario-based and participatory design. The processes they describe have been used extensively to develop a variety of computer systems, though not for online communities per se. These books also describe the procedures used to accomplish design, but do not take into account such things as the highly distributed, variable, and sometimes partially unknown user population with which some online community developers must contend.

Human-Computer Interaction, Second Edition (Dix, Finlay, Abowd, & Beale, 1998), *Human-Computer Interaction* (Preece et al., 1994), *Interaction Design* (Preece et al., 2001), and *Designing the User Interface: Strategies for Effective Human-Computer Interaction, Third Edition* (Shneiderman, 1998a)

These texts provide a general introduction to human-computer interaction. They describe design methods, but are less process-oriented than the three previous books.

A Practical Guide to Usability Testing (Dumas & Redish, 1999)

This book provides good practical advice on usability testing, supported with examples. It does not directly address online communities, but the information provided can be applied to them.

Hosting Web Communities (Figallo, 1998), and *New Community Networks: Wired for Change* (Schuler, 1996)

These books focus on networked communities, both providing a wealth of insight from a community developer's perspective. They offer many useful suggestions about the process of community development and suggest features to include in online communities.

User Analysis and Task Analysis for Interface Design (Hackos & Redish, 1998)
This book offers practical advice on user and task analysis, with many examples. It does not address online communities, but much of the information can be applied to them.

Developing User Interfaces: Ensuring Usability through Product and Process (Hix & Hartson, 1993), and *The Usability Engineering Lifecycle* (Mayhew, 1999)
These texts are strongly process-oriented. They each describe user-centered design, and provide valuable how-to guidance. They do not deal with online community design per se.

Systems Analysis and Design Methods (Whitten & Bentley, 1998), and *Systems Analysis and Design* (Kendall & Kendall, 1998)
These texts provide a detailed account of the stages of analysis and design for general information systems. They focus primarily on database systems, but the material can be adapted to inform online community design.

8 Selecting Software

When the thing lives for you—start to plan it with tools. Not before. . . . Working on it . . . modify or extend or intensify or test the conception—complete the harmonious adjustment of its parts.

—Frank Lloyd Wright (as quoted in Hoffmann, 1978, p. 15)

The aim of this chapter is to present the software options available for online community developers. It discusses key features of generic software and provides evaluation guidance. This chapter also indicates the level of developer expertise needed to successfully implement the various options. It is important to point out that the material in this chapter is written at an introductory level. It is intended for those who need a better understanding of different types of software, not technical experts. And because products date very quickly, specific product references have been avoided.

Contents

The Information Age
Mark Kostabi 1995 © Kostabi World

Online community developers are responsible for building or selecting software that encourage a thriving community. Thus they need to stand with a one foot in each of two worlds, "the world of technology and the world of people, and try to bring the two together" (Kapor, 1996, p. 4). It is not as simple as choosing state-of-the-art software; developers must provide the appropriate usability. "[T]he tendency of those involved in building [software] is to create visually compelling worlds that look good, but do a poor job of fostering social interaction. Many of these systems have more in common with lonely museums than with the vibrant communities they set out to create" (Kollock & Smith, 1996).

There are many issues developers must consider. What functionality does the software provide, and how does it relate the community's needs? How well does the usability support basic user tasks, and how does it affect sociability? How important is it that users be able to search archives? Will the community need tools to support special roles, such as moderation? Can the software support community growth—that is, can it scale up to support more users?

Logistical issues need addressing, too. How or where can developers access software? How much technical expertise do they need to implement it? How much does it cost? How popular is it? Will users need special software or hardware to complement it? Should the services of a software provider be considered?

Three Routes to an Online Community

The sheer volume of software that is available today for building online communities can be bewildering, particularly because there is no central repository. Moreover, the quality and quantity of free software changes rapidly. What was available as freeware one day may not be six months later. And as to commercial products, developers must add concerns about costs to the quality issue.

If you are an online community developer, there are three primary routes you can take to build the community, as introduced in *Chapter 7*. Each route has advantages and drawbacks, and whichever you select will require making trade-offs. A central consideration will, of course, be your level of expertise.

The three ways of developing an online community are to program it yourself, "glue" it together, or become a Web "homesteader." We'll discuss each in turn.

1. *Program it yourself.* If you have strong technical expertise, enough time, and the appropriate equipment, by programming your own community software you will gain maximum control over its design and maintenance. Numerous tools are available to support HTML, VRML (virtual reality modeling language), Perl, Java, JavaScript, CGI scripts; a host of Web development tools; and Web pages crammed with how-to information. These tools comprise an important and far-reaching topic, but one that is outside the scope of this book.

2. *Glue it together.* Whether you purchase or acquire it free from the Web, bulletin boards, Web page templates, chats, and other useful software make building communities very convenient. Assembling these modules in a Web site is becoming a popular way of achieving this task, and has much to recommend it. The price you pay for this approach is loss of a unified look and feel. Developers must accept the design decisions made by others. Worse, what are called the *seams* between components may show, which annoys users and causes usability problems. Furthermore, such freeware carries the additional risk that it may change or cease to be maintained, though making an informed choice can reduce these risks. Obviously, following this route requires considerably less expertise and time than if you were to progam these elements yourself. Nevertheless, you still need sufficient knowledge to download software, link to another server, coordinate modules, build a Web site, and more.

3. *Become a Web Homesteader*. Web services such as Xoom.com, geocities.com, communities.msn.com, and theglobe.com, invite people to create their own community or subcommunity on their sites. This generally involves creating Web pages using templates, selecting chats and bulletin boards, and building email lists using their software. You will need little technical skill, and the community can become functional very quickly. The drawback is, of course, lack of control. You cannot change or import other software. On the other hand, selecting a reputable host can help to ensure the community's long-term existence. Many of these host sites offer free membership in return for the advertising revenue they earn on the community sites.

Whichever route you choose, you still have to decide which software and services to use. The following factors will help to focus your thinking:

- *Developer expertise*. What level and how much technical expertise will you need to set up and maintain the community?

- *Equipment*. What equipment will you need to develop and maintain the community software? What equipment will community users need? Will it have to be accessible to users with old or low-power equipment?

- *Scalability*. Will the software impose any restrictions on the size of the community that can be supported, either due to technical or commercial constraints? For example, could the software host a million people if necessary? Are there tools to support administrators and moderators of large communities? Does the host site limit the number of people who can belong to communities on its site?

- *Usability and implications for sociability*. Does the software have good usability, support high skill retention, and promise low error rates and high productivity? (Shneiderman, 1998a.)

Software Options

New software is made available on the Internet every day. Some of it can be downloaded and used as it is; other programs can be glued together with still other software and Web pages to form an online community. Some of this software, such as list-servers, has existed for many years, but most of it has been developed more recently. This section describes the most popular of these, in addition to listservers.

Listservers

One of the most straightforward ways of creating an online community is by setting up a listserver that coordinates email delivery to a group of users. Starting a new list can be done in two ways: the list can be hosted by a company or institution with listserver software (e.g., Majordomo, listserv, listprocs), or you can purchase the software and support the list yourself. When someone else sets up the management procedures, the burden for you, the community developer, is lightened. Assuming the host is reliable, taking this route requires a shorter time commitment and, overall, is the easiest way to proceed. The specifics vary depending on the list management program and the host, but the basic steps to set up any list are:

1. Choose a name for the community and for the list.

2. Write a charter containing the list's purpose and policies.

3. Formulate a welcome message for new subscribers, then delineate straightforward instructions for posting to the list, getting help, unsubscribing, and sending comments to the list owner.

4. Start a FAQ page and other companion Web pages. This step is not mandatory, but is strongly recommended.

5. Follow the instructions provided by the host administrator to institute the list. Some hosts do the initial setup, while others require you to do it yourself, usually by editing a configuration file.

6. Test the list thoroughly before opening it to the community.

Once the list is established users will have to register—that is, subscribe—to the listserver. This process can usually be made straightforward: (comm-1@umbc.edu)

1. Request to subscribe to the list by typing: `sub <listname> your-first-and-last-name`; for example, `sub comm-1 Jane Doe`.

2. To unsubscribe, type: `Unsub <listname>` in the first line of a message sent to the listserv address e.g `unsub comm-1`.

Listservers work in different ways, but share these parameters:

- Requesting service from the listserver provider usually involves specifying the name and address of the list.

- If the *To address* field is used, generally it prompts a reply to the entire list.

- If the *From address* field is used, generally it prompts a reply to an individual who sent the message being answered.

- Messages can be forwarded individually or in collections known as digests. Digests are sometimes chosen for moderated lists.

The elements to consider when considering a listserver community include:

- *Developer expertise*. Listserver functionality is well understood by many users, which makes them a safe, reliable option. The major decision here, then, is whether to host your own listserver or to have it hosted on another machine. The latter is a straightforward procedure, whereas the former requires knowing how to mount listserver software and run a server.

- *Equipment*. Listservers require no special equipment for community members, because they use email.

- *Scalability*. There are no special issues. Lists can be very large especially if set up with the intention of broadcasting information. However, while this is not a problem for list owners, it may be for users.

- *Usability and implications for sociability*. Because they are asynchronous, listservers are well suited to broadcasting messages and discussion. However, when the number of messages posted each day exceeds 15 to 20, some participants may feel overwhelmed. There is a choice of software, but the program of greatest import—the email reader—is not under the developer's control. Another disadvantage is that digests can be annoying because their use makes it difficult to reply to individual messages. Finally, members have to register, which discourages casual visitors and may help to create a sense of security and belonging, two major advantages.

One good source for developers interested in using listservers for their communities is *Liszt*, *www.liszt.com/*, an enormous directory of mailing lists, newsgroups, and Internet relay chat (IRC) channels. In 1999, Liszt contained more than 90,100 mailing lists. There, developers learn how to add or remove a list from the Liszt directory, and frequently asked questions (FAQs) provide advice—for example, how to deal with spam. The directory can be searched either by specifying keywords or by selecting from a topic menu. Typing `architecture`, for example, produced seven lists.

UseNet News

UseNet News is a collection of discussions on numerous subjects, hosted on Internet-connected servers, although they can also be hosted on servers that are not part of the Internet. UseNet's original protocol was UNIX-to-UNIX Copy (UUCP), but today, the Network News Transfer Protocol (NNTP) is used. In contrast to a listserver, community UseNet participants have to go to UseNet to read messages. Some 30,000 UseNet newsgroups exist, often just referred to as newsgroups. UseNet newsgroups can be found at *www.liszt.com/news/*. Most are open communities, meaning that anyone can post without registering. This also means that flaming and spamming frequently occur. UseNet is classified into 10 broad categories:

alt (alternative newsgroups)

comp (computer newsgroups)

news (UseNet news)

sci (science newsgroups)

talk (UseNet talk groups)

biz (UseNet business newsgroups)

misc (miscellaneous newsgroups)

rec (recreation newsgroups)

soc (social issues newsgroups)

all (a catch-all group)

If, for example, you chose the `comp` category, you would find more than 900 UseNet groups that discuss computers, each listed with a one-line description and a note indicating whether it is moderated. Using the UseNet reader allows you to email a reply, check the posting history of the sender, view the thread that the message is part of, bookmark it, view it as text, and more. And by typing `DejaNews`, you can search for newsgroups. If a newsgroup does not exist on the topic you want (unlikely), you can create one.

The main decision for a developer is whether to have his or her community assigned to one of the most well-known categories or the more generic `alt` category. The decision requires making a trade-off between ease of creation and speed of propagation—that is, how rapidly the community is "built" on the tens of thousands of news servers all over the globe. Launching a new group in the well-known categories can be a drawn-out and somewhat involved process, taking as long as two or three months, but once complete, most servers will add the new community fairly quickly. In contrast, creating a new alt group can take just a couple of weeks; the bad news is, it may take a long time for a significant number of servers to get around to adding the group, and they may need encouragement from their own users. Also, some smaller servers do not carry alt groups.

To get into the main hierarchy you must submit a formal proposal, (called a Request for Discussion, or RFD), to the moderator who posts it for discussion to news.groups. Several rounds of revisions to the RFD may be requested. Finally, the UseNet Volunteer Votetakers (UVV) appoints a vote-taker who posts a Call for Votes (CFV), which gives people a chance to formally register their support or disapproval. If the proposal passes, the moderator initiates the setup of the new group.

Less involved, proposals to the alt hierarchy are made to justify the new group. They are posted in alt.config, Comments. Providing the proposer acknowledges them, and there are no serious objections, the group is created.

Messages to UseNet groups are read via a newsreader, which may be standalone software, such as Forté's Free Agent, or part of a Web browser, such as Netscape's Collabra or Microsoft's Outlook Express. The factors involved in developing a UseNet community are:

- *Developer expertise.* You need sufficient expertise to run a server or to access someone else's server. And you need persistence if you want to get into the main hierarchy.
- *Equipment.* No special equipment is necessary for community members.

- *Scalability*. There are no special issues. Many UseNet newsgroups have thousands of members. Unlike listservers, users go to the UseNet community to read messages so their personal email cannot be bombarded with messages.

- *Usability and implications for sociability*. UseNet messages are composed as asynchronous text, similar to email except that users go to the community as we have said, which has both advantages and disadvantages. Many UseNet communities are open and not moderated, so inappropriate messages and spam are sent.

Chats

Internet Relay Chat, IRC, is the best known and oldest chat program on the Internet, developed in Finland in 1988 by Jarkko Oikarinen. By mid-1999, there were more than 45,520 IRC channels on 27 IRC networks (*www.liszt.com/chat/*).

Unlike email and UseNet, chats traditionally are synchronous text systems, though many now allow users to represent themselves using avatars. Different channels enable people to participate in different conversations at the same time. On large networks, such as Efnet, more than 2,000 channels can exist. Typing the hash symbol (#) tells you how many available channels there are worldwide (Figure 8.1), and typing the ampersand (&) tells you about the local channels.

Once you are in a channel, you will see chat activity similar to that shown in Figure 8.2. In a typical IRC, a dozen or more people may be registered at the same time. Each participant selects an alias to identify him- or herself, and as each sends a message, it appears on the screen. Unlike email and UseNet News, IRC users don't have time to reflect and compose because the activity happens in real time,

There are currently 147999 users on 37750 channels on 27 networks.

	No. of Channels	Last Contacted
Undernet	14153	*Jul 14 03:17*
EFnet	8596	*Jan 20 13:01*
IRCnet	8571	*Jan 20 04:56*
GalaxyNet	2282	*Jan 20 11:43*
BeyondIRC.net	613	*Jan 20 13:44*
AUSTnet	499	*Jan 20 13:09*
StarLink	473	*Jan 20 12:08*
BrasIRC	401	*Jan 19 07:59*
SuperChat	328	*Jan 20 13:04*
Newnet	323	*Jan 20 13:52*
AfterNET	322	*Jan 20 12:21*
ChatNet	270	*Jan 20 12:14*
DALnet	259	*Jan 20 11:37*
GrIrcNet	193	*Jan 20 13:49*
Red Latina	143	*Jan 20 13:06*
FEFnet	82	*Jan 20 11:40*
SorceryNet	78	*Jan 20 13:31*
EICN	61	*Jan 20 11:24*
WarpedNet	34	*Jan 20 11:11*
SubNet	29	*Jan 20 13:31*
QNet	20	*Oct 6 1998*
k0w	17	*Oct 13 1998*
Multinet	2	*Jan 5 1999*
BSDNet	1	*Jan 20 13:20*
AlterNet	1	*Jan 20 12:41*

Figure 8.1   Available channels

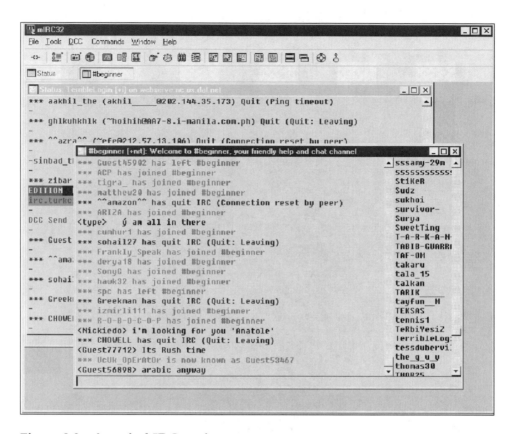

Figure 8.2   A typical IRC session

so messages are short and conversations move very quickly, with old messages scrolling off the top of the screen as new ones arrive. And several conversations may be occurring at the same time, whose comments interweave on the screen. Channels disappear when the last person has logged off.

Some channels have an operator whose comments are prefaced by the "at" symbol (@). He or she decides how strictly to moderate the channel. At the top of each channel is its name, possibly along with introductory information, a statement of purpose, and a moderation policy. Participants invoke lists of commands like those in Figure 8.3 to contribute to chats. In newer chats, the channels are referred to as *rooms*, an analogy whose origin is attributed to America Online (AOL), used there to evoke a spatial metaphor.

To run a chat, you need a chat client to connect to an IRC. For example, mIRC is a client for Windows that can be downloaded. Using a chat is straightforward, making the learning curve short even for Internet novices. Next to the talk window is usually a smaller window listing the participants who are currently logged on, so users can see who is involved, as well as those who are not actively participating—the lurkers. Also, there are usually options for speaking privately to a particular individual, via what's called a *back-channel*.

A wide variety of chat software now exists ranging from single-line text chats to elaborate 2D and 3D graphical environments populated with avatars, which are playful and enable participants to hide, disguise or enhance their real identity. Avatars can

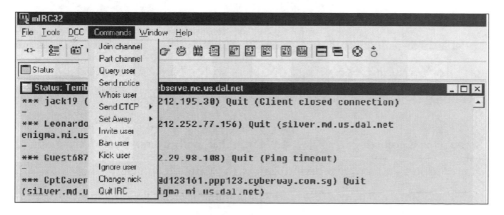

Figure 8.3   The basic commands for IRC

contribute a sense of presence (*Chapter 5*), which in turn can help to motivate a feeling of community. As bandwidth continues to increase, the sophistication of these graphical chats will improve. Beneath the surface, however, many chats on the Web are like IRCs. TalkCity.com, for one, lists chats categorized under a number of topics, all of which are easily accessible. Hosted chats are identified with an H next to them and a number in brackets next to the name of the chat indicates the number of participants at that time. A window at the bottom of the screen enables private conversations. Changing channels, leaving a chat, and getting support are also easy.

In WorldsAway.com, users can construct their own avatars by selecting from a variety of bodies and heads. Construction kits for designing avatars, available on the Web, can be imported into some chat environments. Chats that are defined by a URL rather than assigned to a server, appear to the user as if they move around with chosen Web pages.

Note: Chats that make use of graphics may cause access problems for users with slow modems and/or low-memory computers. Some chats, such as VirtualPlaces.com, address this problem by offering a low-bandwidth text version along with a downloadable high-bandwidth client version that displays thumbnail-sized GIF images for avatars. Offering two versions for users with different technical capabilities is becoming a common tactic for getting around these limitations (Figallo, 1998).

Activeworlds.com (Figure 8.4) combines a chat with avatars and a 3D graphical environment. The screen is divided into four windows similar to those shown in Figures 8.5 and 8.6. The window on the right in Figure 8.5 advises newcomers how to navigate Activeworlds.com; pop-up menus guide them to select their status as either a

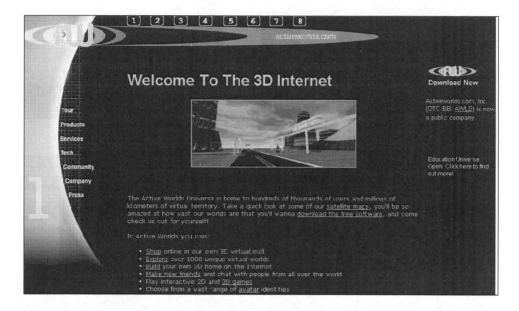

Figure 8.4   Activeworlds.com welcomes users

Figures 8.4–8.8 are reproduced by permission of Activeworlds.com, Inc.

tourist or citizen. At various times, depending on which world the user opts to inhabit, additional information is made available. Also in Figure 8.5, in the upper middle window, is a 3D picture of the world, where participants' avatars roam. Participants use arrows to direct their avatars. As they encounter other characters, their comments appear close to their "bodies." One problem is that over-writing of comments occurs, which can be annoying. Comments also appear in the lower middle window, beneath the graphical world. Conversations here are threaded, and threads often interweave. Participants who register and pay fees are able to build within the environment, and unlike in early MOOs, programming skills are not needed. Players can select from directories of objects. A player can, for example, select a home and various artifacts with which to adorn it, to make it unique.

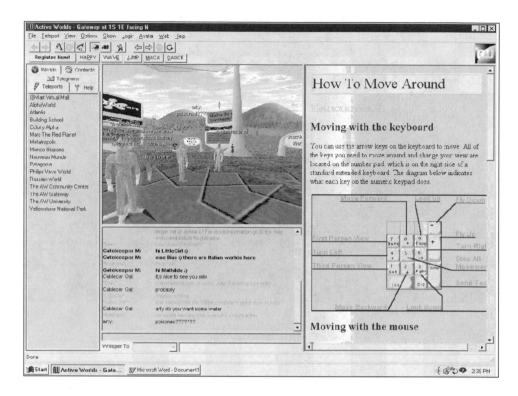

Figure 8.5   Chatting in Activeworlds.com

The left-hand window in Figure 8.5 offers a choice of different worlds to visit. They include: Yellowstone National Park (see Figures 8.7 and 8.8), the planet Mars, a university, a shopping mall, and others. News is presented in another window. Using cursor keys, participants move their avatars through the environments, usually accompanied by sound effects, if they choose. Note that the university and shopping mall are similar to some communities that are being developed for distance education and e-commerce. The addition of an online catalog, online billing, and a delivery system make commercial transactions possible.

Figure 8.6   The graphical gateway to Activeworlds.com

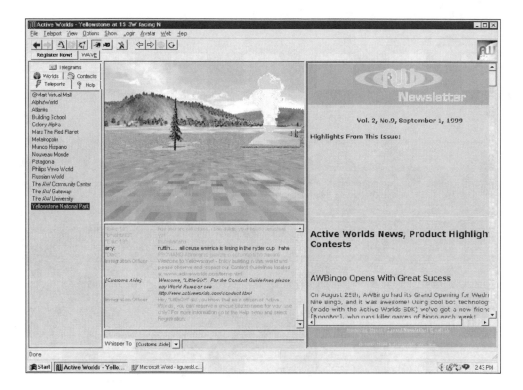

Figure 8.7   Yellowstone National Park as experienced in the Activeworlds environment

Web-based chat services are available mainly as downloadable applets and clients. Clients can be downloaded to users' PCs, from which it communicates with the chat server. Some of these are programs that have to be downloaded, while others are *plug-ins*, smaller programs that work with specific browsers or Java applets on a user's PC. In the case of the latter, problems may occur if the client is not compatible with the setup of the PC; and people using different clients may see different chat screens.

Some chats also make tools available to moderators to help them monitor user activity and to tailor the environment. Using such tools, moderators can, for example,

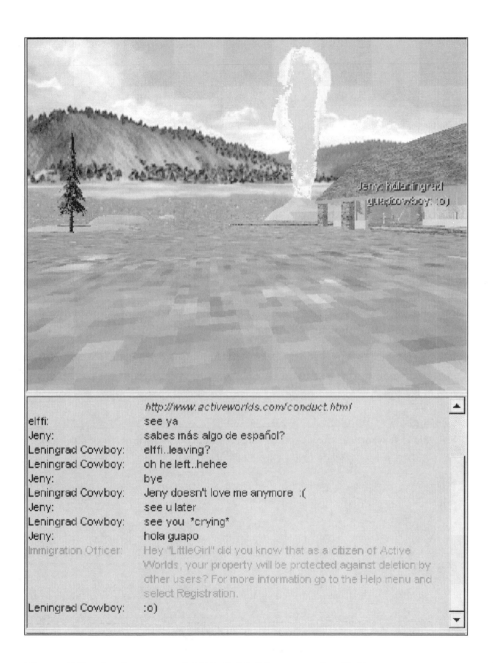

Figure 8.8 A close-up of Old Faithful geyser in Yellowstone, courtesy of Activeworlds.com

restrict access to rooms, impose filters, and prevent users from customizing avatars. Some also have *bots* that carry out predetermined activities such as enforcing rules. Other chats, such as ichat.com, can be adapted for guided tours, which may prove attractive to e-commerce entrepreneurs. Imagine going on a guided tour of a retail clothing store: After you tell your "tour guide" your size, color and style preferences, you are taken to see a selection of goods that you might find attractive. Or you might choose to go on a virtual bicycle ride through the Loire Valley, for a walk in Yosemite National Park, or to explore the Galapagos Islands.

Here are the factors to consider for developing a chat community:

- *Developer expertise*. Chats can be implemented in a variety of ways depending on the developer's expertise (Figallo, 1998):

  - IRC is well established and provides a reliable service. To use it developers need to establish a channel and direct people to it. Though relatively low in cost, its scope for extending features is limited.

  - Hosting a community on an existing hub is a technically easy option; but, as with IRC, extending the system is limited. In addition, there may already be a chat on the same subject at another host site.

  - Forming a partnership with a hub service also precludes installing the service, but it may be difficult unless the developer can guarantee a reasonable volume of traffic, so that the hub benefits from advertising revenue.

  - Installing your own server gives maximum control, but requires technical expertise, and may be expensive.

- *Equipment*. Deciding how to launch a chat forces developers to assess their equipment and that of the user community. Two versions of the system may be necessary, a text version for those with slower connections and lower-power machines, and a graphical version for those with fast connections and state-of-the-art equipment. To date, it is not clear how much added value comes from graphical chat environments, which may also impact the equipment issue.

Advocates claim they provide a broader experience, generating a stronger sense of presence and engagement. And in fantasy environments and general chit-chat environments, avatars and graphics may be attractive and motivating for users.

- *Scalability*. Developers must have a firm grasp of how large the community is and how much it is likely to grow. And they must know its design. Chats that use avatars can become very crowded with as few as 10 on the screen at once. Obviously, text-only chats can handle more participants.

- *Usability and implications for sociability*. In general most first-time users have no trouble learning to use chat but developers should ensure that it is easy to start new channels, hold private conversations, enter and leave discussions, archive discussions, and other tasks.

Real-time auditoriums

Real-time auditoriums are chats that can be configured to handle thousands of people, though they rarely attract their maximum number. If everyone were to type their message when they pleased, it would quickly become chaotic, so auditoriums are managed by moderators who filter the messages to display for all to see. Often, a special guest is invited, to whom questions are directed. Depending on the event and the software in use, attendees may be able to participate in other ways; for example, they may be able to communicate more freely with others in the same "row", hold break-out sessions, or have private conversations with individuals (Figallo, 1998). Some auditoriums also have voting procedures that allow participants to register their opinions. Such systems point the way to a future that makes widespread use of more online political forums.

Many of the same issues need to be addressed when selecting a real-time auditorium as for an ordinary chat. In addition developers must confirm that the chat has tools for event moderators that enable them to filter and channel questions and form subgroups. Facilities should also be available to support voting, to show slides, and the like.

Instant messaging

Instant messaging systems such as ICQ (an acronym for "I seek you"), allow groups to stay in contact while working on other things. That means ICQ runs in the background. ICQ also makes it possible for users to engage in one-to-one conversations while taking part in chat room discussions. It is increasingly common to see instant messaging and chats used in this way.

Instant messaging communities are set up by users who register on a server that is connected to a network of servers across the Internet. The new user gets a Universal Internet Number (UIN), that enables others in the community to recognize who is online. The ICQ software checks a list of contact names, and whenever someone logs on or off, it is reported to the community. Discussions (referred to as chats) are initiated by clicking on an icon that represents an individual or a group (see Figure 8.9). Members tell one another about themselves by creating an ICQ home page that resides on the user's hard drive and is only accessible to others when the person is online.

Users create a home page by, first, selecting the ICQ Services button (see Figure 8.10) and then following the sequence of options until the ICQ Homepage Factory wizard appears. There users see three tabs: Main, Design, and Advanced. The Main tab contains the modules that represent different areas of the user's home page: Home, Chat, Messages, Personal Details, Favorite Links, File Server, and Guestbook. ICQ provides some default text and graphics for these pages, but users can replace these with their own HTML text. The Design tab enables users to customize their ICQ home pages, using ICQ's default collection of graphics, backgrounds, and headers, or by importing others. The Advanced tab gives users greater control over the page, including how other users interact with them. Users can specify their IP address, set passwords, and get statistics on who visited the page.

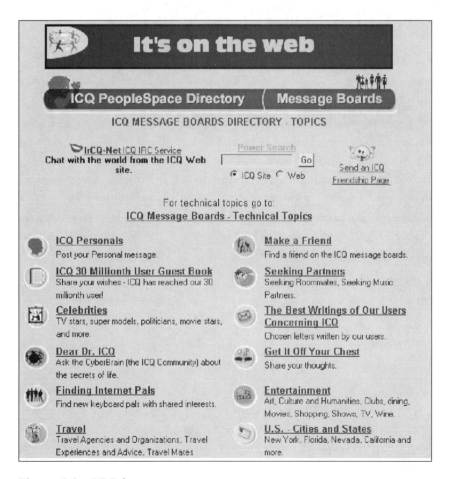

Figure 8.9   ICQ home page

Figure 8.10   An example user's ICQ home page

When developing an ICQ community, consider these factors:

- *Developer expertise.* An ICQ community can be developed using ICQ-provided tools and services. The easiest way to form an ICQ community is by creating an ICQ Interest Group or by joining an existing one. The ICQ Interest Groups are located on the ICQ server. Another way to is to create an ICQ user list and post it on the Directory of User lists. To use this option, you must first download the List template before people can be added to it. Furthermore, all clients need to download and install the ICQ software.

- *Equipment.* No specific equipment is required unless you will be including advanced features, such as sound cards and speakers for voice services like ICQPhone.

- *Scalability.* There are no limits to the number of people who can join an ICQ community.

- *Usability and implications for sociability.* From the client point of view, there are two modes: Simple Mode, the default for new users, and Advanced Mode. However, some server features, such as User Group and User List can be easily set up. The ICQ Members Directory, People Navigator, or ICQ Networks enable users to find their friends easily. Future developments will enable ICQ users to connect with pagers or cellular phones.

Bulletin boards

The Web version of traditional bulletin boards has revived their popularity. Along with chats, bulletin boards are becoming an essential element for conducting e-commerce and for supporting many other Web-based communities. Many bulletin boards are available free on the Internet. Two well-known systems are Hypernews, one of the oldest bulletin board systems, and Discus.

The following describes features found on most modern bulletin board systems:

- Basic systems that are available free generally allow users to obtain alternative views of messages. One view presents messages in the chronological order, that is, time of receipt. Another view *threads* messages, that is groups them by related topics.

- Template forms are available for composing messages, which can be sent to public or private topic areas.

- Participants can search for new messages, using pull-down menus that enable them to find messages by topic and by date. Figure 8.11 shows a list of messages from drkoop.com. Notice the icons for navigating through messages; the arrows indicate the direction of movement through the messages. Many bulletin board systems also provide icons that can be included with messages to indicate content, such as a question mark for a question, or a dialog bubble to indicate a comment etc. Emoticons (*Chapter 3*) may also be available for signaling emotional intention.

- Another common—and helpful—usability feature is that messages that have been read are distinguished from those that have not been read.

Commercially available bulletin boards offer even more features, including a range of tools to support moderators and for additional security. Some enable users to provide extensive profiles. They can upload pictures of themselves (images are stored on the discussion board server) and specify additional personal information, such as home page URL, age, and so on. The board administrator can configure fields for this

```
- ▼ General (270)
    Welcome (DKC-Todd) 08/21
  + How useful is this site? (hrrw) 08/29
  + health care reform (LindaC) 09/30
  + Morinda Citrifolia (commentrep) 10/12
  + CROHN'S DISEASE (YORKIDOLL) 11/05
    Child development chat (DKC-Sandy) 11/18
    health issues for children (DKC-PHYLLIS) 12/16
  + lower back pain (pan) 12/25
  + psoriasis (christopher) 01/04
  + Aspartame (KyaraB) 01/07
  + No Topic (Gena) 01/08
    BURN SURVIVOR CHAT (DKC-TK4BILL) 01/08
  + Bell's Palsy (Desgnr) 01/11
  + Body Heat (NJS) 01/12
  + DIETING (LAMBI) 01/13
  + Difficulty Swallowing (lunastar) 01/16
  + Adverse side effects of Biaxin (Laurenz) 01/19
  + TURNING BACK THE CLOCK (DKC-Margo) 02/05
    Tackling Your Demons! (DKC-Margo) 02/09
    WAS GRANDMA RIGHT? Old Remedies for New Ills. (DKC-Margo) 02/09
  ▼ Next ▬ Bottom
+ Request a New Conference (13)
+ Feedback (11)
+ Alternative Medicine (88, 1 New) NEW
```

Figure 8.11   List of messages from drkoop.com

Reproduced by permission of drkoop.com

information, or users can define custom fields. Users can also specify preferences such as to skip the preview when posting and to use the text-only view when searching for new messages; they can specify favorite topics when searching new messages, do a keyword search, invoke the tree view, and do a spell check.

Commercial systems may also offer enhanced features for composing messages. For example, Discus Pro allows attachments to be uploaded in any format, such as

Microsoft Word and Excel documents, audio files, binaries, or images. The attachments are stored on the discussion board server and are linked directly from the messages. The board administrator can disable attachment uploading or limit file sizes. Users can initiate private discussions and ask to be notified when replies arrive to topics they initiated.

Discus Pro and others allow moderators to configure the system so that users can register themselves, thereby reducing the administrative burden. Some systems also provide archiving support. Moderators can set limits on the number of messages that remain in the main board; when that limit is reached, old messages are either deleted or archived. Message-queuing facilities make it possible to organize messages for review by moderators. Log analysis tools enable moderators to analyze activity on the board. Some boards also provide facilities for identifying user IP number so that problem visitors can be banned from discussions. Support is also provided for making backups of all or part of the board. Many other features are also becoming available.

Developing a bulletin board community involves these considerations:

- *Developer expertise*. Downloading and installing a bulletin board on your own server may prove more difficult than the instructions lead you to believe. Technical skill and patience are needed. Most bulletin board systems use Perl CGI scripts, and are designed for tailoring, so knowledge of Perl is a requirement. Developers should evaluate the online documentation that specifies the steps to follow to download the product and key features, to determine whether the product uses frames, how it works with well-known browsers such as Netscape and Internet Explorer, and the like. Developers who do not want to install their own systems will find many companies that host bulletin boards, but they should realize that this option implies some loss of control.

- *Equipment*. No special equipment is needed for most bulletin board systems.

- *Scalability*. Many commercial bulletin board systems are now designed to cater to a large number of discussions involving thousands of users. Thus, the main limiting factor may be one of management, not technology, though better tools for moderators now available help; still, the number of messages that any one person can read will be limited.

- *Usability and implications for sociability*. Modern bulletin board systems offer many desirable usability features, such as those discussed. Clear instructions for composing and editing messages, and techniques for searching for new messages and in archives are particularly important. The ability to send attachments is likely to become increasingly popular (to send personal photos, spreadsheets, and URLs for home pages), as will being able to hold private discussions. Alternative views of the board which show threading and possibly other relationships between messages make following discussions easier.

Web Homesteading

More often, online communities are composites, of Web pages, chats, bulletin boards, instant messaging, databases, and others. These composite communities are designed to have a consistent look and feel among all the modules. Developers can choose from already well-populated sites offering numerous facilities to empty platforms into which developers "pour" their own content.

The homesteading advertising model

Homesteading sites invite others "on their land" to increase traffic and, ultimately, to generate advertising revenues. Consequently, developing a community on one of these sites (e.g., Yahoo.com, Xoom.com, GeoCities.com) is free or low-cost. Developers need little expertise to follow this route, but, naturally, control over their community is limited.

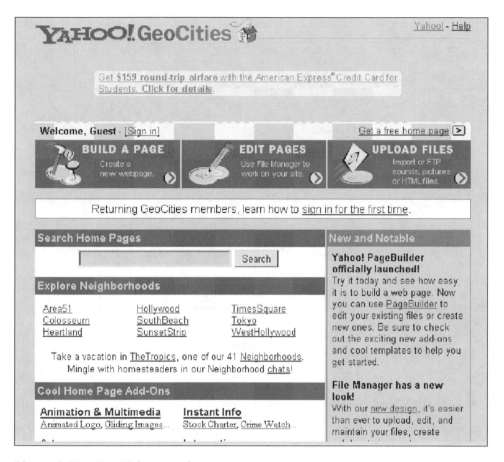

Figure 8.12   GeoCities.com home page

Reproduced by permission of Yahoo! Inc. © 2000 by Yahoo! Inc. YAHOO! and the YAHOO! logo are trademarks of Yahoo! Inc.

The GeoCities.com site, for example, hosts hundreds of small communities that are clustered in neighborhoods, which contain *avenues* (see Figure 8.12). Each GeoAvenue contains information about a particular topic, such as travel, arts and leisure, shopping, and many more. Clicking on an avenue brings more choices. For example, the GeoAvenue on Arts and Leisure leads to a collage of pictures and another set of choices. I am going to France this summer, so I clicked on France next. This took me to a short introduction, highlighted by a picture of the Arc de Triomphe. A counter told me that I was visitor 2642. More choices let me visit Web pages created by different people; or I could choose to go to chats and bulletin boards covering a variety of topics.

To add a Web page to GeoCities, users have to register, by completing a form, which entitles them to free email and their own Web site. Web templates make this task easy, even for novices. There are no financial costs (advertising pays for beginners' Web pages), but users relinquish control over Web page design and communications software, and they become one of many GeoCities participants. More experienced Web page developers can, however, buy access to more sophisticated tools.

The Globe functions similarly. Created in 1994 by two Cornell University juniors and a few high school students, the first employees were recruited from the student union and paid with pizza. As at GeoCities, you have to register, but immediately you advance to the Globe's Homepage Builder with its menu of options for constructing your own page. Selecting Page Wizard under the Create Pages menu takes you to a variety of templates that are similar to MicroSoft's PowerPoint. By following a sequence of easy numbered steps, you select your template and color scheme then add your own information. No knowledge of HTML is required. If, however, you know HTML, you can select Custom HTML, rather than Page Wizard, to write your own code. Also, like GeoCities, the Globe has chats on a variety of topics; it also enables you to create and send postcards, develop an address book, or receive a personal horoscope. The Globe also shares a disadvantage with GeoCities: there is little or no sense of real community and little scope to create one.

The Mining Company is another commercial community that provides design templates. If you have considerable expertise in a particular area, such as vintage cars, you can take a qualifying test to become a guide. Guides take people on site tours and are paid a percentage of the advertising revenue from the site, proportional to the amount of Internet traffic that the guide hosts. This arrangement supports partnerships that can benefit individuals or small companies by encouraging community among the traders.

These are the factors to consider for developing a Web homesteading community that is supported by advertising:

- *Developer expertise*. You need virtually no technical expertise. The host company provides easy-to-use templates to develop Web pages. Some allow you to link to a discussion forum, but many do not. The trade-off for choosing this route is that you have no control over the design and it is difficult to generate a sense of community.

- *Equipment*. No special equipment is required.

- *Scalability*. Successful providers host hundreds of community developers. To date, it is not clear how they will manage if a particular community becomes very active.

- *Usability and implications for sociability*. Host-supplied templates make creating and using these systems straightforward, but functionality tends to be limited with little opportunity for tailoring the system.

Shells

An increasing number of companies (e.g., CommunityWare.com, Axis.com) provide a suite of generic communications software, typically containing chats, bulletin boards, instant messaging, listservers, and Web templates, which you assemble as you wish to build your own community. Simply, you select the components and put them together yourself. Developing a community using a ready-made shell may be an attractive option for those with limited technical expertise but who need to develop an independent community, rather than "stake a claim" on someone else's homestead.

If you are considering developing a community using a shell, keep the following in mind:

- *Developer expertise*. You need little technical expertise to build a community using a shell, though count on spending more time and effort than by homesteading. The host company will make it easy to select components and put them together, and will maintain the system on its server. Just be aware that there is a limited range of choice and scope to tailor the system.

- *Equipment*. Generally, no special equipment is required, as most shells are hosted on the server of the company that provides them.

- *Scalability*. Successful providers host many community developers, but how well they will manage if one or more become very active remains to be seen.

- *Usability and implications for sociability*. The major drawback of shell systems is that you probably won't be able to change the interface if you find usability problems. On the other hand, participants will have seamlesss integration between modules. Developers with limited technical expertise will, therefore, be better able to design intuitive online communities by using a shell than by importing modules with different interfaces and no common look and feel.

Summary

The aim of this chapter was to identify the key features of generic software currently being used to build online communities. The details of specific products and their cost will undoubtedly change, but their main features will not change as rapidly. The following factors should influence which products you decide to use: how much technical skill you need; whether you will have to invest in special equipment either to provide the service or to enable users to participate; whether the product can support community growth; and how well designed the user interface is.

Developer skills are particularly important. Obviously, those with strong technical skills and the resources to set up their own servers will have broader choice and greater control. That said, keep in mind that having a wide range of choices does not necessarily equate with *making* good choices. Ensuring that all users will be able to participate in the community with the equipment they own, and that the software is intuitive, straightforward, and pleasant to use is as important.

Further Reading

Hosting Web Communities (Figallo, 1998)
This book contains a wealth of valuable information about online community development, plus many useful pointers to features to look for when buying software products.

Internet 101: A Beginner's Guide to the Internet and the World Wide Web (Lehnert, 1998)
As the name suggests, this is an introductory text. It describes all the main software types and how and why they are used.

9 Guidelines: Sociability and Usability

My experience of the world is that things left to themselves don't get right.

—Thomas Henry Huxley, *Aphorisms and Reflections* (as quoted in Murphy, 1978, p. 6)

Knowing the principles of sociability (*Chapter 3*) and usability (*Chapter 4*) is essential for developing full-functioning online communities. Subsequent to that knowledge are guidelines that help developers apply these principles and keep them focused. Guidelines do not dictate to developers how to design a community; they support the developers' decision-making process. Guidelines also help to direct formative evaluations during community-centered development. The aim of this chapter is, therefore, to present guidelines that meet those goals.

Contents

A Marriage of Convenience
Mark Kostabi 1992 © Kostabi World

Careful social planning, sociability, and well-crafted software, usability, can't guarantee a successful online community, but without them, almost certainly a community will fail. Guidelines support developers to implement good sociability and usability. They are established to direct and focus developers toward their goals and what they should check when they evaluate online different communities.

Guidelines for interface design have been well established (e.g., NIST; Preece et al., 1994; Shneiderman, 1998a), some specifically for Web design (e.g., Lynch & Horton, 1999; Nielsen, 1995, 2000). As yet, no specific guidelines exist for online communities, but applicable advice can be found in the aforementioned texts (e.g., Figallo, 1998; Schuler, 1996; Schuler & Namioka, 1993). This chapter draws from many more to synthesize current available knowledge and to propose guidelines that will help online community developers.

Before we begin, however, let's review three points:

1. Community-centered development helps keep the community's needs central to the decisions and choices that are made. No clear formula for developing successful online communities has been defined (Kollock, 1998), but the community-centered development process (*Chapter 7*) paves a path to follow.

2. Communities are dynamic; they continually change and evolve, influenced by participant personalities, the activities of the group, and sometimes external influences. For instance, what may be important early in the life of a community may not be as significant later on.

3. "Technology isn't the most important factor in [online] communities. Members are" (Hagel & Armstrong, 1997, p. 172). Developers may have little or no control over community members, but they can do much to get a community off to a good start, by making sure software has good usability and by planning social structures.

Guidelines for Sociability

As repeatedly stated, sociability focuses on social interaction. Communities with good sociability have established social policies that support the community's purpose and that are understandable by community members, socially acceptable, and sufficiently practical so that they can be implemented easily. Sociability is not, however, permanent; it will change as the community evolves and matures. Maintaining the purpose, the focus, of the community is particularly important (Figallo, 1998).

Chapters 1, 3, 5 and *6* discussed sociability from different perspectives. *Chapter 1* asked and attempted to answer what is an online community? *Chapter 3* discussed sociability more broadly and addressed the following questions: How does a community communicate its purpose? What is the impact of different personalities and policies (e.g., membership regulations, behavior guidelines, conversation monitoring, etc.)? How should emotion, content, and online activities be represented? How can privacy and security be assured? *Chapters 5* and *6* discussed evidence that shed more light on most of these issues. This section extracts key principles, using the "purpose, people, and structure" foundation from *Chapter 3* and presents them as guidelines.

To review, for clarity and practicality, sociability and usability are discussed separately, but they are closely related and impact one another. For example, deciding whether to have a registration policy and what its content should be is a sociability concern; determining how to present the policy (deciding which font type and size and interaction style to use) are usability concerns.

Purpose: Defining it clearly

To begin, the community needs a name. Assigning the community a meaningful, concise, easy-to-remember name and defining the community's purpose clearly is important so that newcomers know what to expect. For example, DSOAG is meaningful only to those who already know what it means. The full name, Down Syndrome Online Advocacy Group, is necessary to inform people what that acronym stands for. A short statement of purpose defines the intention of the group: "Our focus is Down Syndrome research and its funding, so please stay on that topic." The home page further elucidates the purpose of the community. The home page of drkoop.com (Figure 2.2) also has a clear title, statement of purpose, symbol of the American Medical Association, and a picture of the well-known Dr. Koop.

The guidelines for this stage are:

- Give the community a clear, meaningful *name*.
- Write a concise, clear *statement of purpose*.
- Provide *additional information* on a Web page that supports—does not contradict—the statement of purpose.

People: Access, roles, and effective communication

Decisions about who is eligible to join the community, the roles members take and the way people communicate are decisions for the community. But developers of new communities will have to provide initial frameworks so that users know what to expect.

Access

If a community is intended to have open membership, you, the developer, must make sure that it really is open to everyone, that there are no hidden barriers to entry. Consider whether level of education, gender, cultural background, or type of equipment will prevent some users from access. For example, there may be symbols or phrases that invoke strong cultural feelings or cause offense. Or the system may be set up to preclude users with old or low-power equipment from joining. You may have to provide two versions, one for those with high-end equipment and another for those without these capabilities. The guideline here is:

- *Provide a clear statement* about technical and other access requirements.

Role-playing

As in offline life, online people generally take on different roles as the community develops—except in commercial communities where managers assign roles as needed. Well-known roles include moderators, community administrators (who may not be visible in the community), and specialists or experts who participate in question-and-answer sessions and provide advice. All of these roles are extremely important. The moderator's responsibilities often include initiating and guiding discussion, as well as acting as troubleshooter when there are interpersonal problems. Consequently, the moderator can have a major impact on content and interaction. Deciding whether to have a moderator is, therefore, an important consideration, and may require an outside resource or a volunteer. Similarly, the question of whether to bring in experts can only be answered after careful consideration. The guideline for this element is:

- *Decide whether moderators and experts are needed.* Plan how to manage their contribution to the community and associated policies. Base this decision on the purpose of the community and makeup of membership. Policies for moderation are discussed later in this chapter.

Effective communication

A healthy alternative to setting rules is to encourage people to communicate more effectively, to reduce misunderstandings and to prevent frustration. However, in the absence of a personal presence, problems arise (*Chapter 5*). Pictures, icons, links to personal Web sites, personal stories, and avatars help to remind users that a real person exists behind the electron trail. Emoticons also help to convey personality. Some communities, such as Systers.com, a community for women working in computing fields, insist that participants provide information about their true identity. New users must complete a form stating their name, gender, and reason for wanting to join the group.

Guidelines that help in this regard include:

- *Support personal presence (Chapter 5).* Note, this may even involve supporting annonymous personal presence, e.g., in games.

- *Establish common ground* by compensating for limitations of the media (*Chapter 5*). Encourage participants to develop explicit, sensitive, and sensible communication styles.

- *Ecourage empathy, trust, and cooperation (Chapter 5).* Focusing on the purpose of the community will increase familiarity among members, which leads to empathy, trust, and cooperation. Help participants to make their intentions clear by providing emoticons and a menu of gestures.

- *Develop clear policies to encourage all of the preceding guidelines.* All of these measures will help to discourage aggression, flaming, and other inappropriate behavior.

Policies: Registration, governance, trust, and security

Developers who want to influence governance, rather than let serendipity run the show, will have to work with community members to write policies to shape the community's growth. The trick is to achieve the right balance of structure and flexibility to launch the community on a steady course of growth. Too many directives, stated too forcefully, will deter people; not enough will weaken the structure. Phrasing and tone are important, too.

Registration

Some communities deliberately try to restrict access to achieve their purpose. For example, religious, ethnic, and political discussion groups want people who support their philosophies to join. Communities that deal with sensitive issues (e.g., support groups) or whose topic requires particular knowledge or expertise (e.g., usability specialists, anesthesiologists) generally have registration policies. Communities may also use registration to deter casual visitors and to make hit-and-run flaming difficult. The guidelines to follow here are:

- *Consider a registration policy*. This applies in particular to communities dealing with sensitive issues, or that are narrowly focused and require particular expertise, or that do not want casual visitors.

- *Determine whether to allow visitors*. ActiveWorlds.com, for example allows visitors for a limited period, to see if they like the community before paying a registration fee. Free trial memberships are becoming increasingly common.

Governance

Various governance models exist, used primarily by commercial companies, which set the rules. Communities in which participation is voluntary are usually more democratic. Five guidelines are relevant to this topic:

- *Decide either that the community owners will govern the community or that it will govern itself.* Diversity University, for example, has a sophisticated democratic voting process.

- *Decide on the acceptable level of free speech.* Should racist, obscene, blasphemous, or aggressive language be censored? For example, early in its existence, members of the WELL decided that complete freedom of speech was important to them (Rheingold, 1993). Some communities make a statement of what they regard as reasonable behavior. For example, the Down Syndrome Online Advocacy Group simply requests: "Do not communicate to someone else that which you would not want communicated to you" (*www.dsoag.com*).

- *Establish netiquette.* Then enforce it on chats, listserver, and bulletin board communities (*Chapter 3*).

- *Define rules for voting and other processes that require public participation.* For example, Diversity University and UseNet News have strict regulations about who can contribute.

- *Enforce rules.* This is usually a moderator's or mediator's role, who has to make judgments. To avoid controversy, generally a clear statement of policy ensures that everyone knows what to expect.

Trust and security

Trust is important in all communities but in health and e-commerce communities, it is essential. People must be assured that their privacy is protected and that their comments are kept confidential. They also need to be able to easily recognize information provided by professionals, as opposed to that which is the personal opinion of community members. The guidelines to follow here are:

- *Protect confidential information.* At a minimum ask for a bona fide agreement that conversations will not be repeated outside the community. You may also need formal privacy statements, stating that confidential information, such as medical details, contact information, and the like will not be disclosed or sold.

- For communities involved in financial transactions *include a statement to assure customers that their credit card details are secure.*

- *Include a disclaimer* (see Figure 9.1) in health communities and others providing information that could have dangerous consequences if incorrectly interpreted or used.

- In professional discussion groups, *include a copyright statement to protect intellectual property.*

- *Institute a policy or procedure to encourage and support trust.* At eBay, the reputation manager serves this purpose. Other techniques involve providing evidence of credibility—for example, the symbol of the American Medical Association and the photograph of Dr. Koop at drkoop.com convey a sense of authenticity and responsibility. Branding—including a well-known logo or symbol—also helps establish trust in online communities, particularly those associated with e-commerce.

In all these examples, deciding whether to have a policy, and what its content should be, are sociability considerations, involving judgments about how such actions affect the purpose and people in the community. Deciding how to make such policies available is a usability issue if software is involved.

Guidelines for Usability

As discussed previously, online communities use a variety of different software, ranging from a single, free-standing, computer-mediated communications system (e.g., chats, bulletin boards, listservers) to combinations of modules embedded in a

Online Service Agreement

drkoop.com[TM] is an Internet-based online information and communication service (the "Agreement"). BY ACCESSING OR USING DRKOOP.COM[TM], YOU AGREE TO BE BOUND BY THE TERMS AND CONDITIONS OF THIS AGREEMENT. IF YOU DO NOT WISH TO BE BOUND BY THIS AGREEMENT, YOU MAY NOT ACCESS OR USE DRKOOP.COM[TM].

DRKOOP.COM MAY MODIFY THIS AGREEMENT AT ANY TIME, AND SUCH MODIFICATION SHALL BE EFFECTIVE IMMEDIATELY UPON EITHER POSTING OF THE MODIFIED AGREEMENT OR NOTIFYING YOU. YOU AGREE TO REVIEW THIS AGREEMENT PERIODICALLY TO ENSURE THAT YOU ARE AWARE OF ANY MODIFICATIONS. YOUR CONTINUED ACCESS OR USE OF DRKOOP.COM[TM] SHALL BE DEEMED YOUR CONCLUSIVE ACCEPTANCE OF THE MODIFIED AGREEMENT.

1. DISCLAIMER

The information contained in drkoop.com[TM] is presented for the purpose of educating consumers on wellness and disease management topics. Nothing contained in drkoop.com[TM] is intended to be instructional for medical diagnosis or treatment. The information should not be considered complete, nor should it be relied on to suggest a course of treatment for a particular individual. It should not be used in place of a visit, call, consultation or the advice of your physician or other qualified health care provider. Information obtained in drkoop.com[TM] is not exhaustive and does not cover all diseases, ailments, physical conditions or their treatment. Should you have any health care related questions, please call or see your physician or other qualified health care provider promptly. Always consult with your physician or other qualified health care provider before embarking on a new treatment, diet or fitness program. You should never disregard medical advice or delay in seeking it because of something you have read in drkoop.com[TM].

The information contained in drkoop.com[TM] is compiled from a variety of sources ("Information Providers"). Neither drkoop.com nor Information Providers directly or indirectly practice medicine or dispense medical services as part of drkoop.com[TM].

Figure 9.1   Sample disclaimer from drkoop.com

Reproduced by permission of drkoop.com

Web site. Developers contribute to the community's success by selecting or designing software with good usability, which means it supports rapid learning, high skill retention, low error rates, and high productivity. It is also consistent, letting users feel they are in control.

A number of usability issues are common across software types, but details may differ. The rest of this section discusses Web usability and identifies salient usability issues for communications software implemented in online communities.

Web usability

An increasing number of online communities are being integrated into host Web sites, so Web usability is important. Furthermore, from the user's point of view, the Web site and the online community are parts of the same entity, meaning that each component influences the user's impression of the others. The following guidelines were suggested by Web usability experts; they are grouped into three broad categories: *navigation*, *access*, and *information design*.

Navigation

One of the major problems for users of large Web sites is navigating, to find what they need. In badly designed sites, users get "lost in cyberspace." A mark of successful Web sites is adequate and clear navigation support. The following six guidelines encourage good navigation.

- *Avoid using frames.* They prevent bookmarking and disable consistency, because users have no idea where they will end up after clicking on a link. Frames impede users' ability to develop safe and reliable mental models of the site's content and design (Nielsen, 1998).

- *Prevent the occurence of orphan pages.* These are pages not connected to a site's home page, thus may lead users into dead ends. And if users access these pages independently, they cannot get to the rest of the site. This is frustrating and a major maintenance problem (Nielsen, 1998).

- *Avoid designing long pages with excessive white space.* These force scrolling, which users often will not do, preferring to skim the immediately visible portion of pages (Nielsen, 1998). This was more problematic in the early days of the Web. Users are now more tolerant. However, too many links to find a known item is also problematic, so a balance is needed.

- *Provide navigation support.* Give users a clearly defined *site map*, such as the one in Figure 9.2. This map should appear wherever the user is in the site. Guidance in this form helps users to develop correct mental models of how different parts of the Web site relate to one another (Shneiderman, 1998).

- *Refrain from using deep, hierarchical menus.* These force users to burrow down to find what they are looking for. Empirical evidence indicates that broad, shallow

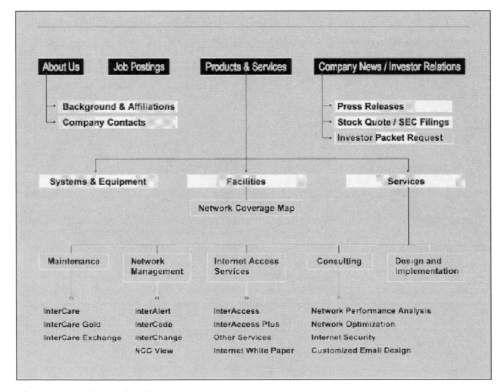

Figure 9.2   Sample site map
Reproduced by permission of Yahoo! Inc. © 2000 by Yahoo! Inc. YAHOO! and the YAHOO! logo are trademarks of Yahoo! Inc.

menus have better usability (Larson & Czerwinski, 1998; Shneiderman, 1998a), by drawing on users' ability to *recall* information rather than remember it. Yahoo's home page, shown in Figure 9.3, is a good example of the latter. On it, many items are at the surface level, and links are logically organized in a compact layout. This design supports usability even though it appears to

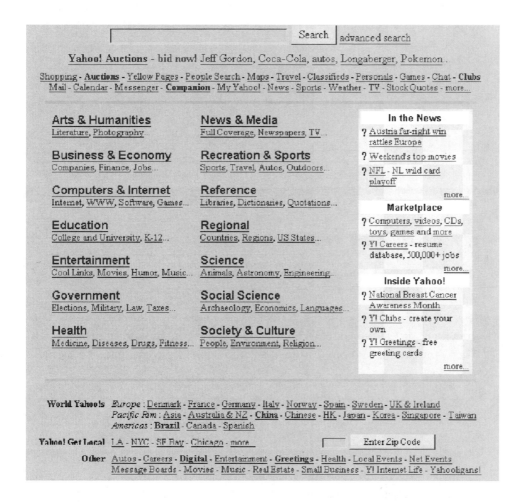

Figure 9.3   Yahoo's home page contains many links

contradict the well-known guideline to allow plenty of white space on paper documents. On-screen, white space is traded-off in favor of fitting more information.

- *Establish a consistent look and feel for navigation and information design*. This is particularly important when the site makes use of several software programs. Moving from one part of the site to another should be straightforward. If it is impossible to achieve this because some modules are imported, users should be alerted to this fact.

Access

Ensuring easy access to Web material can be problematic. Browsers may balk at minor errors typed in URLs, and many users do not have state-of-the-art equipment or high-speed Internet access. These three guidelines lead to good access support:

- *Refrain from complex URLs*. Lengthy Web addresses that include unusual characters lead to typing errors, which in turn result in unsuccessful searches, and then frustration (Nielsen, 1998). For example, the following URL is difficult to type without making errors: *www.cmaisonneuve.qc.ca/~lan/sbk/CW98/MALcolmZ/laughrt.2.html*.

- *Use standard link colors* (Nielsen, 1998). Links not yet followed are generally shown in blue; those that have been clicked are usually shown in purple or red. This color pattern has become something of a standard, so changing it may cause confusion.

- *Design to prevent long download times*. Naturally, a user's tolerance will depend on how much he or she wants the information, but 15 seconds is a reasonable guideline. Research indicates that user perception of content value and interest is influenced by download time (Ramsay, Barabesi, & Preece, 1998). Furthermore, graphics do not necessarily add to comprehension, as many designers assume (Sears, Jacko, & Dubach, 2000). Avoiding gratuitous graphics and animation helps to reduce download times (Jacko, Sears, & Borella, 2000) and ensures that users with low-power equipment can access the material.

Information design

Information design, which comprises content comprehension and esthetics, contributes to the user's understanding of the community and its purpose; it also indicates to the user whether the site is professional, reputable, and, hence, can be trusted. The following five guidelines support good information design:

- *Remove outdated or incomplete information* (Nielsen, 1998). Not doing so is the fastest way to give a poor impression to users.

- *Present text effectively.* Though a number of design rules for paper-based text are applicable online, others are not. Long sentences, paragraphs, and documents are no-no's. Break lengthy material into discrete, meaningful chunks to make it easy to read (Lynch & Horton, 1999).

- *Avoid excessive use of color.* Online, color is useful for indicating different kinds of information (e.g., cueing (Preece et al., 1994)). A change of color should signal a change in information type. For most sites, soft colors are recommended for backgrounds, with contrasting colors for text. Stay away from primary colors for both background and text. And keep in mind that a small percentage of people are color-blind. Green and red used together are particularly problematic for these people. Of course, specific audiences have different color expectations and preferences, and this must be a design factor too. *Wired* magazine, for example, favors bright, bold colors and wild background patterns, to appeal to its target audience, composed primarily of technical people, many of whom are young males.

- *Limit gratuitous use of graphics and animation.* Apart from increasing download times, too many graphics and animation can become distracting and, hence, annoying (Lynch & Horton, 1999). What may be cute and amusing on the first few visits to the page may become tiresome on subsequent visits. Here, too, however, the target audience's demographics must be taken into account.

- *Aim to achieve consistency.* This applies both within pages (use of fonts, numbering, terminology, etc.) and within the site (navigation, menu names, etc.), and is important for usability and for successfully designing aesthetically pleasing sites.

For example, instituting a simple convention such as starting all menu names with a capital will go a long way toward making the site look professional. And be sure to use the same menu names throughout the site, to improve navigation.

Communications software

Chapter 8 discussed the functionality offered by various computer-mediated communication (CMC) software programs and highlighted some of their differences. Here, usability guidelines are divided into seven categories of tasks: *downloading software, registering and logging in, communicating, finding people and information, ensuring readability of instructions, getting help,* and *providing tools to support moderators and other role-players.* In the main these guidelines describe generic usability issues, which must be addressed in most types of communications software, although a few specific issues that affect only certain types of software are also addressed.

Downloading software

If community members need to download software, the two guidelines that follow will help to ensure that the process is straightforward:

- *Provide (or confirm that the third party has provided) a clear statement of the technical details for running the software.* This is particularly important for Internet connections (e.g., modem speed), operating system and memory requirements, and any additional software needed. Figure 9.4 shows a sample of such a statement.
- *Include clear download instructions.* Explain to community members exactly what they have to do, and provide feedback as they go through the process.

Quick Facts	
Company:	ICQ
Version:	99b beta 3.19 build 2569
Release date:	August 16, 1999
File size:	5MB
Approx. download time:	23 min. at 28.8 kbps
Downloads:	**70,822,671**
License:	Free
Minimum requirements:	Windows 95/98/NT
Uninstaller included?:	Yes
Download Now	

Figure 9.4   Sample of details for downloading software

Registering and logging in

Many CMC systems require users to register before they can join discussions and to log in each time they participate. Two guidelines help to ensure these procedures are well designed.

- *Compose registration and login procedures* with as few steps as possible, and describe them clearly, as in the sample in Figure 9.5. Use forms to ensure that only relevant information is submitted, and so that it can be entered directly into a database. (Additional information about designing forms is provided in *Chapter 10.*)

- *Include a help capability*. Users forget their passwords, so you must enable them to retrieve this information easily and securely.

Communicating

Design choices that relate to the community's purpose, as well as policies for social interaction and communication tasks strongly influence usability. The following eight guidelines encourage good communication:

- *Develop accurate conceptual maps for users with different levels of experience.* Clearly word instructions and procedures for doing such basic tasks as reading,

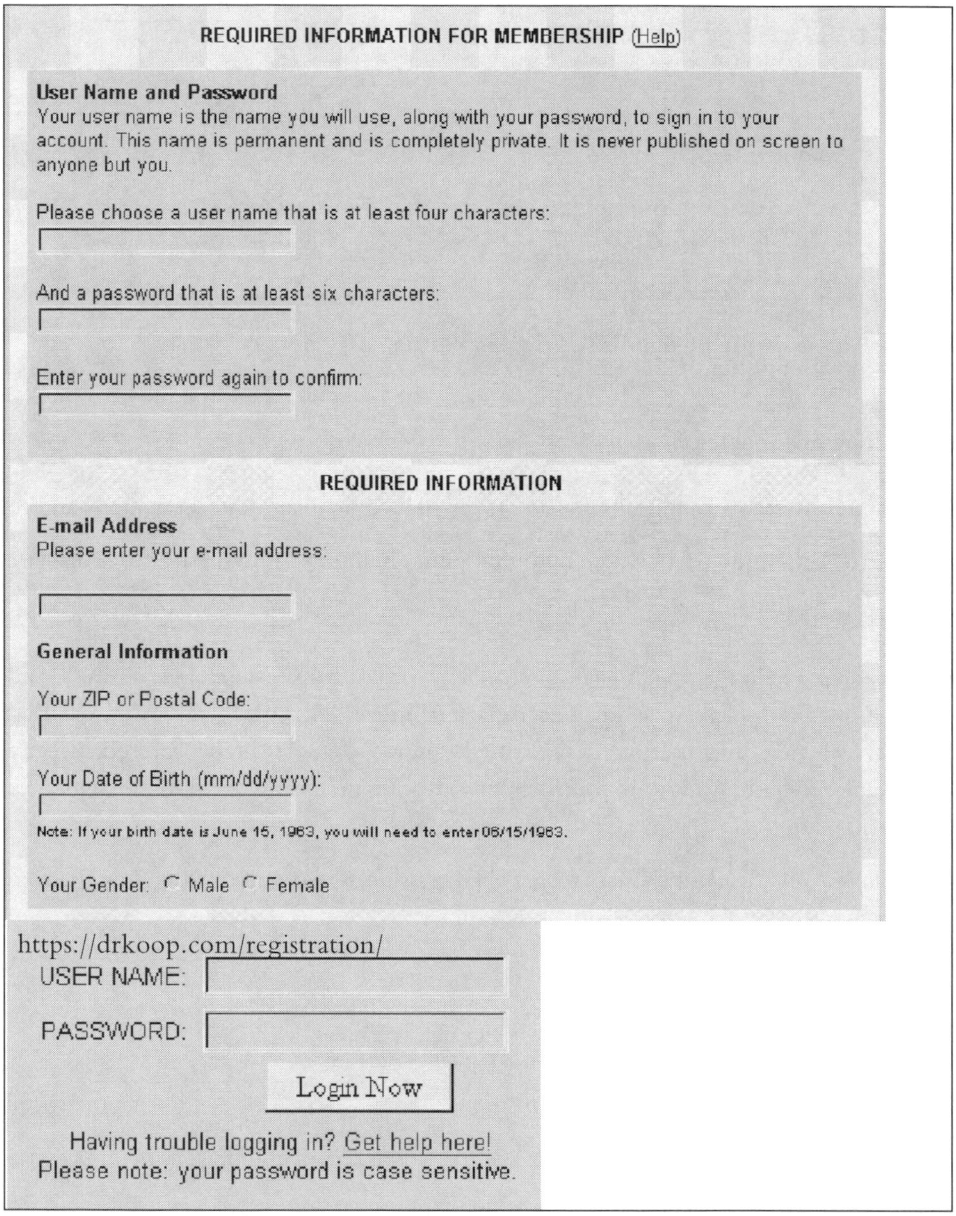

REQUIRED INFORMATION FOR MEMBERSHIP (Help)

User Name and Password
Your user name is the name you will use, along with your password, to sign in to your account. This name is permanent and is completely private. It is never published on screen to anyone but you.

Please choose a user name that is at least four characters:

And a password that is at least six characters:

Enter your password again to confirm:

REQUIRED INFORMATION

E-mail Address
Please enter your e-mail address.

General Information

Your ZIP or Postal Code:

Your Date of Birth (mm/dd/yyyy):

Note: If your birth date is June 15, 1963, you will need to enter 06/15/1963.

Your Gender: ○ Male ○ Female

https://drkoop.com/registration/

USER NAME:

PASSWORD:

Login Now

Having trouble logging in? Get help here!
Please note: your password is case sensitive.

Figure 9.5   Sample registration and login procedures

Reproduced by permission of drkoop.com

composing, and sending messages. These are often provided as "getting started" information (see Figure 9.6).

- *Provide editing facilities.* This means supplying various fonts and symbols, a spell-check capability, and templates for sending messages, among others. Figure 9.7 shows a sample message template.

- *Enable the communication of emotion and intent.* For example, include a dictionary of easy-to-understand icons that can be included in messages to clarify their meaning.

- *Support different levels of experience.* For example, provide information about advanced editing features in a separate place, so that inexperienced users are not overwhelmed. MUDs and MOOs, in particular, can be complex, so include a set of basic commands, to which users can add as their experience grows. Predefined

Getting Started

Welcome to this discussion board! This document gives you the basic knowledge that you need to use this board effectively. If you experience any difficulties with the board, contact one of the moderators listed under the Contact link from the Main Menu.

- Reading Discussions
- Contributing to Discussions
- Searching the Board
- Getting an Account
- Where to get further information
- Rules and "Netiquette"

Reading Discussions

Anyone with WWW access can read discussions on this board. To read discussions, navigate to the discussion of interest by single clicking on the links from the list of topics and subtopics. You can navigate backwards using the navigation bars at the top of each page.

Contributing to Discussions

To post a message to an existing discussion, fill in the "Add a Message" box at the bottom of the page. You may use formatting codes or basic HTML tags to improve the appearance of your post. At the discretion of the moderators, the discussion may allow public posting or may require a user account (username and password). Follow the instructions on the form to supply the necessary credentials for posting.

Where available, you may click on a "Create New Conversation" button to start a new discussion. This will add a subtopic with the subject you specify and start a conversation with the initial message that you specify. After filling in the subject line, post a message as described above.

Searching the Board

Figure 9.6   Basic user information for getting started in a community from www.discusware.com

Reproduced by permission of DiscusWare

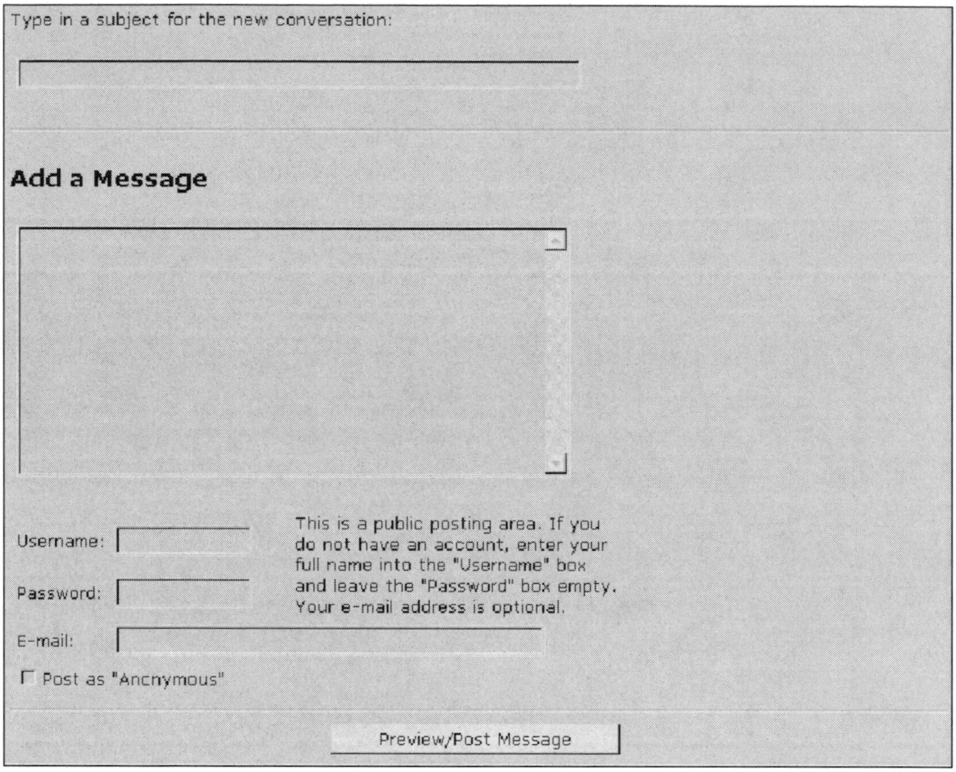

Figure 9.7   A bulletin board message template from www.discusware.com
Reproduced by permission of DiscusWare

modules and templates for programming also support novice programmers (Curtis, 1997).

- *Protect user rights.* If privacy, security, and copyright are issues in the community inform users about the mechanisms being implemented to protect them. Figure 9.8 shows a clearly worded, itemized privacy policy.

- *Make communications easy to follow.* This means, for example, show as many lines of "conversation" on the screen as possible, and ensure there are sufficient channels available in chats. And keep in mind, as populations increase, scaling up may be a problem.

Privacy Policy

Recognized by the industry for our commitment to safeguarding consumer privacy on our Web site, we operate under a strict set of privacy principles:

- The only information drkoop.com obtains about individual visitors to its Web site is information supplied voluntarily by visitors.

- In cases when drkoop.com may need personal information to provide visitors with services tailored especially for them, or to inform them about new features or services, visitors are asked explicitly for that information.

- All identifiable information provided by members (name, email or home address) will not be disclosed to anyone unless members specifically request drkoop.com to do so.

- Only statistical information of our members as a group (usage habits, demographics) may be shared with any partner of drkoop.com; no identifiable information will be shared at any time.

- drkoop.com employs strict security measures to safeguard online transactions; personal information is stored in a secured database and always sent via an encrypted Internet channel.

How to Reach Us

If you ever feel uncertain about whether this site is following the privacy policy we have described here, please notify us by e-mail to feedback@drkoop.com. We will make every reasonable effort to find and correct the problem promptly.

Figure 9.8   A privacy policy from drkoop.com

Reproduced by permission of drkoop.com

- *Clarify the relationship between avatars and conversation.* On-screen, message crowding and overlapping may occur when several avatars are participating at the same time, so alternative ways of viewing messages may be necessary.

- *If graphical representations are used to indicate user activities, provide histories, enhance users' presence, and so on*, make sure that graphics, if used, communicate information as intended (Figures 3.1, 3.2).

Finding people and information

The amount of information available over the Web is monumental, so tools to support searching are essential. These three guidelines will help to choose appropriate search mechanisms:

- *Enable keyword searching.* This method is very common, and usually can be invoked either by relevance or by using Boolean logic.

- *Distinguish messages that have been read from those that have not.* Figure 9.9 shows how this can be accomplished even in the absence of color.

- *Identify relationships among messages.* This will aid user understanding of content, and help them to find information and communicate. Threading is the typical method of achieving this in bulletin boards. Replies to messages are prefixed by the abbreviation Re: and placed directly beneath the original message. Indenting is also used to further define the relationship among messages (*Chapter 2*). Other ways of associating messages are by topic, chronological order, and name of originator.

	Re: Cookies for Wednesday	Dr. Jennifer Preece	Sat 3:31 PM
	Re: The database for Ebay transactions.	Ross	Sun 9:27 PM
	Online Communities Website	Dr. Jonathan Lazar	Sun 10:24 PM
	FW: COMPUTER SCIENTIST (seeking ...	Olufikayo Abiola Akintola	Sun 11:53 PM
	Interesting reading	Donne Andrews	12:39 PM
X	Undergraduate Project	diane.hawkins@exim.gov	3:43 PM
	Undergraduate Project	diane.hawkins@exim.gov	4:03 PM
X	Re: update	Gabriel Tekle-Haimanot	4:30 PM
X	Re: Undergraduate Project	diane.hawkins@exim.gov	5:01 PM
	problem	Zhuhui Chen	6:15 PM
	This message is unread.	**Zhensen Huang**	**6:25 PM**
	This is also an unread message.	**Zhensen Huang**	**6:26 PM**

Figure 9.9   Distinguishing between read and unread messages

Screenshot reprinted by permission of Microsoft Corporation

Ensuring readability of instructions

Similar rules for Web page design apply to the wording of instructions, as these three guidelines indicate:

- *Clearly word all instructions*. Use the same typography conventions and terminology throughout.

- *Provide relevant help*. User errors are bound to occur, no matter how well designed the system. Anticipate common user errors, then write help content to guide users to correct them.

- *Give feedback in a timely fashion*. And make sure that users will understand it. Do not use technical terms or codes. The message "Error 12057 cannot continue" will be meaningless to almost all users, for example.

Providing tools to support moderators and other role-players

The responsibilities of moderators, administrators, and other role-players will, obviously, differ across applications. For example, learning communities not only have to support students, they also must supply tools for keeping student records, distributing quizzes, facilitating discussions, and the like. Here are four guidelines for choosing appropriate tools.

Guidelines:

- *Support changes in population size*. One example is to spawn new discussions.
- *Enable moderators*. Supply them with tools to identify spam and flames, to record messages, to automatically archive or to do whatever is necessary.
- *Institute automated registration*. This is relevant especially to large communities.
- *Collect metrics on community activity*. Doing so will inform future development and support decision making. More on this in *Chapter 10*.

Checklist for Sociability and Usability

Probability, it need not be said that users view usability and sociability differently from developers and managers. Simply, users want to know whether they can find and do what they want, when they want, and that their interactions are comfortable. The eight questions that follow raise the typical concerns expressed by most users. The answer to these questions provide *heuristics* for developers and managers. In conjunction with guidelines, they are useful for guiding the development process and planning evaluations.

1. Why should I join this community? (i.e., What are the benefits for me?)

2. How do I join (or leave) the community? (i.e., What do I do to become a member?)

3. What are the rules of the community? (i.e., Is there anything I shouldn't do?)

4. How do I get started reading and sending messages?

5. Can I do what I want to do easily? (i.e., Can I make the software do x or y?)

6. Is the community safe? (i.e., Will my comments be treated confidentially? Will my personal information be maintained securely?)

7. Can I express myself as I wish?

8. Why should I come back? (i.e., What makes being a member of this community worthwhile in the long term? What's in it for me?)

Table 9.1 summarizes the key usability and sociability features for each of these questions.

Guidelines for Moderators

Moderators generally learn by apprenticeship, that is, by watching those with experience (McMann, 1994); or they must learn "on the fly." They must learn to achieve a

Table 9.1   Checklist of Eight Heuristics

User Questions	Usability Concerns	Sociability Concerns
1. Why should I join this community?	Does the community have a clear and meaningful name? Is there a clear description of the community's purpose? Is the content attractively presented (design—color, graphics, etc.)? Will the site be updated regularly?	What title and content will communicate the community's purpose effectively and attract people?
2. How do I join or leave?	Are the instructions for registering clear-cut? Is it a short procedure? Is there a statement ensuring privacy and confidentiality?	Should this be an open or closed community? How sensitive are the issues and participants? Do we want to control who joins?
3. What are the rules?	Are policies clearly and concisely worded, and appropriately positioned?	What policies are needed? Should a moderator guide and enforce rules? Do we need disclaimers or other statements of intent?
4. How do I read and send messages?	Has appropriate support been defined and provided (e.g., templates, emoticons, FAQs, single messages or digests for listservers, etc.)?	Is support needed for newcomers? Should the system facilitate sending private *and* group messages?
5. Can I do what I want easily?	What capabilities will best meet communication needs (e.g., different formats for information, such as Web pages, FAQs, content variation; search facilities,	What is the best way to ensure that the community is a congenial place, one where people can do what they want to do?

Table 9.1   Continued

User Questions	Usability Concerns	Sociability Concerns
	effective help at the appropriate level; private communication, etc.)?	What are the communication needs of the community?
6. Is the community safe?	What are the best ways to protect personal information, secure transaction processing, support private discussion, and protect members from aggressive behavior?	Will the community need a moderator to ensure appropriate behavior? What level of confidentiality and security is needed?
7. Can I express myself as I wish?	Will users need, want, or expect emoticons, content icons, a seamless link to private email, Web pages, and so on?	What kind of communication capabilities does a community with this purpose require, and how should they be supported?
8. Why should I come back?	How often and by what method should content be changed (e.g., news broadcast, provocateur to stimulate discussion, etc.)?	What will entice people to return on a regular basis?

balance: exerting too much control deters participation; too little can result in loss of focus, frustration, and aggression. A survey of 73 listserver moderators showed that filtering content to keep conversations on track took 32 percent of their effort; facilitating and promoting discussion took 29.3 percent; and preventing flaming took 14.1 percent (Collins & Berge, 1997). Other tasks included being an administrator, editor, and expert guide. *Chapter 3* detailed the moderator role; in this chapter, we discuss how to support moderators.

In person, facilitating discussions effectively requires skill and experience. Online this task may be even more difficult (Feenberg, 1989) because of the absence of tacit clues, such as body language and facial expressions (Collins & Berge, 1997). However, online moderators can learn valuable lessons from "real-life" facilitators. As with most social interactions, there is no guaranteed formula for successful facilitating, but the collective experience of both online (Berge, 1992; Collins & Berge, 1997; Salmon, 2000) and offline facilitators suggests the following guidelines:

- *Suspend personal opinion.* This recommendation was made almost universally.
- *Know the players.* This is difficult to do in all but small closed communities. However, in most communities, only a fraction of the population regularly participates, so it is possible to get to know the most vocal.
- *Foster candor and trust.* Encourage people to show respect for each other's comments. People can be surprisingly open online, so this may be relatively easy to achieve. The downside is that people may also become too outspoken and aggressive toward others.
- *Maintain a constructive tone.* Don't be sarcastic or lose your temper. It's the moderator's job to maintain civility, not engage in bad behavior.
- *Foster a group dynamic.* When necessary, remind participants of the aims of the group. One of the main jobs of a moderator is to filter out comments that are not relevant, to keep the discussion on target (Collins & Berge, 1997).
- *Think ahead of the group.* This means anticipate where the discussion may be headed; or, if it appears to be going nowhere, be prepared to suggest ideas that will get it going again.
- *Form subgroups.* When a number of people appear to be branching in several interesting but different directions, be prepared to split participants into subgroups; but enable them to rejoin the main discussion at a later time. Knowing when to spin off subgroups is likely to become an increasingly important skill, as the population of the Internet expands and communities become very large.

- *Foster group ownership.* Encourage members to acknowledge the contributions of others, to reciprocate when possible, and to acknowledge the benefits of being in the community. This will help to build group commitment.

Many moderators devise moderation policies, often in consultation with the community, which they make public. This helps to protect the moderators if community members should disagree with their actions, which may occur, for example, when a moderator decides not to circulate a participant's message. Public moderation policies are particularly important in communities prone to intense debate, such as political and religious communities and some MOOs. Diversity University, for example, has a detailed policy. A clearly defined moderation policy is also valuable for coordinating the tasks of two or more moderators.

The moderator's job can become very time-consuming (Berge, 1992), especially as the popularity of online communities grows. Tools that support moderators without taking control from them will become increasingly important. The concept of a "mediator" provides another way of dealing with this problem. Mediators, as the name suggests, are on call to help resolve problems reported by community members, but they do not review each message. Commercially developed medical communities often have mediators that serve a collection of communities.

Guidelines to Help Participants Communicate

Needless to say, not everyone writes well, yet writing is necessary to communicate via the Internet. And for people who don't write well, online, the absence of body language and facial expressions poses real problems. (See *Chapter 5* for a discussion of establishing common ground and empathy via various media.) To guide those participants, it may help to show how messages can be misunderstood, then offer an alternative, to facilitate better communication. Distance education specialists from the British Open University have devised templates to encourage clear communication among students (Zimmer & Alexander, 1996) and to prevent flame wars (Kayany, 1998). This is of particular importance in support and education communities in which interpersonal trust plays a big role in their success (Fox, 1996).

Bob Zimmer and Gary Alexander (1996) aim to convert cycles of aggression into positive, open, and empathic communication (*Chapter 5*). Their ideas are based on the work of the well-known psychotherapist Carl Rogers (1959). Using four short, straightforward templates, they encouraged students in a study to confirm that they understood the intent of the person sending a message before they responded to it. This strategy helps recipients to avoid responding inappropriately, and perhaps defensively and antagonistically. Students were encouraged to use these templates, listed here, in their own messages as appropriate:

- Here's my own experience and what I want to do:
- [Name], I'd welcome knowing what you think I mean, to be sure my feelings are accepted.
- [Name], Tell me what you want to do here, so that I can see your point of view.
- [Name], What I think you mean in essence is . . . . My own view differs in this way. . .

These templates were made available from the computer desktop to be copied into messages or turned into macros for inserting by a single keypress. Explanations and examples were provided to explain to students why understanding each other is so important. When the students (adults taking a course on renewable energy), were interviewed about the templates, they spoke very positively about their value and the associated training. Zimmer and Alexander also provided an electronic Face-Maker program that enabled the students to create pictures of themselves to send with their messages. This helps students to get to know each other and to create a sense of presence in their electronic environment.

The use of emoticons is another way to make an author's intentions explicit. Jokes can be misinterpreted when there are no facial and auditory cues to accompany them, so inserting an appropriate emoticon in the text signals that the comment is not to be taken seriously. Many MUDs, MOOs, and chat environments provide easy-to-insert comments and icons. Acronyms, such as LOL (for laughing out loud) serve the same purpose (*Chapter 3*). In addition, well-known rules of netiquette (*Chapter 3*) have evolved to prevent misunderstandings. Examples include: Do not copy a message to the whole list when it is intended for a particular person; include contextual informa-tion in replies so that the receiver knows to what the comment refers; and do not send very short replies, such as yes, no, or me too. Experienced members also can help newcomers learn by serving as role models.

Guiding community members to learn how to communicate effectively online will help developers ensure the growth of harmonious and satisfying communities, and will also make the moderator's job easier.

Summary

Sociability is concerned with supporting social interactions online. A key way to achieve this is by planning policies that encourage development of congenial and appropriate behavior: Usability has to do with making interfaces consistent, controllable, and predictable, which in turn makes them easy and satisfying to use. By focusing on sociability and usability, community developers can influence the potential success of online communities. They can help guide the process of community evolution, which is shaped to a great degree by the relationships and interactions of its participants.

In contrast, user concerns generally span both sociability and usability, as they want to do what they want, when they want, efficiently and easily.

Chapter 10 expands this material by discussing methods for evaluating usability and sociability.

Further Reading

The Role of the Moderator in a Scholarly Discussion Group (SDG) (Berge, 1992), *Moderating Online Electronic Discussion Groups* (Collins & Berge, 1997), and *E-moderating: The Key to Teaching and Learning Online* (Salmon, 2000)
Written by experienced moderators, these three publications provide considerable support and insight for moderators. The book by Gilly Salmon focuses on moderating distance learning, and provides a wealth of valuable tips on how to be a successful moderator. There are also case studies and descriptions of student experiences of their moderators.

Web Style Guide (Lynch & Horton, 1999), *Designing Web Usability: The Practice of Simplicity* (Nielsen, 2000), and *Web Site Usability: A Designer's Guide* (Spool, Scanlon, Schroeder, Snyder, & DeAngelo, 1997)

These texts provide guidance on usability for successful Web site design. The text by Jakob Nielsen is particularly comprehensive and should be read by all Web developers. The Lynch and Horton book focuses on typographic design.

Human-Computer Interaction (Preece et al., 1994), *Designing the User Interface: Strategies for Effective Human-Computer Interaction (Third Edition)* (Shneiderman, 1998a), and *Effective Color Displays* (Travis, 1991)

These books on human-computer interaction give general coverage of usability; they do not specifically address online communities. Shneiderman's text discusses usability of Web site design, while the book by Travis provides valuable information about using color.

"The Rogerian Interface: For Open, Warm Empathy in Computer-mediated Collaborative Learning" (Zimmer & Alexander, 1996)

This paper discusses how users can be trained to find common ground online. It introduces techniques used by the British Open University for online education.

www.naima.com/articles/ (Kim, 1998)

Amy Jo Kim is a Web community developer. Her Web site presents a short but important list of guidelines for developing successful online communities, which are explained in her new book, *Community Building on the Web* (Kim, 2000).

10 Assessing Needs and Evaluating Communities

They value it differently: their formal analysis is different: but behind all that, the essence to which they are responding is the same.

—C. P. Snow, *The Two Cultures and a Second Look* (1969, p. 94)

The aim of this chapter is to introduce a range of techniques for assessing community needs and for evaluating sociability and usability. It presents a framework for thinking about evaluation and offers guidance to developers, managers, students, and researchers on selecting appropriate techniques.

The Connection
Mark Kostabi 1984 © Kostabi World

Contents

Is it possible to predict whether an online community will be successful? Certainly, taking the time to assess the participants' needs beforehand can get developers off in the right direction. But after the community has been launched, can its success be accurately determined? Knowing how many people visit the community each day is one measure of its success. However, what if many of these people are just passers-by, not active participants? Counting the number of "hits" then would give a false impression of the site's success. Reading messages is another way of evaluating success, to learn the benefit people get from belonging to the community. Classifying these messages into types—for example, questions, answers, empathic comments, complaints, and so on—provides more information.

There are many techniques for evaluating the success of an online community, and deciding which to use depends on who needs the information and what they want to know. Information needed by a community member or developer is different from that needed by a researcher or company manager.

Evaluation is concerned with gathering information regarding the effectiveness of sociability support and usability design during various stages of development, including after the community is fully functioning.

- *Usability evaluation focuses on interaction design.* Software with good usability supports rapid learning, high skill retention, low error rates, and high productivity. It is consistent, controllable, and predictable making it pleasant and effective to use. Interfaces with these characteristics are easier to learn, more effective to use, and generate greater satisfaction.

- *Sociability evaluation focuses on social planning and social processes.* Sociability is concerned with producing social policies that support a community's purpose, and that are easy to understand, socially acceptable and practicable. Communities with these characteristics are more agreeable, well organized, and socially predictable.

Certain evaluation techniques are better for understanding sociability, while others are more appropriate to usability; therefore, combinations are needed during development, post-launch, and throughout community evolution. Evaluation is related to needs assessment, in that both help developers learn what the community wants. In practice, it is useful to evaluate whether the community's needs have been correctly understood during early development. Furthermore, some of the same techniques used during needs assessment are also used in some kinds of evaluation. Interviews, questionnaires, observation, and ethnographic approaches are commonly used for both purposes (see *Chapter 7* and the case studies in *Chapter 11*). This chapter, therefore, discusses techniques for needs assessment as well as for evaluation.

Evaluations conducted to inform community development and evolution are known as *formative evaluation*, because they influence how the community develops (see *Chapter 7* on community-centered development). Evaluations also play a validation, or *summative* role. Summative evaluations demonstrate to management or to a funding organization, for example, that the money they invested in the project has been well spent. Let's say that a senior marketing manager of an e-commerce company has heard that online communities draw customers and increase sales. After investing in online community development, she wants to track exactly how much impact the community is having, to determine whether the investment was worthwhile. Evaluations are also done for research purposes, to validate a theory or predictive model.

Many evaluation techniques have been well documented (e.g., Preece et al., 1994; Denzin & Lincoln, 1994; Robson, 1993, 1994) but they cannot directly be transferred to study the Internet (Sudaweeks & Simoff, 1999); they need to be adapted, and new ones need to be developed (Jones, 1999a). Conducting research on the topic of Internet communities requires an interdisciplinary perspective, which brings together methods used in a variety of paradigms (Rice, 1989). To that end, the evaluation techniques discussed in this chapter represent a small selection of techniques that are or could be used to evaluate online communities. They are drawn from *positivist* and *interpretive* paradigms and survey research. Positivists believe there are immutable structures to be discovered, explored, and analyzed so their approach is generally *quantitative*, involving statistical validation. In contrast, interpretivists prefer to become immersed in situations, to allow insights to emerge during the process of investigation. Their studies are generally *qualitative*, guided by research questions. That said, it is necessary to point out that even this neat, well-established dichotomy is breaking down, and combinations of approaches are proving valuable for providing different perspectives.

Social context is at the heart of the concept of community, therefore, ethnography (the study and systemic recording of human cultures) is a valuable approach to evaluating online communities, and it is covered more fully here than experimental methods. The use of questionnaires, in particular online questionnaires, is becoming increasingly important as well, most specifically for evaluating e-commerce communities, because they are comparatively inexpensive to design and analyze. In contrast, though data logging and metrics give precise numeric results, they can be difficult to interpret.

This chapter reviews evaluation methods that can be used by:

- *Developers*, to influence formative development of communities, including the collection of community requirements prior to starting development.

- *Managers* to assess the business impact of online communities.

- *Researchers*, to answer fundamental research questions.

To begin, an evaluation framework is introduced; next, ethical issues are discussed; then a brief overview is presented of the five categories of techniques that are discussed in more detail later in the chapter. The chapter ends with a summary of the strengths and weaknesses of the methods, as viewed from the perspectives of developers, managers and researchers.

Evaluation Framework

Evaluation studies are more likely to provide useful information when they focus on answering a question. Even exploratory studies and ethnographic studies, when researchers are open to what the community reveals, are guided by questions. The questions provide the goals for the evaluation, which in turn influence the choice of methods used. Logistical considerations, such as time allotted for the study, costs, evaluator skills, and other factors also influence this choice. The triad of *goals, questions, and metrics* (GQM) (Basili, Caldiera, & Rombach, 1994) forms a general framework for thinking about evaluation (Preece & Rombach, 1994).

- *Goals comprise the overall aim of the evaluation.* They will vary according to who is doing the evaluation and why. The same community could be evaluated with different goals in mind; or developers might evaluate the community at various times during the design phase.

- *Questions direct the focus of the evaluation.* They are influenced by goals, but they provide more specific guidance for the evaluation. There may be many questions for each goal. For example, the goal of an evaluation could be to determine whether distance learners taking the same class were benefiting from an online student community. This would be determined by asking more specific questions, such as do the students learn more as a result of interacting online with other students? Do they enjoy the learning experience more?

- *Metrics are used by evaluators to quantify answers to questions.* Skillful evaluators decompose questions into a series of subquestions. Invariably, different methods are used for each type of question.

Five Approaches

Books about evaluation can be confusing to readers because different disciplines and scholarly paradigms use different terminology. For example, as already discussed, evaluations are said to be qualitative or quantitative. Qualitative evaluations produce data, such as in the form of comments and descriptions, that are not numeric measurements and so cannot be statistically analyzed, unless they are converted into a form that can be counted. In contrast, the data from quantitative evaluations are numeric in form and can be statistically analyzed. In addition to the qualitative-quantitative dimension, data can be objective or subjective (see Table 10.1).

Two other terms commonly used in evaluation discussions are *field studies* and *laboratory experiments.* Field studies, also referred to as *naturalistic,* are undertaken in

Table 10.1   Qualitative-Quantitative and Subjective-Objective Dimensions

Evaluation Type	Qualitative Data	Quantitative Data
Subjective	Ethnographic data, for example, interviews, observations, artifacts are interpreted by ethnographers.	Questionnaires, for example, take subjective input, then express it using numeric rating scales.
Objective	For example, content analysis categorizes user comments, seeking to identify patterns and frequencies.	For example, usage logs generate data that is statistically analyzed.

natural settings. The data collected is usually qualitative (e.g., descriptive). Yet another term that is popular in educational research is *action research*, used to describe ongoing evaluation (for example of a new teaching technique) during which improvements are made; in other words, there is no discrete evaluation phase. This approach has been successfully used to evaluate educational communities in distance learning (Hiltz, 1994; Hiltz & Turoff, 1993). Laboratory experiments are used in research and have been adapted for usability testing, which is discussed later.

The terminology used in the context of the topic at hand, online community evaluation, is generally associated with one of five approaches, which are briefly introduced here and discussed in more detail later in the chapter:

- *Reviews involve one or more reviewers, who comment on the software and sociability of the community.* They give subjective opinions and make suggestions for improvements. Their reviews are often guided by heuristics, in which case they are known as *heuristic evaluations* (Nielsen & Mack, 1994). The review approach has been used extensively in software development. It is particularly valuable for evaluating usability, and to some extent sociability planning, throughout development.

- *Surveys, done either by questionnaires or interviews.* Both formats seek to elicit the subjective opinions of the community, but each requires different skills to achieve this goal. Surveys are frequently used to assess community needs, gather demographic data, and answer research questions, and often are used to evaluate established communities. Questionnaires can be delivered online or in-person, which makes them valuable for doing online community work.

- *Observation involves watching and monitoring the activities of a community.* Observation is usually considered subjective, but, depending on the techniques used, some interpretation of the findings is necessary. Ethnography (which is considered a special form of observation in this text) has been used successfully by online community researchers, and hence is regarded as a valuable approach for gaining a general understanding about a community.

- *Experimental, quasi-experimental, and usability testing are derived from scientific experimental procedures in which hypotheses are tested under controled conditions.* But, because people and the conditions in which they interact cannot be controled, experimentation is of limited value. In contrast, usability testing does not depend on controled conditions, so these techniques are most applicable to testing software usability during development. However, as described later, they have some broader applications.

- *Data logging and metrics both involve the accumulation of numeric data.* Data logging provides a way of quantifying online activity that is popular with managers. Metrics are measures, or counts, used to quantify activity in communities.

Before we discuss these approaches in greater detail, we must first address some general issues that are relevant to all of them, namely: the ethics of Internet research, pilot studies, and awareness of goals and perspectives.

Ethical issues

Because an astounding amount of information, much of it personal, can be collected easily and inexpensively from online community evaluations, this activity poses many questions of an ethical nature, chief among them questions of privacy, confidentiality, informed consent, and appropriation of personal content (Sharf, 1999, p. 245). It is all too easy online to abuse the rights of others and infringe their privacy, even without intending to do so, therefore it is especially important to safeguard these interactions.

The following list provides brief practical suggestions that are applicable to any study of these ethical issues.

- Consider at the outset whether your study could damage people in any way. Are the aims of your study beneficial to the community? If not, reconsider pursuing it further.

- Tell the community what you are going to do, and why, and reassure participants they will remain anonymous. You may also want to remind the community from time to time, to reach any newcomers.

- Assure the community that personal information they provide will be kept confidential.

- *Never* disclose someone's identity in a report; use fictitious names or numbers.

- Avoid including a quote, comment, or description that might reveal a person's identity.

- Inform participants that if, at any time, they wish to end an interview or withdraw from the study, it is their right to do so.

- If you belong to a university, hospital, or federal agency that has a human subjects policy, be sure to follow the correct procedures. This probably means informing the research office and completing a form. If you work for another type of organization, find out if it has any regulations, before starting the study.

Some researchers share their reports with the community or with the community developer. I have done this with a bulletin board developer, who not only was interested and supportive of my work but also corrected some inaccuracies and provided additional information that enabled me to improve the report. And if you intend to quote sensitive material, it's wise to ask permission in advance from those who made the comments, even though they will be presented anonymously. Yes, this takes time, but it serves to engender trust among the community members, whose comments often add pertinent information that lends credence to your report (Sharf, 1999).

Preliminary checks

Observing (i.e., lurking), *reviewing archives*, and *participating* in a community are good ways to get to know a community before formally studying it. Although not a pilot study in the scientific sense, these activities can serve a similar purpose. They enable evaluators to focus their questions and decide whether they are appropriate.

The next steps are to do a pilot study, then plan the main study. A pilot study is a small-scale version of the larger study plan. The aim of a pilot study is to try out a technique, confirm that the questions in a survey are clear, or check that an experimental procedure works. Pilot studies enable developers to learn about problems in advance, so that they can correct them before conducting the main study. It is advisable to do as much checking as possible. Depending on the situation, you may even want to perform several pilot studies and make necessary changes after each. Also, ask for input from colleagues.

Goals and perspectives

Determining how many questionnaires to collect, messages to sample, subjects to involve, and when to stop is always an issue. Usually, it depends on what you are trying to achieve; in other words, what are the *goals* of the study and which *questions* will lead to fulfilling those goals (i.e., the GQM framework introduced earlier in this chapter).

As noted previously, there are three different perspectives to consider—those of the community *developers*, *managers* of organizations, and *researchers*. Each has different goals that will affect the choice of evaluation methods.

Community developers

The main reasons that community developers want evaluations are to:

- *Collect user requirements*. Typically, observation, interviews, and surveys are used.
- *Verify that requirements have been addressed as thoroughly as possible*. Typically, evaluations are done throughout the development process. The goal is to confirm that appropriate software has been selected, and that the usability and sociability are optimum. Many informal reviews are often done as well.

At all stages of community development, as well as after the community has been launched, it is important to conduct evaluations. Developers may have overlooked or inadequately addressed certain requirements, or the community's needs may have changed. Or new people may have joined, who change the dynamic of the community. Software may have to be upgraded to meet requests from the community, or simply because better software has become available. External events may also have an influence. For example a host Web site may have changed its advertising policy, prompting managers to ask whether more traffic is coming to the site, how long they stay, and how this impacts sales; developers will want to know how this activity impacts the attitude of the original community. Practically, increases in population may require more channels for chats; or new discussions may have to be spawned on a bulletin board. What will be the effect of these alterations, and how should they be done?

Many goals underlie the questions community developers ask when they evaluate. Most, of course, are concerned with making the community as satisfying as possible for members. The checklist in the previous chapter can be used to guide most evaluations, but more detailed questions may also be needed. In general, however, any evaluation is better than none, but more is usually better. Review evaluations typically involve just a few people—five or six is common but one- or two-person reviews are done, too. Often, the more people who agree to complete a survey the better. However, larger numbers also equate with additional time, effort, and cost. For most types of evaluation, the number of responses needed—whether from a survey or interview—is the number that results in representative feedback about the community. Obviously, evaluations done for development purposes will not have the same goals as those of researchers, so statistical significance is not necessarily the point.

Organization managers

Managers of e-commerce organizations may request developers to do the evaluation, or they may hire independent evaluators. Sensibly, if managers provide the budget for developing an online community in the belief that it will attract customers and, hence, bolster sales, they will want to have proof of return on their investment, asking: Has the strategy been effective? Should a similar one be adopted to support other products or services? Or they may want to know the effect of a change in advertising policy, as mentioned above, or of a site redesign.

In short, managers are not concerned with the details of usability and sociability; they want to know the effect on sales. Consequently, metrics are usually important to managers, as are customer opinions, which are usually collected using survey techniques. They often want statistically significant samples of respondents, before they regard the results as authoritative.

Students and researchers

The aim of research is to discover new knowledge; therefore, evaluation type research must be rigorous. The procedures have to be carefully managed and reported so they can be replicated and/or referenced by other researchers. The level of rigor necessary for such research is usually higher than for development and management purposes.

The evaluation methods detailed in the following sections are discussed in relation to these three perspectives. As stated, to date, little has been written about the role of evaluation in online community development or for determining the commercial implications of e-commerce communities. Fortunately, many techniques used in usability evaluation can be adapted for some forms of community evaluation (see discussion and comparison of methods in Preece et al., 1994). The role of ethnography, metrics, and surveys in online community research has received more attention (Jones, 1999a).

Reviews

Reviews are widely used in software engineering and for evaluating usability (Nielsen, 1993). Reviewing styles vary, however. Three types are useful for developers of online communities: *expert*, *community*, and *heuristic* reviews. Reviewing is more important during development than in research and manager evaluations. Expert reviews have the advantage of being quick and inexpensive, as they do not require special facilities.

Expert reviews, as the term suggests, use specialists to assess usability, sociability, and community activity. Experts also role-play to determine how typical community members would react, then provide feedback to the developer. Reviewers generally suggest fixes as well as pointing out problems. Guidelines, such as those given in *Chapter 9*, provide heuristics to guide the review, in which case it is a heuristic review.

For community reviews, members of the community are asked to comment on the development of the community. Though they generally are not experts, their input is important to confirm whether developers are meeting the community's needs. Conducting this type of review also encourages a sense of ownership.

Most reviews are done on-site, early in design, but the technique does lend itself to remote reviews, whereby reports are sent to developers via email.

Surveys: Questionnaires and Interviews

Surveys can be done either by questionnaire or by interview; both techniques have been used extensively in human-computer interaction (Preece et al., 1994; Preece, 1993), evidenced by the number of books written about interviewing techniques and survey design (Oppenheim, 1992). Today, not surprisingly, an increasing number of surveys are being conducted via email and the World Wide Web. This route offers several advantages to online community developers, managers, and researchers. There are many similarities between digital and paper-based surveys, as well as some interesting differences, which are discussed below.

Digital questionnaires

The questionnaire format is commonly used to collect basic demographic data and the subjective input of respondents. The advantages of using electronic, or digital, questionnaires, include[1] (Lazar & Preece, 1999a,b):

- It is easy to gather the input of a large number of people.
- Responses are usually returned quickly.
- Costs are lower; there are fewer—or no—copying and postage expenses.

---

[1] This section is adapted from a paper by Jonathan Lazar and Jenny Preece with permission from Jonathan.

- Data can be transferred immediately into a database for analysis.

- Electronic questionnaires take less time to analyze.

- Errors in questionnaire design can be corrected easily (though of course it is better to avoid them in the first place).

Few disadvantages have been reported but there is some evidence suggesting that response rates may be lower online than with paper and pencil questionnaires (Witmer, Colman, & Katzman, 1999).

There are two types of electronic questionnaires: email-based (Thach, 1995) and Web-based (Bertot & McClure, 1996). The main advantage of email is that you can target specific users; the main disadvantage is that you are limited to text. Web-based questionnaires enable greater format flexibility; you can include graphics, boxes for choices (see Figure 10.1), pull-down menus (see Figure 10.2), help screens, and other amenities can be included to guide respondents. In addition, Web-based surveys enable immediate data validation; and you can design for restrictions, such as to enable only one response or one type of response, such as numerical. This cannot be done in email. For these reasons, Web-based questionnaires seem more promising for online community evaluations (Lazar & Preece, 1999b; Schmidt, 1997).

In Figure 10.1, notice that respondents check the appropriate answer, whereas in Figure 10.2, a pull-down menu displays alternatives. The menus take less space, and users are less likely to make errors using them. On-screen questionnaires also require a tighter layout, so respondents are more willing to fill them out, as opposed to paper questionnaires that often run for several pages.

> # General Demographics Questionnaire
>
> ## Click here if the survey is not working properly.
>
> | Part 1: Background |
> |---|
>
> How did you find out about the GVU's Tenth WWW User Survey?
> *(Please check all that apply.)*
>
> ☐ Followed a text link from another Web page
> ☐ Followed a graphical banner/icon from another Web page
> ☐ Found GVU site using a search engine
> ☐ Saw postings to WWW related newsgroups
> ☐ Received email from www-surveying mailing list
> ☐ Was told URL by friend
> ☐ Read about it in a newspaper/magazine
> ☐ Remembered to participate from last survey
> ☐ Other sources
>
> How long have you been using the Internet (including using email, gopher, ftp, etc.)?
>
> ○ Less than 6 months
> ○ 6 to 12 months
> ○ 1 to 3 years
> ○ 4 to 6 years
> ○ 7 years or more

Figure 10.1   A Web–based checklist questionnaire from www.gvu.gatech.edu

Printed by permission of Georgia Tech Research Corporation, © 1996–1999, Atlanta GA 30332

Four steps are recommended to successfully implement a Web-based surveys (Lazar & Preece, 1999b):

1. *Design the survey on paper.* Many guidelines for designing paper surveys also apply to Web-based surveys. In any case, probably you will need to use both paper and electronic surveys to reach all community members (Lazar, Tsao, &

Please indicate your agreement/disagreement with each of the following statements.

Not Answered ▼	There should be new laws to protect privacy on the Internet.

Not Answered
Agree Strongly
Agree Somewhat
Neither Agree or Disagree
Disagree Somewhat
Disagree Strongly
No Opinion

Not Answered ▼	I support the establishment of key escrow encryption (where a trusted party keeps a key that can read encrypted messages).

Not Answered ▼	Web sites need information about their users to market their site to advertisers.

Not Answered ▼	Content providers have the right to resell information about its users to other companies.

Not Answered ▼	A user ought to have complete control over which sites get what demographic information.

Not Answered ▼	Magazines to which I subscribe have the right to sell my name and address to companies they feel will interest me

Not Answered ▼	I like receiving mass postal mailings that were specifically targeted to my demographics

Not Answered ▼	I like receiving mass electronic mailings

Figure 10.2   A   Web-based   questionnaire   with   pull-down   menus   from www.gvu.gatech.edu

Printed by permission of Georgia Tech Research Corporation, © 1996–1999, Atlanta GA 30332

Preece, 1999; Patterson, 1997). Consult key texts on questionnaire design for guidance (e.g., Oppenheim, 1992; Preece et al., 1994; Preece, 1993). Run pilot tests as often as necessary with subjects from the target population to verify that the wording is unambiguous and that the style of questions is consistent.

2. *Commit to an implementation methodology.* If the questionnaire will be used for community needs analysis, it is important to confirm that all potential respondents have online access when the survey is being conducted. A Web-based survey is only valuable when a sizable number of the survey population have access. For an existing online community this will not be an issue, but for new communities, this may be an impediment. For those without Web access you will need to prepare a paper version that mimics as closely as possible the Web version. Developers of the Blacksburg Village, Quiz Bowl, and Down Syndrome Online Advocacy Group communities report successfully employing this dual-version approach. (See the case studies in *Chapter 11.*)

   You must also define the survey population. Normally, a random sample is drawn so that the results are indicative of the whole population. However, this may be difficult, if not impossible, to do for a Web-based survey if the size and demography of the population are not known. The absence of a population definition has been a criticism of several online surveys, including Georgia Tech's Graphics, Visualization and Usability (GVU) survey which has been surveying the demography and activity of the Internet twice yearly since 1994. The policy that GVU employs is to make as many people as possible aware of the survey to encourage a wide variety of participants. GVU does this by publicizing the survey using banner advertisements, via other popular sites, in newspapers, and in other media. A similar policy (Harper, Slaughter, & Norman, 1997) is used by the developers of the Questionnaire for User Interaction Satisfaction, QUIS, whose introduction screen is shown in Figure 10.3 (Shneiderman, 1998a). However, these efforts do not avoid biased sampling, as participants are self-selecting.

3. *Turn the paper design into a digital design.* This involves a number of steps. First, make the survey error-proof, by providing clear, thoroughly tested instructions and by designing to prevent input errors. That is, you should

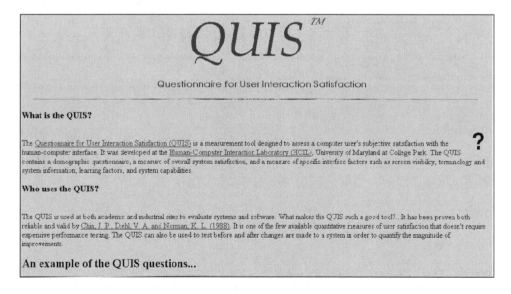

Figure 10.3   Introduction to an online survey

Permission given by University of Maryland. Excerpt from Questionnaire for User Interaction Satisfaction (QUIS™) © 1989, 1993, 1998. All rights reserved

engineer out errors; for example, if respondents are to check just one box, design the system to reject more than one.

Second, make sure the survey is accessible from all common browsers and is readable on different-size monitors and various network locations. Do not require special software or hardware to access it. Even having to download software will deter novice users.

Third, make sure respondent information is captured on each submission, to preclude the same person submitting several surveys. This can be done by recording the Internet domain name or the corresponding IP address of the respondent, which can be transferred directly to a database. Another way is to access the transfer and referrer logs from the Web server; these provide information about the domains from which the Web-based survey was accessed. Of course, people can still submit from different accounts with different IP addresses, so additional identification information may be needed.

Fourth, once implemented, user-test it with members of the community.

4. *Publicize the survey to the target population.* Some researchers stress the importance of inviting people to participate prior to release of the survey (Witmer et al., 1999). It is also important to target the questionnaire at those who are interested in its topic, obvious as this may sound. Some evidence suggests that lack of interest in the topic is a greater deterrent to completing an online questionnaire than a paper questionnaire (Witmer et al., 1999).

Although questionnaire design is a well-established technique for conducting evaluations (Oppenheim, 1992), do not underestimate the problems that may arise as a result of implementing it via new media, such as the Web and email.

Interviews

Interviews provide similar types of information as questionnaires. However, the skills needed to successfully implement the two techniques differ. The intricacies of interviewing in-person or over the telephone are well understood (see for example,

Robson, 1993; Preece et al., 1994). Three primary interview protocols are described here: *structured, open*, and *semi-structured*; a fourth, *focus groups*, is also briefly introduced.

Structured interviews are the most similar to questionnaires. Their questions require a specific answer or a selection from a prescribed written list of options. Structured interviews are easy and quick to use where people would probably not be willing to stop to complete a paper questionnaire, such as in airport terminals.

Open questions mean that interviewees are free to answer as fully or as briefly as they wish. Open questions often provide very rich data because respondents may mention factors not considered by the interviewer. But there is a cost; open interview data is difficult and time-consuming to analyze. Nevertheless, open questions can be very useful early in development, to establish the community's needs.

In semi-structured interviews, the interviewer starts with a general, but preplanned question, then probes until no new relevant information is forthcoming. For example:

> I have noticed that you often post on *this* bulletin board. Why? ⟨answer⟩ And why do you like it? ⟨answer⟩ Tell me more about x. ⟨answer⟩ Anything else? ⟨answer⟩ Is there anything more you want to tell me? Thanks.

For consistency, it is wise to write a basic script for guidance, to ensure that the same topics are covered with each interviewee. Semi-structured interviewing suffers from the same problem as open interviews — they are tedious to analyze. Consequently, they are best used to collect basic information early on. This technique is, however, more systematic than open-ended interviewing. Often, you may find a combination of structured and semi-structured interviewing is the way to go.

Focus groups are a form of group interview that allows for the discussion of diverse issues leading to immediate feedback that confirms or refutes hypotheses. Focus groups are commonly used for political and marketing purposes. An agenda is decided upon, and a coordinator is present to facilitate and motivate and monitor discussion, as necessary, whether to prompt quiet people to participate or to rein in the more outgoing. When done well, a focus group can be a very productive way of obtaining information. Participants are selected to represent typical users. The discussion is usually recorded for later analysis, during which participants help interpret the data.

Conducting interviews

An important admonition when composing interview questions is do not preempt answers. For example, if instead of "I have noticed that you often post on the bulletin board," you write "you seem to like this bulletin board. . ." it will sound as if you *assume* this is the case. A surprising number of people will give an answer they think the interviewer wants to hear, whether or not it is accurate. Though less problematic with questionnaires, it can be a major problem in face-to-face interviews where the physical presence and body language of the interviewer can influence how an interviewee responds.

A second piece of advice is, when there are silences during interviews, don't be too quick to interject, and when you do, use a neutral probe such as, "Do you want to tell me anything else?" Then give the person time to think. Most important, be polite at all times and try to put people at ease. No one wants to feel as if they are being interrogated. Finally, thank them for their time.

In summary, interviewing techniques can be conducted in traditional formats, face to face or by telephone, or using state-of-the art technologies, including desktop video conferencing systems such as Microsoft's NetMeeting, or possibly a synchronous chat focus group, or email, depending on the nature of the study. However, experience using these new media is limited and success is open to question. Note that chat environments tend to be most suitable for short responses, so short, unambiguous questions are usually best for an online focus group; questions requiring more reflection would be better via email.

Observation

There are many ways to observe, both on- and offline. Just watching what is happening in a community is an essential first step for most developers and researchers. Online, if you watched a chat in Active Worlds for an hour, you would probably see a variety of avatars moving around the screen amid a sequence of messages, in the form of greetings, requests for help, flirtations, and others. Casual observing in an online community enables researchers and developers to formulate questions for a later in-depth study. It is a preview observation.

Observations are somewhat difficult to capture and document however, because humans are not good at remembering numerous details for long periods. A form of recording is needed. Taking notes is one option, but tends to be unreliable. In face-to-face situations, video and audio recording are often used. Though easy, these forms of data collection are time-consuming to analyze. It often takes a minimum of five hours to analyze one hour of video, sometimes much longer—there are reports of ratios as high as 100 : 1 (Preece et al., 1994). Fortunately, there are ways of logging most activity in online communities. Communities in which communication is asynchronous and uses archived text provide an immediate source of data. Special logging techniques are needed for other types of communities.

A variety of qualitative observation techniques exist, which emanate from various research paradigms, each having different theories and practices; for example, phenomenology from philosophy, ethnography from anthropology, grounded theory from sociology, ethnomethodology from semiotics, discourse analysis from linguistics and qualitative ethology from zoology (Morse, 1994). Each has its preferred evaluation approaches (Denzin & Lincoln, 1994). But because ethnography is one of the most widely adapted techniques for studying online communities, the remainder of this section focuses on it, while touching on a few other useful techniques.

Ethnography and participant observation

Anthropologists and ethnographers continue to debate the definition of ethnography. However, it is generally agreed that, in practice, ethnography is a form of social research that has a substantial number of the following characteristics (Atkinson & Hammersley, 1994, p. 248):

- A strong emphasis on exploring the nature of particular social phenomena—as opposed to testing hypotheses about them.

- A tendency to work primarily with unstructured data, that is, data that has not been coded at the point of collection in terms of a closed set of analytic categories.

- Investigation of a small number of cases, often just one in detail.

- Data analysis that involves explicit interpretation of the meanings and functions of human actions, in which verbal descriptions generally dominate; quantification and statistical analysis play at most a subordinate role.

- Methods that rely at least in part on participant observation. This raises issues for researchers (which are less significant for developers) such as how much interaction and what kind of relationship the researcher has with the community, how this affects the community, and how the researcher's biases influence the way data is interpreted and reported.

These characteristics relate well with the nature of much online community evaluation and research, which is frequently best approached by a cyber-anthropologist and ethnographer. Ethnographers attempt to interpret and make sense of human activity (Walsham, 1993) using whatever data helps them to attain this goal. Typically open-ended interviews, known as *ethnographic interviews*, are a central source of data. These interviews may be recorded in notes, on tape or video, and be supplemented with diary entries, annotated notebooks, photographs, and artifacts, as appropriate. In other words—anything that helps to tell the story.

Ethnography has become important to the study of human-computer interaction, computer supported cooperative work, and online communities, to learn how groups interact with technology. It is often used in conjunction with other techniques such as data logging and discourse analysis to gain different perspectives on a problem. This combo technique is known as *triangulation*.

There are many examples of ethnography in online communities research. A particularly potent example, is Nancy Baym's "Interpreting Soap Operas and Creating Community: Inside an Electronic Fan Culture" (1997). Baym participated in a soap opera online community for over a year before writing about it. The following quotes illustrate how she approached the community, then adapted interviewing and questionnaire techniques to support her observations and collect additional information.

> As a longtime fan of soap operas, I was thrilled to discover this group. It was only after I had been reading daily and participating regularly for a year that I began to write about it. As the work evolved, I have shared its progress with the group members and found them exceedingly supportive and helpful (Baym, 1997, p. 104).

Baym, like many researchers, opted to tell the community what she was doing and share her findings with them. By being open with the community, she benefited from their support. They may also have helped explain some of her findings. She summarized her data collection methods as follows:

> The data for this study were obtained from three sources. In October 1991, I saved all the messages that appeared.... I collected more messages in 1993. Eighteen participants responded to a questionnaire I posted. Personal email correspondence with 10 other ... participants provided further information. I posted two notices to the group explaining the project and offering to exclude posts by those who preferred not to be involved. No one declined to participate (Baym, 1997, p. 104).

Baym used her data to examine, one, the group's technical and participatory structure, with particular emphasis on the spatial and temporal separation of group members; two, emergent traditions; and, three, performance.

Although ethnography is primarily a research tool, the approach and philosophy underlies contextual inquiry (discussed in *Chapter* 7), in which a thorough understanding of context, from an insider's perspective, helps to inform community-centered design (Beyer & Holtzblatt, 1998), particularly for community needs analysis and during the early stages of development. As well as being a useful research technique, ethnography is a potentially valuable technique for community developers.

The remainder of this chapter addresses a number of observation methods that can be used either within an ethnographic paradigm or to provide alternative perspectives. Some of these techniques are most suitable for face-to-face work with prospective community members. Others involve analyzing data collected online (e.g., content analysis, data logging, and metrics); still others could be adapted for use on- or offline. Although many are suitable for research, some could provide information for developers and even for managers.

Think-aloud protocols

Think-aloud protocols are verbal descriptions of what a user or pair of users is thinking and doing while interacting with a computer. This technique has been used to gain insights into how people use computers and the problems they encounter with interface designs. Typically, as a user (or pair) performs a task, he or she describes what he or she is doing and why. The descriptions are captured on tape or video.

A well-known problem with this technique is that the subject must speak, use a mouse, and problem solve at the same time. This often causes cognitive overload, and many users stop speaking out loud. With two people working together this is less of a problem because they talk to each other about what they are doing.

In the context of online communities, think-aloud protocols can be useful for assessing the usability of online community software during participatory design and development.

Participant diaries

Participant diaries can be used to inform online community developers and researchers in a variety of ways. For example, diaries that document sociability or usability problems can provide valuable input for community development. Conveniently, this activity can be done by participants when they wish; it does not have to be scheduled. The major problem with diaries is that people get lazy or forget to make entries, so incentives are needed to encourage them; and the process must be straightforward and not time-consuming.

In another study, J.P. Robinson and G. Godbey, the authors of *Time for Life: The Surprising Ways that Americans Use Their Time* (1997) used time diaries in which, at the end of each day, participants were required to specify how much time they had spent on various activities. This data was then analyzed to ascertain the impact of television. Robinson and Godbey intend to extend this study to investigate the impact of computers on people's lives, similar to the study by Kraut and his colleagues (Kraut, Scherlis, Mukhopadhyay, Manning, & Kiesler, 1996) discussed in *Chapter 1* and elsewhere. Variations of this approach could also be used to investigate how people spend their time online in greater detail.

Metrics and Data Logging

Because online data can be logged easily, developing metrics to quantify and describe activity in online communities is an appealing approach for community developers, e-commerce managers, and researchers alike. Developers want to know how communities evolve once they are populated; managers of e-commerce companies are eager to learn how online communities might improve their sales, and whether a business case can be made to support their continued maintenance; students and researchers want to track trends in community development and relate them to specific research questions. Despite this strong interest, however, little has been written about metric development and the logistics of logging data to track online community activities. That is due to change, because an increasing number of large-scale studies are being successfully conducted that would be impossible without data logging (Nonnecke & Preece, 2000a,b; Rafaeli, Sudweeks, Konstan, & Mabry, 1998; Smith, 1999; Whittaker, Terveen, Hill, & Cherny, 1998).

The important first step to take before using data logging and metrics is to revisit the goals and the questions of the study. A variety of metrics can be collected to describe community demographics, activities, discourse, and content, and to compare the effects of changes in software design.

Metrics that describe community members

Collecting basic metrics about community participants is the first step in quantifying activity and planning for future change. Factors include: number of members, basic demographics (e.g., gender, age, residence etc.), and length of membership.

Metrics that measure community activity

Quantifying community activity provides a more detailed picture of its members, by tracking changes and cycles (Smith, Farnham, & Drucker, 2000; Nonnecke & Preece, 2000a,b). For example, metrics might show there is more activity in the evening than during the day, on weekends, or during the week. As the community evolves, metrics can show how activity patterns change. Offline, cycles are determined by people's need to eat, work, and sleep; annual cycles are punctuated by holidays and festivals. How do such offline activities impact those of online communities? Do online communities develop their own, separate, cycles of activity? If so, what drives them? Does behavior online change with experience; for example, a recent study showed that gesturing via avators declined (Smith et al., 2000).

Metrics that can be adapted to answer some of these questions include number of messages sent over a certain period of time, number of messages per person, frequency of visits, and others (Smith & Kollock, 1999). For example, in a study of 109 listserver discussion groups, data logging was used to establish that 147,946 messages were posted over a three-month period by over 19,000 of the 60,000 members (Nonnecke & Preece, 2000a,b).

Comparative studies that use metrics

Metrics to assess the influence on an online community of changes to software, sociability, and external events (such as advertising) would be of use, in particular for e-commerce entrepreneurs. For example, they could be used to learn how introducing a moderator or new software (e.g., a chat, a new version of a bulletin board, etc.) would affect community activity.

In a study of an online interactive art museum, University of Southern California researchers analyzed server logs over a seven-month period, tracking who visited the site via their unique Internet address (McLaughlin et al., 1999). They recorded when people came to the site, what they requested, how long they looked at each page, which browser they were using, and where they were from. The researchers used Webtrends, a commercial analysis tool, to analyze the data. The researchers were able to determine the number of successful sessions per day and when those sessions took place. Among the findings, they discovered that the site was busiest in the evenings during the week.

Data collected from logs complements data extracted from other sources, to gain a fuller picture of what is happening. For example, information from the data log in the interactive museum study was used with data from a questionnaire to ascertain when it was most opportune for a museum curator to participate in chats.

Metrics can also be collected using content and discourse course analysis techniques, as described a little later in this chapter.

Experiments, Quasi-Experiments, and Usability Testing

The objective of experiments is to study the changes that occur in one or two pairs of variables in controlled laboratory conditions. Experimental evaluation was the cornerstone of early work conducted in human–computer interaction. It provides a way of analyzing small differences in the design of interface components. For example, experiments can be used to examine the efficacy of two menu designs or dialog boxes for particular users to do a certain task. For a number of years, this topic has received little attention from software designers (Gaines, Chen, & Shaw, 1997), but the current trend to include online communities in e-commerce sites is helping to change this. In general, however, the role of experimental evaluation is less significant in online community development because many principles of interaction design are already well documented. Moreover, networked environments are complex and do not lend themselves as easily to scientific reductionism. Finally, many books have already been written on designing and running experiments (e.g., Robson, 1994) and on usability testing (e.g., Dumas & Redish, 1999; Nielsen, 1993). For these reasons, these topics will only be touched upon here.

The basic tenet of experimentation is that a *hypothesis* is formulated, and stated, from which an experiment is constructed to either prove or disprove the hypothesis. Two kinds of variables are identified: the *independent variable* is manipulated by the experimenter, for example, an interface feature; the *dependent variable*, for example, the time it takes to perform a particular task, is influenced by the independent variable, but not vice versa. When designing the experiment, the researcher has to make a number of very important decisions, including:

- How to control other variables not of central interest that if left uncontrolled could bias the results; for example, selecting subjects and defining the experimental task.

- Which experimental design to use.

- The kind(s) of data to collect, and how much of it; how to analyze the data and present the results.

Selecting appropriate *subjects* is crucial. As closely as possible, subjects need to be matched in terms of critical characteristics, such as gender (equal numbers in all experimental conditions), age, experience (particularly experiences that are similar to the experimental condition), and culture. A standard is that the pool of subjects should be representative of the general user population that will participate in the community.

The experimental *task* should also be representative of the community's activities. If the purpose of the community is to discuss a particular topic, to provide emotional support, or whatever, the experiment should involve that activity. When determining the task, it is also important to decide the kind of data to collect and how to analyze it. Asking advice from a statistician may be useful in this regard before starting. It may also be a good idea to conduct a pilot study to unearth any major problems with the experimental procedure before doing the full-blown experiment.

There are several experimental designs from which to choose, and the availability of suitable subjects and the type of task will strongly influence the choice. Three well-known designs are: *independent subject design*, *matched subject design*, and *repeated measures design*. In independent subject design, a single group of subjects is gathered and allocated randomly to the experimental conditions. In matched subject design, subjects are paired (often male-female to eliminate gender bias) and then randomly allocated to the experimental conditions. In repeated measures design, all subjects appear in both conditions, meaning that only half the number of subjects is needed, making this design popular. However, in this design, it is important to ensure that the order in which subjects perform tasks does not bias the results. For example, if there are two tasks, A and B, half the subjects should do A followed by B and the other half should do B followed by A.

Usability testing (Dumas & Redish, 1999) is an applied form of experimentation used by developers to ensure that the software they are developing is appropriate for the target population. Unlike experiments, usability testing does not focus on controlling variables; it takes a broader view. For example, a group of typical online community users might be asked to compose and send a message to the group. By logging their activity, the developers could record the time that it takes each person to complete the task and the number of incorrect keypresses each makes in the process. This data will inform them about the ease of use of their product.

When all the subjects can be gathered in the laboratory, usability testers can control the tests, to verify that each is doing the test, to accurately record the time it takes. When testers must rely on the subjects doing the test off-site, inevitably, inaccuracies are incurred. For example, a subject might be distracted by his or her children coming into the room or the doorbell ringing; or he or she may give in to temptation to take a break. So, though distributed testing can be done, it involves risks; however, by increasing the number of subjects, the effects of these risks can be reduced. For example, e-commerce developers could compare the behavior of two groups, each comprising several hundred customers. Software would direct the participants to the appropriate interface, and their behavior would be logged. The log would detail any problems that the users experienced with the software.

The process of usability testing is well documented, but the techniques need to be adapted for online communities.

Quasi-experiments may be possible to conduct with entire online communities as has been done in some studies of computer-supported cooperative work (Olson & Olson, 1997). For example, if two communities with similar purposes use different software, it may be possible to examine the impact of the software's design on the frequency and type of communication in the two groups, or the impact of major changes in sociability, such as the introduction of a moderator or a new registration policy. Of course, interpreting and reporting findings must be done conscientiously so as not to assume cause-and-effect relationships that may result from other differences between the communities. Experiments are carried out by students and researchers, though developers may perform usability evaluations, which do *not* have a control group. The developer's goal is to inform design, rather than to publish statistically valid results.

Note: To become a skillful experimenter or usability tester requires experience, and those interested should read much more about the profession, and consult with experts in the field. Additional reading sources are provided at the end of the chapter.

Additional Techniques for Students and Researchers

Two additional techniques that may be useful for students and researchers are content analysis and discourse analysis, both of which make it possible to examine the content and meaning of online discussions. Findings are often compared with those from in-person studies.

Content analysis

Content analysis is a systematic, reliable way of coding content into a theoretically meaningful set of mutually exclusive categories (Williams, Rice, & Rogers, 1988). Online discussions, such as those in bulletin boards (Preece, 1999a) and chats, can be analyzed qualitatively, to develop an understanding of different types of content, or quantitatively, to determine the frequency of various topic categories. To do this, a planned strategy for sampling messages is needed. Depending on the aims of the study, sampling is either random or extracted at fixed intervals.

One of the most challenging aspects of content analysis is determining meaningful content categories that are *orthogonal*—meaning they do not overlap in any way. Content categories are determined by the research question. Deciding on the appropriate level of granularity at which to make the analysis depends partly on the research question and partly on practical considerations. This issue can be illustrated by a study in which a student wanted to analyze text from a listserver discussion group for evidence of gendered communication (Tannen, 1990). Though the category descriptions were clear, the student did not know if she should analyze whole messages, paragraphs, sentences, words, or utterances. Eventually, she decided to work with whole messages, because in this particular discussion they were short.

The content categories and level of granularity of data analysis must be reliable, so that they can be used by other researchers with the same result. This is generally achieved by training a second researcher to apply the categories. When training is complete, both researchers analyze the same sampling of messages. If there is a difference between the two analyses, either training was inadequate or the categorization did not work well, and further work will be needed to establish where the problem lies and to rectify it before repeating the test. When a high level of reliability is reached, it can be quantified by calculating the *inter-researcher reliability* rating. This is the percentage of agreement between the two researchers, which is the number of items that both categorized in the same way, expressed as a percentage of the total number of items examined. Note that transcribing and coding messages by hand and calculating an inter-researcher reliability rating is time-consuming. Fortunately, computer programs make analysis easier and more accurate.

An example of the use of content analysis is a study that examined the content of messages from a large sample of listserver and UseNet communities over a period of several months (Rafaeli, Sudweeks, Konstan, & Mabry, 1998). The study detailed the sampling technique used, coding, the computer analysis, reliability, and the researchers' policy on ethics. Content analysis has also been used to analyze messages in a patient support community (Preece, 1999a). The results of this study indicated that over half the messages had empathic content. These outnumbered requests for and offers of factual information and other messages.

Content analysis provides information about the makeup of messages; it does *not* attempt to interpret deeper meaning or intent, and pays little or no attention to the context of messages. Consequently, the value of this technique in online community research is limited.

Discourse analysis

Discourse analysis focuses on the meaning rather than content of discourse and pays greater attention to the context. It is more strongly interpretive than content analysis. Discourse analysis regards language as not only reflecting psychological and social life but as constructing it (Coyle, 1995).

An underlying assumption of discourse analysis is that there is no objective scientific truth. Language in the form of discourse is a "social reality." Language is viewed as a constructive tool, and discourse analysis provides a way of studying how people use language to verbally describe their worlds (Fiske, 1994). Discourse analysis assumes that all linguistic material has an *action orientation*, which means that it is used to perform particular social functions such as justifying, questioning, and assuring, which are achieved by employing a variety of rhetorical strategies (Coyle, 1995). The role of the discourse analyst is to understand these strategies. Discourse analysis has been used to address the question "what is the function of this text?"; what meaning and impression it conveys.

Discourse analysis may involve taking a very fine-grain approach, whereby individual words are analyzed. This is referred to as *conversational analysis*. More often, discourse analysis involves looking at whole texts. But there are no hard-and-fast rules about sampling discourse. What is important is to obtain sufficient amounts of discourse to give a true indication of the message(s) contained in the text. Analysis could involve a few or many scripts, depending upon the variability of the content. The absence of methodological procedures can make discourse analysis intimidating to those not trained in its use. In many respects, successful discourse analysis depends upon scholarship, how carefully researchers examine and describe their analysis and interpretations. Being guided by a hypothesis is useful; conversely, it is also important not to read too much into a text. Some analysts believe that a useful approach is to look for variability in texts either within or between individuals (Coyle, 1995).

In the two text extracts that follow, Andrew Coyle illustrates how a slight change in wording can change the message in the text (1995).

> Discourse analysis is what you do when you are saying that you are doing discourse analysis. There is no set methodology. In many respects, discourse analysis depends on how carefully you interpret the text and describe your interpretations by backing them with reference to the linguistic evidence in the texts.

> According to Coyle, discourse analysis is what you do when you are saying that you are doing discourse analysis. There is no set methodology. In many respects, discourse analysis depends on how carefully you interpret the text and describe your interpretations by backing them with reference to the linguistic evidence in the texts.

By adding the three words "According to Coyle" in the second extract, the viability of the statement changes, depending on what the reader knows about Cole's work and reputation. It is up to the analyst to determine and describe the meaning of the two samples.

To review, discourse analysis is a way of describing the meaning and intent of communication in a community, whereas content analysis focuses on what is discussed. Content analysis lends itself well to computer analysis. Discourse analysis does not: instead, care must be taken to understand the meaning of a message. This involves examining both the language and context of the message. Discourse analysis is, therefore, time-consuming, but it can produce valuable insights.

An interesting example of discourse analysis was an in-depth study done of two UseNet group messages (Denzin, 1999). This study was concerned with understanding how online personae relate to offline personae, as well as the use of gendered conversation. This study pointed out, as others have (Turkle, 1995), that online community communication is different from "real-world" communication.

Without doubt, discourse analysis is a powerful analytical method for students and researchers seeking to understand the underlying meaning of online discussions; however, experience is needed before effective use can be made of it.

Table 10.2   Different Approaches for Evaluating Usability and Sociability

Approach	Needs Assessment	Usability Evaluation	Sociability Evaluation
Reviews	Plays no role in the development of a new community, but could inform redesign of software.	Useful for collecting formative feedback from experts during development. (Used extensively during the development of case studies in *Chapter 11*.)	Experts can offer suggestions for planning policies. (Used extensively during the development of case studies in *Chapter 11*.)
Surveys and Interviews	Surveys can be sent to potential participants either online or off (e.g., Quiz Bowl case study, *Chapter 11*). Interviews are useful for eliciting information from core community members (e.g., DSOAG case study, *Chapter 11*).	Used extensively during development, and by managers to assess usage and user satisfaction. Online surveys are inexpensive. Surveys can be used both for formative and summative evaluation.	Interviews are useful for defining the community's purpose, and for determining acceptability of policies and other parameters early in development. Surveys can be used both formatively and summatively to evaluate sociability.
Observation	Useful for identifying problems that may occur when changes are made to an existing community.	Used for informing development. Ethnography is well-suited for longitudinal studies of the activity in a community.	Ethnography is important for understanding social interaction in a community and for detecting problems. It can be used formatively or summatively.

Table 10.2   Continued

Approach	Needs Assessment	Usability Evaluation	Sociability Evaluation
Metrics and Data Logging	Plays no role in the development of a new community; however, valuable input could be collected to inform software redesign or when social policies change.	Useful summative measure of overall success, and for comparing how changes in software or sociability affect participation. Particularly popular with managers.	Applies as for usability.
Experiments and Quasi-experiments	Not applicable.	Used in research. Usability testing can be done in labs and, to a limited extent, online, to formatively evaluate designs.	Quasi-experiments can be done summatively to compare two communities or groups within a community.

Summary

A major point of this chapter is that traditional evaluation methods must be adapted for Internet research, and new methods must be devised, before online communities can be studied effectively. Web-based questionnaires, data logging, and metrics are promising approaches for e-commerce managers who need to justify online community development budgets. Tools to support these techniques, such as templates for questionnaire design, and data collection and analysis tools are also needed. Furthermore, many methodological issues require research—how to sample

Internet populations; what length of questionnaire is effective; under what conditions are people more likely to complete questionnaires; and so on.

Improved techniques are also needed to specifically address the evaluation of online communities from all perspectives: development, management, and research. Surveys are proving to be particularly valuable because they can be distributed on- and offline. Both online and telephone interviews of online participants are likely to increase. In contrast, though ethnography provides a natural approach for studying online communities, and has already been used extensively, it does not provide the quantitative results that developers and managers seek. However, in the future, better data logging tools and metrics promise to satisfy this need.

Triangulation, in which different techniques are used to provide a global picture, is a good approach for evaluating online communities. The benefit of triangulation is that different techniques provide different lenses through which to examine the problem (Morse, 1994, p. 224). For example, the combination of in-depth interview techniques and data logging is already providing useful results in research (e.g., Nonnecke & Preece, 2000a,b).

In some online community evaluations, the same data may be analyzed in different ways. For example, interview data might also be analyzed quantitatively using content analysis. However, when two different techniques are used, they should not interfere with each other. For example, an ethnographic study could be conducted to evaluate the sociability of an online community, in conjunction with a separate experimental study to evaluate a particular aspect of software usability.

Many factors will affect the choice of evaluation methods. The goals of the evaluation and the specific questions to be addressed are central considerations; logistics are important, too. Some approaches are more suitable for assessing a community's needs; others are better for evaluating usability or sociability (see Table 10.2). Often, usability and sociability are evaluated together, using surveys. Similarly, although ethnography focuses more on sociability, usability issues may also be revealed.

Further Reading

Handbook of Qualitative Research (Denzin & Lincoln, 1994)

This edited book is a bible for qualitative researchers. It contains detailed descriptions of discourse analysis and many other techniques. Though it does not target the Internet and online communities it does deal with the key paradigms of research in this field. The chapter by Denzin and Lincoln provides an excellent overview of qualitative research, in which the differences between these approaches are thoroughly discussed.

A Practical Guide to Usability Testing (Dumas & Redish, 1999)

This book provides an excellent introduction to the practical issues that have to be addressed in planning and carrying out usability tests. It is not written for online community developers and managers, but they can apply much of the advice to their work.

Doing Internet Research: Critical Issues and Methods for Examining the Net (Jones, 1999)
To date, this is the only book that addresses Internet research per se. It is a collection of many useful articles that cover important research techniques. For example the chapter by Dr. Norman Denzin provides a good introduction to discourse analysis, and Dr. Nancy Baym's chapter is a good introduction to ethnographic research using a combination of techniques.

"Designing and Implementing Web-based Surveys" (Lazar & Preece, 1999b)
This article provides an introduction to the advantages and challenges of Web-based questionnaire design.

Usability Engineering (Nielsen, 1993)
This book discusses a range of techniques used to evaluate usability, including standard usability testing.

Human-Computer Interaction (Preece et al., 1994)
The final part of this five-part book describes a range of usability evaluation techniques that will be useful for evaluating software usability for online communities, and for collecting requirements prior to development of the community.

Experimental Design and Statistics in Psychology (Robson, 1994)
This book provides a concise and clearly written introduction to experimental design.

Real-World Research (Robson, 1993)
This is a good resource for any real-world research, in particular for interview and questionnaire design. It provides many good practical hints. However, because it was

written before the advent of the Internet and online communities, it does not address the special issues required for this research.

Research Methods and the New Media (Williams et al., 1988)
Despite its publication date, this book still contains much useful information about evaluating new media.

www.cc.gatech.edu/gvu/user_surveys/
Anyone interested in Web-based surveys is strongly encouraged to view examples of Georgia Tech's Graphics, Visualization and Usability WWW User Surveys. GVU started its study in January 1994, and has now completed more than ten surveys. The site also offers advice on sampling, gives fascinating comparisons of changes in Internet demography over the years, and much more.

www.cs.umd.edu/hcil/quis/
The Questionnaire for User Interaction Satisfaction (QUIS) is a widely used evaluation tool. It is constructed using a hierarchical approach, in which overall usability is divided into subcomponents that constitute independent psychometric scales.

11 Development Case Studies

It is the manners and the spirit of a people which preserve a republic in vigor.

—Thomas Jefferson (as quoted in Risjord, 1994, p. 49)

This chapter presents case studies of community-centered development to exemplify much of what we have discussed so far. Different issues are emphasized in each case, depending on the logistics of the development process.

Contents

Epicurean Epic
Mark Kostabi 1993 © Kostabi World

This chapter details the development of two online communities, noting both the challenges to and the solutions for each of them. The overall aim of the chapter is to demonstrate how community-centered development is practiced. In both communities, the developers worked closely with members to understand their needs, to select appropriate software, and to develop good sociability and usability; in short, they formed very close partnerships.

These two cases were chosen because their development history has been well documented. Large commercial online communities, as well as some hosted by Xoom.com, Convene.Com, and others also look for ways to involve users and verify their understanding of user needs. They may rely on experienced usability consultants to review their products during development. Having watched thousands of users and reviewed many products these experts are able to role-play typical users (often using heuristics; *Chapters 9* and *10*) before launch. Then they log or survey thousands of users interacting in the community to confirm that the policies they devised are working as planned and that there are no serious usability complaints.

Down Syndrome Online Advocacy Group[1]

This case study describes how the Down Syndrome Online Advocacy Group (DSOAG) was revised by two information systems masters students at University of Maryland, Baltimore County, Judah Buchwater and Beth Hanst, in close collaboration with members of the DSOAG community. One of the parents of a child with Down Syndrome founded DSOAG with the goal of "bridging the gap"

---

[1] Permission to cite the facts of this study was granted informally by the project team.

between parents of children with Down Syndrome and the Down Syndrome research community. Several other Down Syndrome Web sites exist, but they are support groups, or have a marketing orientation. The primary goals of DSOAG are to (Lazar, Hanst, Buchwater, & Preece, 2000):

- Support interaction among scientists involved in Down Syndrome (DS) research and parents of children with Down Syndrome.
- Inform visitors of the process by which funding for health-related research is allocated by U.S. lawmakers.
- Inform visitors wishing to make monetary donations to Down Syndrome-related organizations of legitimate channels for doing so.

A secondary aim is to provide a centralized site with links to other resources provided by other Web sites and online communities.

The project began with a core group of community members explaining ideas about Web site design, which was already in progress when the project team entered the scene. The role of the team was threefold: to evaluate the community's design concept; work with members to ensure that their ideas were representative of the larger community; finally, develop an online community with good usability and sociability to support the extant offline and online communities. Needless to say, it was imperative that the project team acquire a basic, yet thorough, knowledge of Down Syndrome and its impact on children, their parents and family, and the community. They also had to become familiar with the legislative issues involved and research work. Finally, because these parents of children with Down Syndrome already had many Internet resources related to these issues, the team had to learn about these and decide how best to integrate links to them.

Community needs assessment and user task analysis

The project started in the fall of 1998, when the project team members were introduced to two parents of children with Down Syndrome who were eager to develop an online community to support research into the condition. At that time, a Web site already existed that had been designed by one of the parents, and the second parent moderated an AOL chat room that provided support for 180 parents of children with Down Syndrome. Of those parents, 88 percent lived in the United States, with 43 percent living on the East Coast. Seven members lived outside of the United States. The geographic locations of members were evenly divided among cities, suburbs, and rural areas.

The development team began by learning about the needs of parents by recording interviews with the two parents already active online (Lazar et al., 2000). The team also talked with other parents of children with Down Syndrome who attended a Buddy Walk in Washington, DC. From these meetings, the team discovered that the majority of these parents belonged to offline support groups; a number also belonged to regional and national support groups. Many reported difficulties in attending group meetings, which required too much time away from home or caused scheduling conflicts. Parents living in rural areas had a particularly difficult time getting to meetings. In addition, parents complained that discussions too often went off topic and that it proved problematic to cater to the differing needs of members. Also, very few parents were able or willing to volunteer to perform leadership and organizational tasks.

The next step for the development team was to develop a survey with the help of core community members—the developer of the original Web site, the moderator of the

AOL chat, and others. Email addresses were obtained from the chat room moderator, who was careful to ensure participants' privacy. Before distributing the survey, the team sent a note explaining its purpose and assuring parents that their participation was voluntary and would be kept confidential.

The survey, distributed by email, comprised 15 questions covering the following topics: access to equipment; demographic information about each participant; Internet experience; usage and opinions of the DS chat room, listservers, and other software; comparison of benefits of meeting online and offline; and preferences for the design of the new online community.

A total of 78 (43 percent) responses were received from the 180 subjects, considered a good response rate for online surveys. Many of the answers were detailed and carefully worded, which gave the development team confidence that the quality of information collected was high. Excerpts from the developers report follow:

- Respondents listed these benefits of chat rooms in order of importance:
    Talking to other parents of children with DS.
    Finding information about DS, including medical information and
    information about educational opportunities for children with DS.
    Providing and receiving support.
    Collecting information about education for children with DS.
    Having the service available from home.

- Respondents rated these following features as most useful for the Web site:
    Links to Web sites concerning research on DS.
    Listserver where questions are answered by qualified experts.
    Summaries of current research related to DS.
    Online letters to "sign" and send to legislators.
    Advice column with questions answered by qualified experts.
    Links to libraries/bases of knowledge about DS.
    Moderated question-and-answer sessions with medical doctors.

      Moderated question-and-answer sessions with researchers.

      News items about DS.

      Information about funding for DS research.

- Respondents requested Web content in these areas:

      Adult clinics and residential facilities; teen and adult vocational information.

      Educational support.

      Local DS group links.

      Links to other subjects (e.g., augmentative communication, sex education, sensory therapies/games, exercises).

      Periodicals.

      Funded legal support.

Selecting technology and planning sociability

The DSOAG site was being hosted by an Internet service provider, which had proven satisfactory, so there was no reason to change this. Initially, the team considered using a Web homesteading shell for the purpose of easy maintenance. However, due to limitations of the shell for Mac and AOL users, the team opted to use the chat room and bulletin board features provided free by a company called Top Choice. Although some features of this product were considered confusing, they offered better usability than many "shareware" chat rooms and bulletin boards. The revised Web pages were constructed using LiquidFX Professional, a Web authoring environment developed by Psylon (*www.psylon.com*).

Key sociability issues considered at this stage included: the need for a moderator, registration, and by-laws to direct online behavior. These are discussed in the following section.

Designing, implementing, and testing prototypes

The development team and community representatives decided to make the following resources available from the DSOAG home page:

- Basic information about DS, identified by the question What is Down Syndrome?

- Research News, with a link to Dogpile.com, a site that routinely searches the Web for updates on specified topics and reports the findings.

- Link to research funding, with links to other key sites.

- Link to Lawmakers page, with further links.

- Links to related research sites.

- Link to page on alternative medical treatments, where researchers and clinicians are invited to submit suggestions, which are reviewed and, potentially, added to the site.

- Links to chat rooms on AOL and other support communities. (The group also wanted a chat room for medical researchers where experts would be invited to host chats and answer questions.)

- Links to listservers. (Medical researchers at the National Institutes of Health (NIH) agreed to participate asynchronously in discussions about Down Syndrome.)

- Links to bulletin boards. (The community decided not to develop its own bulletin board for asynchronous communication. Instead, they linked to other sites.)

- Link to a Contact Us page, which contained registration forms for joining the community and Web pages where researchers and scientists could post descriptions of their work.

Sociability and usability design

The design team was particularly concerned that the community site have good usability and sociability. They considered each of the following topics in turn.

Conceptual map

Before starting the redesign, the team analyzed the original site and found it hard to conceptualize. None of the pages presented a clear overview or offered information about navigation, which was controlled by buttons whose labels had no descriptive quality, such as Next or More Info. Furthermore, the positions of the navigational buttons varied from page to page.

To facilitate navigation and promote consistency within the site, the developers reserved 25 percent of the display area on the left-hand side of each page of the site for a navigational menu containing the same links to Web pages and other features of the DSOAG (see Figure 11.1), in the same order. To distinguish the current page

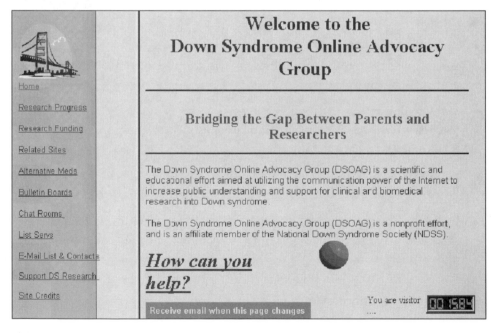

Figure 11.1   Home page of the Down Syndrome Online Advocacy Group.
Reproduced with permission

from the hyperlinks to other pages, the name of the current page was colored red and was not underlined.

Aesthetic features

Most of the pages on the original Web site required the user to scroll, which research has indicated users resist (Nielsen, 1998). The revised design was formatted for a 640×480 pixel screen, to greatly reduce the need for scrolling. These other formatting decisions completed the aesthetic redesign:

- *Background.* The turquoise-blue background and multicolored fonts used for the original site did not seem appropriate to the scientific research theme of DSOAG. In the redesign, the navigational panel was colored aqua, with the balance in white, to draw the visitors' attention to this menu. The aqua color was kept light enough to provide sufficient contrast between the red, navy, and magenta colors of the navigational links.

- *Graphics.* To support the site's theme, "Bridging the Gap between Parents and Researchers," a bridge icon was added to the top left corner of each page. The bridge symbol also became an identity symbol of the community. And where the original Web site featured a number of blinking icons and cartoon-style graphics, some of which included animation, the overall tone of the redesign was more professional.

- *Fonts.* The Arial typeface was chosen for the navigational links and text in the body of each page. For contrast, Times New Roman was used for the title of each page. Readability of the two fonts was tested and found to be acceptable. To reduce eyestrain and to complement the aqua panel, navy blue was chosen for the links and body text. Magenta was chosen to indicate an already clicked-on link because it was clearly visible over the aqua panel and did not clash. Red was chosen for the subtitle of each page, to accentuate the red element in the bridge icon.

Usability

The useability features that were addressed in the redesign included:

- *Consistency*. The appearance of pages and the meanings of words and actions within a Web site should be consistent (Nielsen, 1993). The original site lacked consistency in appearance and navigational functions. To remedy this, each page was revised to the following format:

    The bridge icon appears in the upper left corner.

    The left quarter background of the screen is aqua. The remaining screen background is white.

    A complete list of navigational links appears on each page, and the order of the links is the same from page to page.

    Titles, unclicked links, and body text are navy blue.

    Subtitles and the current page title in the navigational menu are red.

    Visited links are magenta.

    Times New Roman (serif) font is used for titles and subtitles.

    Arial (sans serif) font is used for navigational links and body text.

- *User control*. Straightforward organization and clearly marked navigational paths help users to form a conceptual map of the site and contribute to their sense of control. Links to external sites can induce the "lost-in-hyperspace" syndrome, so a message reminding visitors to use the Back button on the Web browser is repeated with the links. Use of graphics within the site is limited to the bridge icon, plus blue lines above and below page titles, so users do not have to wait for fancy graphics to load.

- *Clearly marked exits*. Users should be able to leave a page or undo an action without difficulty (Nielsen, 1993). When navigating within the DSOAG site, visitors do not need to use the Back button. Pages that are accessed only through other pages, such as the Lawmakers page and the form for joining the DSOAG mailing list, include return links to the previous page.

- *Browsers*. Due to inconsistencies among browsers, the same Web page may appear differently depending on the browser through which it is viewed; code that functions well in one browser may produce unusable results in another. Therefore the DSOAG Web site was designed to appear and behave consistently when viewed either with Internet Explorer or Netscape Navigator, the two most commonly used browsers.

- *Plug-ins.* Requiring the addition of plug-in applications decreases a site's transparency. It also increases the complexity of the interface, placing an additional burden on the user's cognitive load. Plug-ins may also necessitate the use of a particular browser (Benyon, 1997). To minimize the negative effects associated with plug-ins, for DSOAG, the TopChoice facilities were favored over other Web homesteading shells.

- *Node load.* For DSOAG, developers tried to place an appropriate amount of information on each page. Overloading any page with content requires users to scroll, which may cause them to skim too rapidly over important information or entirely overlook material presented below the immediate page view (Benyon, 1997). Usability testing done at Indiana University revealed that scrolling was also often required when the Netscape browser was used, and information was frequently overlooked because users were scrolling too quickly (Corry et al., 1997). On the other hand, pages weak in content may cause the user to skip around to find information, thereby disrupting the flow of the site.

- *Frames.* Because some browsers cannot handle frames, and frames do not allow bookmarking, they were not used in the DSOAG Web site.

Sociability

The DSOAG developers and community members consulted with the broader community about sociability issues, and decided on the following features:

- *Registration policies.* New members would be asked to register, to deter the casual visitor. Registration also provided a way to get contact information from new community members, so that they could be notified about events.

- *Conduct policies.* After lengthy discussion the community decided to keep rules to a minimum. Only the following two by-laws were written:

  Do not communicate to someone else that which you would not want communicated to you.

Our focus is Down Syndrome research and its funding, so please stay on that topic.

Finally, moderators on the site have the right to reject posts to the listserver and prevent individuals from participating in the chat room, if necessary. The moderator is, thus, a gatekeeper but rarely exercises that right.

Usability and sociability testing

Both online and offline usability testing were conducted for DSOAG. Reviews with other usability experts were also frequently conducted to get feedback on interface design decisions. A usability questionnaire was distributed to the DSOAG mailing list, of 201 email addresses; the response rate was, unfortunately, low, which was surprising because informal verbal and email feedback had been very positive. Perhaps people felt they had said everything already!

Refining and tuning sociability and usability

A variety of changes were made to the DSOAG community site following usability testing. These included:

- Links to external resources were placed higher on the page so that they are not missed when users fail to scroll.
- Pages were placed in a table to control horizontal spreading, because they appeared different in different browsers.
- Fonts and font highlighting were standardized. Some subtitles were added.
- Terminology was standardized, and abbreviations were written in full.

- A message was added to alert users that personal information could not be secured.

- A brief statement was added to describe the differences between AOL and DSOAG chat rooms.

Welcoming and nurturing the community

As noted, the original community was already active, with more than 180 participants, so getting the community started was not a problem. Nevertheless, the community decided to increase its membership by emailing invitations to related sites.

DSOAG continues to be maintained by the original core team of community members who worked on its development. In particular, the father who started the original site continues to be involved, and his dedication and technical skill are undoubtedly helping the community to be successful. Other members are also stepping forward to help; it is envisaged that some of them will eventually take over responsibility for its maintenance. Responses from members of the community continue to be enthusiastic; over a year later, DSOAG continues to evolve into a thriving community!

Quiz Bowl Community[2]

Quiz Bowl is a college quiz game similar to *Jeopardy* in the United States and *University Challenge* in Britain. The Quiz Bowl community has both physical and

---

[2] Permission informally given by J. Lazar and R. Tsao.

virtual components. The physical component involves competition between teams of students from different universities, who compete at tournaments held on weekends throughout the year. At the beginning of this case study, the virtual component of the community consisted of a listserver (run out of Iowa State University), a UseNet newsgroup, and assorted Web pages. These resources were used to announce upcoming tournaments, report results, and discuss the competition. Theoretical discussions, such as "what makes a good tournament?" also took place. (Note: Other Web-based resources existed in the recent past, but not at the time of this study.)

At the time of the study, community members were complaining about usability problems and the need to consolidate their Internet resources to make them easier to use. The three-person development team, from the information systems masters program at the University of Maryland Baltimore County comprising Dr. Jonathan Lazar, Ronald Tsao, and another colleague, worked to produce an online community that integrated the extant resources, which included a Web site with documents, subject lists, and a bulletin board[3] (Lazar, Tsao, & Preece, 1999).

Community needs assessment and user task analysis

Doing the community needs analysis for the Quiz Bowl community was challenging because the users were broadly distributed, not just geographically, but in their type

---

[3] The description that follows was edited from a paper entitled "One Foot in Cyberspace and the Other on the Ground: A Case Study of Analysis and Design Issues in a Hybrid Virtual and Physical Community" (Lazar, Tsao, & Preece, 1999). Lazar and Tsao did the development work.

of involvement, whether online, offline, or both. Furthermore, they belonged to different factions of the community which influenced who used which resources.

The development team used three approaches to collect requirements: (1) informal ethnographic observation by a member of the project team who belonged to the Quiz Bowl community; (2) informal interviews with users; and (3) surveys. The surveys were adapted for the Internet and for reaching different factions of the user population. The survey formed the major instrument for assessing user needs because some members of the community were reachable only online, others only offline, still others either way. The team needed to establish the following: whether the virtual and physical factions were discrete; how to draw good samples from each; and how to deal with the logistics of reaching both.

Fortunately, a member of the development team was also an enthusiastic Quiz Bowl player, so he was able to directly observe and speak with players. From the data he collected, it became clear that the population was transient. Groups formed at a tournament and then dissolved. While segments of the physical and online communities were indeed separate, a large faction moved between the two and belonged to both. Surveys, therefore, seemed like the most promising way of understanding the needs of this split population because they allow data to be collected from a large number of people in a relatively small amount of time. Moreover, they are particularly economical for online communities, and can be distributed easily to physical gatherings of people. Furthermore, in this case, the same survey could be distributed via paper and electronically.

Developing and distributing the survey

It was important that the two versions be exactly the same, to ensure truly comparable results. The two surveys differed only in distribution media; the paper version was handed out at offline tournaments and get-togethers, and the electronic version was made available on the Web. Unfortunately, there was no definitive list of Quiz Bowl community members and their locations, hence no way to guarantee that the team reached a representative sample of the community. Consequently, the team had to do the best they could.

By passing out paper surveys at tournaments, the developers reached out to Quiz Bowl players who were part of the physical community, but not necessarily involved with the virtual component of the Quiz Bowl community. The electronic survey enabled developers to expand their reach, both in number and geographically.

The developers wanted to design the survey so as to assess how well the current online community was functioning, and to determine what additional functionality, usability, and sociability were needed. Three question areas were targeted:

1. *General demographic information.* This included, for all respondents, gender, Quiz Bowl experience, and academic standing. This information would assist the developers in determining if they had a well-distributed sample.
2. *Offline members.* In particular, developers wanted to know who did *not* use the electronic resources and why.
3. *Online members.* Users of the electronic resources were asked which resources and communication tools they used, the problems they encountered, as well as which now-extinct resources they formerly used.

The survey went through several iterations of reviews with community members. The team also ran a more formal pilot study (Oppenheim, 1992; Preece et al., 1994), involving 15 Quiz Bowl players at the University of Maryland. The final surveys were passed out in paper form first at a tournament at Swarthmore College on October 4, 1997; 34 completed surveys were collected. A second set of paper surveys was passed out on November 8, 1997, at a tournament at the University of Pittsburgh; 16 were collected, for a total of 50 paper surveys.

Online surveys were distributed via email from October 28, 1997, to November 12, 1997, and on the Web (an excerpt of which is shown in Figure 11.2). The online survey was advertised through the listserver used by the electronic component of the community. This resulted in 62 surveys being collected. Based on the domain names of the participants, these represented a good geographic distribution of respondents—surveys came from MIT, Harvard, Boston University, Delaware, Chicago, Michigan, Virginia Tech, Memphis, Northwestern, Stanford, Illinois, Missouri, Randolph-Macon, Case Western Reserve, Carnegie-Mellon, Texas-Dallas, Princeton, Caltech, Carleton, George Washington, Eastern Michigan, Berkeley, and Dartmouth Universities, and the New England School of Law. Many survey responses were sent from Internet service providers, so their origin could not be determined.

The paper surveys and the online surveys together totaled 112.

Survey Responses

The survey responses were broken down into the three question areas: demographics, offline member questions, and online member questions.

I would consider myself a:

____ Novice player.

____ Somewhat experienced player.

____ Very experienced player.

____ I would consider myself a member of the electronic Quiz Bowl community.

____ I would not consider myself a member of the electronic Quiz Bowl community.

____ I have taken part in the electronic Quiz Bowl community in the last six months, by utilizing resources or communication tools.

____ I have not taken part in the electronic Quiz Bowl community in the last six months.

If you answered that you have not taken part in the electronic Quiz Bowl community in the last six months, please answer the next question and return the survey. If you answered that you have taken part in the electronic Quiz Bowl community in the last six months, please skip the next question and go on to the next page.

I do not take part in the electronic Quiz Bowl community because:
(you may check more than one choice)

[ ]   I didn't know about the electronic Quiz Bowl community.

[ ]   I do not know enough about the topics discussed.

[ ]   I do not have sufficient access to technology.

[ ]   I do not like all of the flaming (heated arguments which can become personal and insulting).

[ ]   I do not like all of the spam (messages that have nothing to do with Quiz Bowl).

[ ]   I don't have the time.

[ ]   Someone else on my team takes care of being our "electronic contact."

[ ]   It doesn't interest me.

Figure 11.2   Excerpt from the electronic Quiz Bowl needs assessment survey

Section 1: Demographics

The demographic questions in the first part of the survey helped developers to determine that their sample was diverse and that all groups were represented. All student classes (freshman, graduate student, etc.), both genders, and various levels of experience were represented. In terms of gender, the sample consisted of 83 percent males and 16 percent females; 1 percent did not indicate their gender.

Two questions on the survey addressed the resources and community. One asked whether the person had taken part in the community by using the listserver, newsgroup, or community resources. Fifty-five percent, 62 people, considered themselves to be part of the online component of the community; 41 percent did not.

Section 2: Questions for people not part of the online community

These questions were concerned with finding out why some Quiz Bowl players were not taking part in the electronic Quiz Bowl community. Survey respondents were allowed to select more than one choice to explain why they weren't members of the online community. The two most-cited reasons were that "I didn't know about the online Quiz Bowl community," and "Someone else on my team takes care of being our 'electronic contact.'" In the latter response, the developers interpreted it to indicate that those Quiz Bowl players didn't see how the online community could help them. Subsequently, this information may point to the ways to get more Quiz Bowl players involved in the electronic Quiz Bowl community: for example, advertise the existence of the community, and talk about why it's important to be involved in the online component of the community.

It is interesting to note that no respondents considered access to technology a problem. This is a very important—and positive—finding for the community.

Section 3: Questions for members of the online community

These questions asked which specific resources online members used, and what they thought of those resources.

It is easy to see which resources are most effective. Most effective were the Quiz Bowl listservers, the Stanford Packet Archive, and the NAQT Web page. The listservers are the main channel for communication in the Quiz Bowl community. Both the Stanford Packet Archive and the NAQT Web page were considered well designed.

The rest of the closed questions in this area dealt with the resources that no longer existed, that might exist in the future, or that were rarely used. The Quiz Bowl Archive, which no longer existed at the time of the survey was used by the majority of respondents (50/79). Approximately half of the respondents (37/79) used the Frequently Asked Questions page, which was no longer publicly posted or updated. A large majority of respondents (67/80) said they would be interested in a history of Quiz Bowl as a sport. Only one person used the discussion groups on another Web site.

Findings and evaluation

Based on the responses to the open-ended questions, it was determined that the community suffered from two main usability problems:

- The UseNet newsgroup, was unusable because spamming and aggressive comments often occurred. It was interesting to note that although the listservers at Iowa State University were intended to replace the newsgroup, many community members did not feel that a listserver was appropriate. One respondent said, "The mailing list is just not a productive replacement." The respondents indicated they would prefer a moderated newsgroup or a Web-based bulletin board. One respondent said, "I wish we had a simple non-email-based newsgroup." This problem was cited again and again. Though bulletin boards are available on another Web site, Quiz Bowl players rarely use them because of poor relations with the Quiz Bowl community. Also the other site strongly moderates comments and Quiz Bowl players don't want their opinions censored.

- Community members were unhappy about the demise of the Quiz Bowl Archive, which had served the purpose of a centralized repository of Quiz Bowl information. A full understanding of why the archive is not available requires knowledge of social relations within the community, which is beyond the scope of this discussion. Suffice it to say, the Quiz Bowl community includes three organizations (two for-profit, one nonprofit) that sponsor tournaments throughout the year. These organizations directly compete with each other, and often will not acknowledge the existence of the others. What made the Quiz Bowl Archive so valuable was that it had not been affiliated with any of those organizations, so it could offer information objectively. Without the archive, it became more difficult for members to find resources, since they are scattered, or not even available on the Web anymore. Some survey respondents indicated that they didn't even know about certain resources because they were located in different places. One respondent said that a major problem was the "lack of a good repository of information for FAQs, how to write questions, how to organize tournaments, etc. [The Quiz Bowl Archive at] Papyrus Inc. used to provide such a Web site, but it has been destroyed." Developers recognized the need for better advertising and marketing to new schools and players, to replace this function formerly served by the Quiz Bowl Archive.

These findings were supported by information gathered in informal discussions, and indicated that solutions to a mix of sociability *and* technical problems were needed, as described next.

Selecting technology and planning sociability

The development team set out to solve the two major problems—the ineffectiveness of the *alt.college.college-bowl* newsgroup and the demise of the Quiz Bowl Archive. In the case of the newsgroup, they had to decide whether to implement a Web-based bulletin board or a moderated newsgroup. The team looked at time and accessibility factors. Implementing a Web-based bulletin board would take less time to create than a new UseNet newsgroup. Also, depending on the UseNet hierarchy that the group would be in, it might not be easily available to everyone (*Chapter 8*); for instance, many colleges do not subscribe to newsgroups in the alt hierarchy. But a Web-based bulletin board would be accessible to anyone connected to the Internet. Based on those factors, the team created a Web-based bulletin board, which they made part of the new Quiz Bowl Archive, which they launched to address the second problem. The Quiz Bowl Archive was placed on the Student Activities Web server at UMBC. The new Quiz Bowl Archive includes guides to writing questions and running tournaments; rules; schedules; statistical programs; a list of manufacturers of Quiz Bowl equipment; and a list of all resources available to the community.

Even though there was evidence of severe sociability problems caused by spamming and aggressive comments in the old community (see Lazar et al., 1999), the Quiz Bowl community was adamant that the new online community should not be moderated. They also did not want to have a registration policy. Basic usability issues were also addressed, particularly ease of navigation in the Web site (see Lazar et al., 1999 for further details). There was considerable debate about whether to include an animated graphic of Tycho Brahe, the Quiz Bowl community mascot, on the Web site. Some couldn't imagine the site without Tycho; others said that it was trivial and annoying and spoiled the otherwise clean but elegant design. After prolonged debate, the decision was made to keep Tycho.

Designing, implementing, and testing prototypes

The Quiz Bowl Archive was designed around two technical criteria: backward compatibility and minimum system configurations. Good usability and sociability were also listed as important.

- *Backward compatibility*. This is important in order for Web pages to appear and function correctly on all Web browsers. Web browser programs are written to follow a set of HyperText Markup Language (HTML) tag standards approved by the World Wide Web consortium, as well as tags proprietary to the browser's manufacturer. Using only approved standard HTML tags ensures the correctness of coded pages. The Common Gateway Interface (CGI), chosen over other processing engines/languages, contributes to backward compatibility, because it, too, is standardized on all browsers. The Quiz Bowl Web pages were coded entirely with standardized HTML tags with CGI extensions, then thoroughly tested on Netscape Navigator/Communicator (versions 2, 3, and 4) and Microsoft Internet Explorer (versions 3 and 4).

- *Minimum system configuration*. This must be taken into account when designing for diverse communities whose members have many different systems that could range from very high- to low-end. Four design criteria were applied to the new Quiz Bowl Archive: moderate to low processing power, low network bandwidth connections, small screen sizes, and low screen resolution. A large number of Internet users have less powerful machines, as well as low-speed network connections (Pitkow & Kehoe, 1996), for whom Web pages with slow-loading graphics or processing requirements would not be feasible. (The guideline for small screen size comes from Bertot & McClure, 1996; the guideline for low screen resolution comes from Dix, Finlay, Abowd, & Beale, 1998.) The Quiz Bowl Archive was designed to be used on Intel 80486/66, Motorola 68040/33, and Motorola PowerPC 601/66 microprocessors, with 28,800 to 33,600 Kbps modem connections, 640 × 480 to 800 × 600 screens, and 256 colors or grayscale.

To complete the picture, a discussion board was created using a freeware bulletin board system called WebBBS, though heavily modified for consistency with the rest of the site. It is dynamically created each session through the use of CGI and Perl scripting. All messages are text-based and stored in a data directory.

Each page of Quiz Bowl Online contains the same navigation bar for ease of use and to make the pages flow smoothly. Maximize and minimize buttons are provided for the user's convenience. Finally, the graphics are nonintrusive, and text is clearly legible in 256 colors/grayscale.

Content development

The content for the New Quiz Bowl Archive was supplied by members of the community. The development team sent out a request for resources via the Quiz Bowl listserver. The site also contains a complete list of links to all Web resources that relate to Quiz Bowl.

Refining and tuning sociability and usability

After the Quiz Bowl Archive design was complete, usability testing was performed. Ten members of the University of Maryland Quiz Bowl team took part in the testing. They performed three tasks and filled out a short survey. In addition, three Quiz Bowl players (at the University of Minnesota, Case Western Reserve University, and Yale University, respectively) who belonged to the online community evaluated the Quiz Bowl Archive. Testing at both local and remote sites enabled the evaluators to check factors that might not be as apparent on local sites, such as Web page load time and sufficient file access, to enable users outside the local domain to access the Web pages. Finally, based on user feedback, the number of acronyms was decreased, minor editing changes were made, and additional hyperlinks were added (see Figure 11.3).

Welcoming and nurturing

The Quiz Bowl community overall was pleased with the new site and the additional resources that it offered them. In the first months following the redesign, the discussions, despite being unmoderated, were for the most part, civilized. A problem did arise with the server that supports the bulletin board, but because the listserver runs from a different server, the community has used that instead, as well as the Web site. They do, however, miss the bulletin board.

This problem with the bulletin board server illustrates the importance of maintaining servers. It also speaks to the value of distributing community resources so that the entire community does not shut down when there is a server problem. In addition, this case study demonstrates how life online influences life offline, and the close interrelationship between technical and social issues. In this situation, people simply switched between offline and online groups—frequently. While critics might say that the online component offered only communication, not community, in fact, the online Quiz Bowl community has a clearly defined identity, complete with jargon and social norms. Furthermore, this community is composed of people who feel comfortable regularly moving from the virtual world to the "real" world.

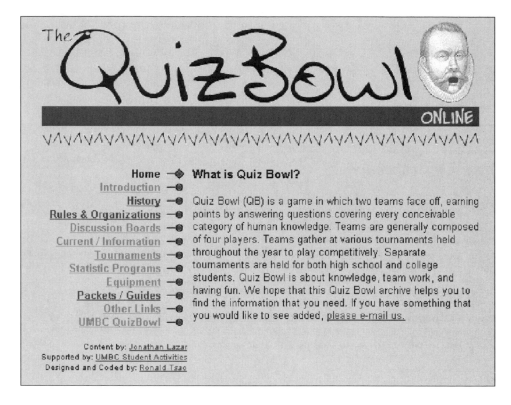

Figure 11.3   Quiz Bowl Online home page

Summary

The two case studies illustrate how community-centered development can be adapted to the circumstances of the particular community and development team. On both projects, there was a strong focus on user participation and community needs throughout development. In both cases, the development teams, all of whom were experienced software developers, who were also working for masters degrees, were pleased, and somewhat surprised, by how much the community wanted to participate in the projects. Members were eager to be involved in the needs analysis and to be consulted and to participate in testing during development.

In contrast, large commercial online communities, such as iVillage.com and Landsend.com, or those hosted by Xoom.com and GeoCities.com, must have more tightly managed development processes. The development teams that produce such sites often are quite large; schedules are tighter and budgets are bigger; and, usually there is less flexibility. But the teams must provide what users want, and they must ensure that usability and sociability are good if they are to succeed in this highly competitive market. They, too, must survey users; Xoom.com, for example, surveys thousands of users. Only those who pay close attention to what attracts people and satisfies their needs will develop flourishing online communities. Good—and bad— news travels fast on the Internet.

Further Reading

"One Foot in Cyberspace and the Other on the Ground: A Case Study of Analysis and Design Issues in a Hybrid Virtual and Physical Community" (Lazar et al., 1999), and "Collecting User Requirements in a Virtual Population: A Case Study" (Lazar et al., 2000)

These articles discuss the issues involved in doing a user needs analysis when some or all of the participants are accessible only via the Internet. The first discusses the Quiz Bowl community project; the second describes the DSOAG project.

Health Online (Ferguson, 1996), *Dr. Tom Linden's Guide to Online Medicine* (Linden & Kienholz, 1995), and *Health Net* (Ryer, 1997)

These three books contain similar introductions to the Internet, with pointers to medical resources, some of which will date quickly. However a few, such as the UseNet communities, are likely to stand the test of time. The books by Linden and Ryer contain useful information about how to integrate knowledge gained from the Internet with consulting with your doctor.

Mindweave: Communication, Computers, and Distance Education (Mason & Kaye, 1989), *Global Networks. Computers and International Communication* (Harasim, 1993), *Learning Networks* (Harasim, Hiltz, Teles, & Turoff, 1995), and *The Knowledge Web: Learning and Collaborating on the Net* (Eisenstadt & Vincent, 1998)

These four books contain useful material about online educational communities and computer-mediated communication in education.

The Virtual Classroom: Learning without Limits via Computer Networks (Hiltz, 1994)

This book describes the author's experience in pioneering the development of a

virtual university on campus. Although dated by Internet standards, it contains a wealth of insight about the way students communicate and learn using technology. It is a classic in this field.

NetGain: Expanding Markets through Virtual Communities (Hagel & Armstrong, 1997)

This book explains how to capitalize on the power of the Internet for business in general and e-commerce in specific. It discusses both business and technical issues, and provides pragmatic advice on developing online communities for business.

"Community Networks: Building a New Participatory Medium" (Schuler, 1994), *New Community Networks: Wired for Change* (Schuler, 1996), and *Community Networks: Lessons from Blacksburg, Virginia* (Cohill & Kavanaugh, 1997)

All these sources tell the story of developing community networks, and are highly informative.

12 Looking to the Future[1]

Our life is composed greatly of dreams . . . and they must be brought into connection with action.

—Anaïs Nin, *The Diaries of Anaïs Nin*, vol. IV (as quoted in Murphy, 1978, p. 5)

This chapter will briefly review the ideas discussed throughout the book, then take a look at the future of online community development. The operative word here is "look." It would be foolish in this arena to try and predict the future. After all, who would have predicted 10 years ago that there would be an Internet and that its influence would be so far-reaching?

Contents

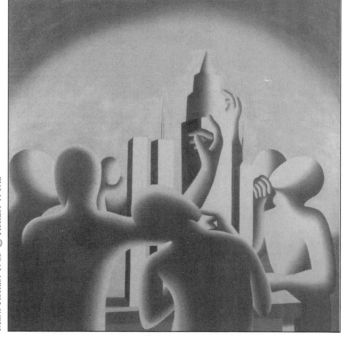

Aspire
Mark Kostabi 1985 © Kostabi World

---

[1] This section draws on reports (Brown, Van Dam, Earnshaw, Eucarnacao, Guedj, Preece, Shneiderman, & Vince 1999a, 1999b,c) from the workshop sponsored by the European Union and National Science Foundation, June 1–4, 1999. The following people contributed: Christoph Busch, Fraunhofer IGD, Germany; Richard Guedj, INT, France; Wendy Kellogg, IBM T. J. Watson Research Center, USA; David Leevers, VERS Associates, UK; Sudhir Mudur, National Center for Software Technology, India; Jennifer Preece (lead author), University of Maryland Baltimore County, USA; Ben Shneiderman, University of Maryland College Park, USA; John Thomas, IBM T. J. Watson Research Center, USA; Deb Roy, MIT, USA; and Junji Yamaguchi, Independent, Japan.

Statisticians claim that the number of people who use the Internet doubles every 52 days. Many are attracted by email, chats, instant messaging and, of course, the World Wide Web. There are more than 25 million AOL users alone. Active Worlds, a graphic chat environment (*Chapter 2*) has more than a million people registered; and during the first quarter of 1998, 450,000 messages were posted to 20,000 UseNet groups. And with the rapid proliferation of thousands of e-commerce, entertainment, education, health, travel, and many other types of sites, ever larger numbers of people are being tempted to partake of all the Internet and World Wide Web has to offer.

How will this amazing trend play out? The pessimists see a gloomy future in which children become addicted to online games, corrupted by online pornography, and tainted by consumerism, while their parents become more estranged from neighbors and community—and their children. The pessimists also envisage a free-for-all of those people on the margin of society, free to spread racial slurs and hatred around the world. Optimists, on the other hand, imagine online communities where everyone, whatever their needs or interests, can find a "home"—seniors, young people, and the physically challenged. The optimists see the Internet as granting access to excellent education for everyone; they predict true democracy through online voting; better quality of life through easily accessible media and legal information; and greater value for consumers thanks to intense competition among e-commerce companies.

Those are the extremes. But what is the reality? It is still too early to tell. Evidence, a lot of it anecdotal, is being marshalled to support both perspectives. Disturbing results from a U.S. Department of Commerce study show that the gap in technology access continues to broaden between low- and high-income families, between poorly and well-educated citizens (National Telecommunications and Information Administration & U.S. Dept. of Commerce, 1999). Fears abound that socializing in "real life" will decline to such a degree that unprecedented numbers of people will be lonely and psychologically impoverished. Results from a small study of Internet usage (some 73 households in the Pittsburgh area) showed a small but statistically significant correlation between hours spent on the Internet and depression (Kraut, Scherlis, Mukhopadhyay, Manning, & Kiesler, 1996), declining involvement in social activities and loneliness (Kraut et al., 1998; Nie & Ebring, 2000). In addition, there is strong evidence of a steady decline in community activities during the last 30 years, which has caused a severe erosion in social capital throughout the United States (Putnam, 1995) and possibly in other technologically advanced nations (see *Chapter 1*). The tide of positive popular opinion about benefits from e-health and e-education (Noble, 1998; Winner, 1995) is also turning. Some are now questioning the efficacy of online education and health. David Noble, appropriately, raises the concern that some online education programs are turning into little more than "digital diploma mills" (1998). Likewise, doctors fear that patients' hopes may be raised—or dashed— incorrectly as a result of receiving unreliable information online.

In any case, the gloom-and-doom reports should not be dismissed, as they alert us to potential problems, and remind us that positive outcomes require energy and dedication. There can be no doubt that the Internet is changing the way we live; and it will continue to do so for the foreseeable future. But we must keep in mind that it, too, will be shaped and transformed by the people—the users and developers (DeSanctis & Gallupe, 1987; DeSanctis, Poole, Dickson, & Jackson, 1993; Poole & DeSanctis,

1990; Hiltz & Turoff, 1993). Refer back to *Chapter 4* about adaptive structuration. As in the real world, life online will present dangers and cause problems, along with offering many advantages. And as in life the goal should be that good triumphs over evil.

How can we make the dream come true? How can we ensure that the Internet makes the world a better place? By using what influence we have, professionally and as citizens of the world. By understanding better how online communities affect people's lives. By becoming informed activists, effective developers, insightful researchers, and discerning users. To be sure, the Internet is an outstanding technical development, but we must recognize that some of the most significant changes that it initiates are social.

At a workshop in the early 1990s to determine the future direction of human–computer interaction Stu Card, a respected researcher from Xerox Corporation, identified four stages in the growth of new disciplines (Card, 1991; Olson & Olson, 1997) that can be applied to online community studies. The first stage is building, evaluating, and reporting on individual cases. Second, as more communities develop, research intensifies; third, gradually, dimensions of success are identified, which eventually lead to the fourth stage, when models, laws, and theories are articulated.

Current research in online communities deals mostly with individual entities. The rapid path of technological development and rapid growth in user numbers make it difficult to track the phenomenon on a broader basis, and hence hamper our understanding of Internet sociability and usability. Research that informs development is urgently needed. But it will continue to be difficult to implement. Online populations are diverse, differing in culture, age, technological experience, education, financial means, and motivation. Little is known about social and business interactions online. But we must find a way, because online communities *must* be well developed, so that they are usable by *all* citizens.

Sociability

To review, online communities with good sociability have social policies that support the communities' purpose, and are understandable, socially acceptable, and practicable. Sociability support will benefit from a deeper understanding of community, culture, and social interaction online. Strong multidisciplinary research teams composed of social scientists are needed to lead basic research initiatives. Computer scientists will be needed to transfer this knowledge into software design that supports social interactions, protects individual privacy, provides security, and encourages universal access (Brown et al., 1999a, 1999b).

Community and culture

Researchers need to understand cultural differences to be better able to support diversity online. Spending time in an online community is part of a much broader community experience, which is still primarily physical for most people. Any kind of community, whether online or off, has complex cycles punctuated by temporal events that may influence the whole community directly (e.g., change in government) or some of its members (e.g., marriage) and unanticipated events (e.g., a sudden death in the family). Howard Rheingold's slice-of-life examination of the WELL (Rheingold, 1993, 1994) marked the start of case study reports based on first-person accounts of "what it is like." Gradually, these eyewitness accounts are giving way to more detailed studies, which often appear in collected editions (e.g., Kiesler, 1997; Smith & Kollock, 1999; Sudaweeks, McLaughlin, & Rafaeli, 1998) and increasingly in journals and conference proceedings. A few sociologists are engaging in research concerned with basic social structures and functions in online communities and their relationship to physical community (e.g., Kollock & Smith, 1996; Wellman, 1997). Work in human-computer interaction focuses on design of social spaces, using knowledge from social sciences to build software that supports social interaction online (e.g., Erickson, 1996; Erickson et al., 1999; Viegas & Donath, 1999). However, topics cited by researchers and developers as needing more research include understanding differences in communities, life cycles, and interaction dynamics.

Understanding dierences among communities

This will require the identification and study of differences among networked and virtual communities and virtual environments—that is, the full "physi-virtual" spectrum of communities (Lazar & Preece, 1998b)—to answer such questions as how do relationships develop, and what is the effect of different forms of sociability? For example, what kinds of governance procedures do they want?

Life cycles

Daily, weekly and annual cycles vary from culture to culture, time zone to time zone. And time zone differences cause severe practical limitations for synchronous communication (Olson & Olson, 2000). What is the effect of these cycles on online communities? Perhaps online community developers can take advantage of the human propensity to structure behaviors around eating, work, and sleep cycles. TV producers appear to understand these cycles well; they can predict maximum viewing times for different sectors of a population. Can software be similarly adapted to support these life cycles?

What role do rituals play offline and how might they be translated online? Some communities have experimented with synchronizing snack times. At an appointed time, participants in different locations take a candy, cookie, or soda break. However, anecdotal evidence suggests that this doesn't contribute much to a sense of co-presence or of community. It seems there is no substitute for "being there" when it comes to sharing a meal! Clearly for some activities, distance does matter (Olson & Olson, 2000).

Interaction dynamics

Interaction dynamics are of course different depending on the number of people involved, and where they are meeting, whether in a four-person face-to-face discussion, a 25-person online classroom, 150 people using a listserver, or several thousand people "in" an online stadium (Eisenstadt & Vincent, 1998). Each forms different social rituals. Offline, for example, the act of going to a meeting signals commitment, and the longer and more difficult the journey, the greater the sense of commitment.

It hardly need be said that handshaking, hugging, and eating are social activities that don't translate well online, though attempts are being made to augment our senses with wearable computers, to empower creativity with well-designed tools, and to better enable people to express their emotional states online. It is more difficult to be angry with a tearful person sitting next to you than with a textual name representing a person that you have never met (Wallace, 1999). Access to information, stories, and monitored data could be useful to both individuals and communities for developing a greater collective intelligence. The term *knowledge management* is often used to describe this kind of information sharing in professional environments and communities of practice (Liebowitz, 1998).

Ethical issues and universal access

Designing software that supports ethical standards and universal access is a challenge for both technical and social scientists. Basic sociological research is needed to inform sociability and usability. For example, what does it mean to have an online democracy? How can we ensure that everyone's interests will be considered and protected (Schuler, 1994)? Participatory design practices help to provide a mechanism for achieving community involvement in design (Schuler & Namioka, 1993), but we need a better understanding of online collaboration and the social processes that uphold it (e.g., Kollock, 1998; Kollock & Smith, 1996). In order to make the features available to support universal access, a number of challenging computer science issues also need solving. Good usability design will be necessary to make new functionality usable by the wide range of users for whom it is designed.

Ethical issues

Awareness of the dangers of participating online
Many users fail to appreciate the potential dangers of participating online. They are unaware that correspondence is electronically stored and can be accessed by tech-

nically savvy people, even though users may think they have deleted it (Erickson et al., 1999). Users also need to be made aware when they initiate insecure communications or operations. Current software does not give adequate feedback about such operations. Dialog boxes, which users generally disable because they are annoying, and tiny icons are insufficient. Better ways also are needed to notify users about unencrypted or encrypted traffic, about potential persistent storage that endangers their privacy, and about actions that might have legal consequences, such as digital signatures.

Codes of conduct for online communities

Protecting individual and group privacy in online communities can be partially realized through improved technology. But policies are also needed to ensure that host operators and maintainers are required to follow fundamental privacy rules. As an analog the Hippocratic oath for physicians could be defined for operators and key persons of online communities.

Research also needs to identify successful models of self-governance in online communities. In a similar vein, a better understanding is needed to determine how cooperation (Kollock, 1998; Kollock & Smith, 1996), trust (Shneiderman, 2000), empathy (Preece, 1999b), and social capital (Putnam, 1995) develop online; how these relationships change over time; and how changes in population size and demography affect them. Contributions from political, social, and IT policy scientists would help to model governance online and to integrate online policies with pre-existing local, national, and international public policies, such as for voting. National and international policies are also essential for dealing with hate-crime and other offensive or derogatory propaganda. The question has to asked: Should this material be allowed online at all? Would it be better to ban it from the Web completely or render it inaccessible using filters (Coste, 2000)? How would such censorship impact free speech and democracy? Issues such as these only scratch the surface of the difficulties facing developers in this area. Clearly, a multidisciplinary approach will be necessary to address broad social problems and their impact on technical design.

Improved environments

Research is needed to understand the impact of digital technology on cultural diversity, environmental issues, conservation of limited resources, and changes in standards of living. This information will help to support appropriate distribution of resources by national and international agencies.

Universal access

Bridging the digital divide (National Telecommunications and Information Administration & Commerce, 1999), requires that we ensure universal access to online communities for people of all ages, cultures, languages, income and educational levels, and physical and mental capabilities. To that end, five broad areas of research have been identified. The first, *multiple interaction modalities*, calls for alternatives to text input and output. The second suggests research into *adaptive interfaces* that can be tuned to a wide range of communication abilities and preferences. Third, research is needed into technologies for supporting *interaction in all languages*, thereby opening the door around the world. Fourth, *translation technologies* are needed for bringing together different language groups. Fifth, software is needed that utilizes low-bandwidth communication systems and machines with low processing power as well as state-of-the-art facilities.

Multiple interaction modalities

Speech interfaces are one example of these modalities. They can bring access to individuals who are illiterate or who suffer from motor control and speech impairments. Speech interfaces are also useful for anyone whose work situations demand that their hands and eyes are occupied with other activities. Speech generation and recognition can occur in various ways (e.g., automatic speech recognition, ASR), and each raises a different set of issues for users. Furthermore, recent advances in computer vision make possible human-computer interfaces based on facial expressions and body gestures. Absence of social presence (*Chapter 5*), and particularly the inability to "read" gestures and conversational cues so vital to understanding human interactions, may portend dire consequences for online relationships (Wallace, 1999). Clearly, better ways of supporting these aspects of interaction in online mass communication environments are necessary.

Adaptive interfaces

Online users also need interfaces that are easy to learn and are customizable to individual parameters, which include: educational levels, preferences for certain applications, age, language, and culture.

Multilingual support

Today, still, digital communications hardware and software are written primarily in English. Future systems will have to support fonts and keyboard mappings for numerous other languages as well. This demand will prove challenging to meet, as many languages have more characters than there are keys in the current standard

101-key board, making a one-to-one mapping impossible. Another issue is that many languages do not read left to right like English.

Likewise, researchers face difficulties addressing how to support multilingual speech-recognition interaction. Currently, speech recognition and synthesis technologies exist for fewer than 20 languages, and these technologies are extremely costly to develop for others. New development strategies are, therefore, in great demand, but may come at the cost of loss of performance. Long term, technologies for numerous languages are needed that may be refined over time. Universal access will have to include speech-recognition interaction, as the majority of the world's population in developing countries is illiterate.

Interlingual support

A major challenge confronting researchers is to design systems that support communication among people who do not share a common language. In addition to enabling machine translation for text and speech, they also should investigate visual languages, visualization techniques (Card, Mackinlay, & Shneiderman, 1999) and greater use of multimedia. Tools that enable communities to dynamically create shared resources (including multilingual, multimedia dictionaries and thesauri to support common codes of communication) will encourage the formation of specialist global online communities.

Software access

Access is another issue. Interfaces must be available to users with low-end as well as high-end equipment. Possible approaches include customizable interfaces (e.g., Active Worlds, discussed in *Chapter 2*), user modeling, and adaptive interfaces.

Usability

Software to support online communities often lacks suitable functionality and usability (Gaines, Chen, & Shaw, 1997). To date, artificial intelligence (AI), speech-recognition systems, large-scale data retrieval, new interaction devices, and others have proven more intriguing to computer scientists. More recently, however, the popularity of online communities has been enticing more computer scientists to work on such technologies as recommender systems (Resnick & Varian, 1997), reputation systems, encryption techniques, visualization, and others. Three technical problem areas are: design, security, and scalability, to produce systems that can handle millions of users.

Design

Theories about culture and social activity online lay the foundation for software design, but research is needed to develop representations that can reveal online behavior in real time, record histories of behavior, store communication and knowledge, explore the nature of interpersonal and mass communication (*Chapters 5* and *6*), and accurately track the number of people participating and with whom. Examples of the use of visualization in chat-type environments are starting to appear (e.g., Erickson et al., 1999; Viegas & Donath, 1999), and a few researchers are also tackling how to represent mass communication (e.g., Sack, 2000), whether via avatars, thumbnail pictures, or other forms.

Revealing behavior

But what will be the impact of revealing individual and group behavior in various circumstances? How can online communities support different kinds of behaviors in conjunction with information? What will be the impact of different types of representation for community dynamics? Online anonymity is a two-sided coin for communities, as discussed in *Chapter 5* (Wallace, 1999). Finally how will the community members react when they can know who is coming and going? At the moment, it is impossible to know who is participating, or when anyone joins or leaves in many online communities.

Representing the content and emotion of messages

The question to answer here is, how should different content be represented? For example, researchers have demonstrated that computer-mediated communication can facilitate the expression of sensitive, personal, or emotional content (e.g., Sproull & Kiesler, 1991). Enabling users to better distinguish among emotional content, personal opinion, and factual information may be essential. A related question is how to help people reveal their mood online. In face-to-face conversation, people modify their comments based on the immediately visible reactions of the other person or persons (Olson & Olson, 2000). Online, it is far more difficult, if not impossible, to ascertain another person's mood. A current but limited solution is emoticons, a crude way of signaling tone and intent of a comment. More expressive are avatars that can become animated and jump and wave.

What other ways might there be to support expression of emotion online? Researchers at MIT are attempting to develop machines with sensors that can detect a user's mood from various physical stimuli (Picard, 1997). But would we want such devices in online communities? Alternatively, if a collective mood of a group could be established by, for example, a voting system, how could it be expressed, and would this encourage better communication online? Other questions that beg research are: How can users just logging on determine the mood and nuances of members already there (Ackerman, 1999)? Or when newcomers join a community, what mechanisms might help them gauge the feelings of the group, the level of conversation, duration of discussion of a single topic, and so on?

Representing large communities online

When large numbers of people want to join an online community it presents specific scalability challenges to designers. What types of features do they need to provide in software to support large communities, their moderators, and administrators? Little attention has been given to scaling approaches and representations for such numbers. How, for example, should—or could—a million people be represented at the interface? What kind of features would support the development of trust in such a large group? Reputation management systems, such as that used in eBay, are one way to accomplish this in e-commerce systems (Kollock, 1999). But what about supporting personal trust among people? Or trustworthiness of online advice and professional information of all kinds?

Implementing broadband networks in online communities

As broadband networks continue to improve, tele-immersion will become more widespread. Those who wish to immerse themselves in 3D tactile environments with stereo sound and vision will be able to do so. The sense of being "in" a room, village, or some other environment with one's online buddies will be possible. Ubiquitous, wireless devices will enable people to continue to connect virtually even as they go through their daily offline activities, from, say, the breakfast table, to the car or train, down the street, and into the office. Educational researchers are already planning to bring high-tech games capability into the classroom (Fowler & Mayes, 1997). Students in London will be able to work in 3D with their peers in Toronto, New York, or anywhere else in the world. Those who don't want immersion will have better tools to create dynamic Web pages, enhanced with real photographs and movie clips. The Web has developed at a phenomenal speed, but technologists believe we haven't seen anything yet.

Security

The success of many—maybe most—online communities will be strongly influenced by how secure they are. Personal information of all kinds must be made secure, which means not only that systems be made secure, but that users *perceive* them as secure. Incorporation of strong cryptographic protocols is essential. These protocols realize classical security requirements such as mutual authentication of communication between trading partners, confidentiality of transactions, authenticity and integrity of goods. Security is a major technical—and marketing—issue for many online communities. Identifying the type and amount of security needed and how to present security procedures to users are sociability and usability concerns.

Two crucial areas require substantial research in the near future to establish a powerful electronic marketplace and gain user trust in online transactions:

- *Resolving conflict of interest between consumers and the vendors and content providers of e-commerce systems.* This dilemma arises because vendors and content providers want to identify their customers using concepts such as globally unique identifiers to recognize digital fingerprints (attached to digital goods), whereas consumers demand privacy protection (Werry, 1999), which requires nontraceable inter-actions. Research is required to figure out how best to resolve this conflict, perhaps using limited pseudonymity and setup of trusted third parties (Brown et al., 1999a, 1999b).

- *Copyright protection.* As content is contributed to online systems the question of intellectual property protection gets more and more crucial. Consequently, adequate copyright protection mechanisms must be investigated and developed. In this context digital watermarking is a promising technology to provide security for content contributors, since it allows an imperceptible (inaudible) mark to be embedded in the content data itself. This mark bears the identity of the copyright holder and, eventually, also the purchaser's fingerprint (Brown et al., 1999a, 1999b). Research is needed on watermarking technology for all kinds of multimedia data, namely images, audio, video and 3D data such as representations of virtual models and virtual environments. While substantial work in the protection of images is already underway, protection of virtual worlds (i.e. the 3D model itself) is lagging far behind.

Scalability

Scalability, touched on briefly in the discussion of handling large communities, is a research priority, and one that presents significant technical challenges and implications for sociability and usability. Software for such entities must have high usability and be able to guide sociability. Questions here include: How should we structure conversations? How do we control online crowds and develop social protocols? What kind of online governance is needed to control inappropriate behaviors, and to ensure fair practices of all kinds? The technical challenges are to design interfaces adequate to support large, diverse populations of participants, as well as tools to support their moderators.

Theory and Methods

As noted throughout this book, most online community theory is borrowed from other disciplines, which researchers adapt to make informed guesses about how it applies to online communities (*Chapters 5* and *6*). In the future, however, new theories and methods relating specifically to the online world (Jones, 1999) will become essential to better inform software design, sociability, and usability.

Most of the theories discussed in *Chapters 5* and *6* were borrowed from linguistics, psychology, communication studies, sociology, and human-computer interaction. Social presence, common ground (Clark & Brennan, 1993), and social network analysis (Haythornthwaite, 1996) appear to support observations from online community investigations, but more theory that speaks directly to developers of online communities is needed. For example, what does critical mass mean to online communities? Can this useful idea be applied quantitatively and, therefore, made useful in practice? What are the effects of influxes and exoduses of people from mass communications systems?

Methods and measurement

Methods

Designing, measuring, and evaluating online communities requires adaptation of well-established techniques, along with the development of new techniques. For example, gathering information about user needs (i.e., user needs analysis) requires gaining access to widely distributed populations, who may not all be online at the time of the analysis. Furthermore, the question of how to bridge wide cultural gaps must be answered. How can developers gain access to representative users? How many users are likely to use the community? If surveys are to be used, how can unbiased sampling be achieved when the user population is unknown (Lazar & Preece, 1999)?

Measurement

Suites of automated tools are needed to measure the success of online communities to answer, for example, how many people are in the community at any time? How many are participating? What topics are being discussed? How involved are conversations i.e., threadedness ? How is participation changing (i.e., real-time measures of community activity)? What sociability and usability problems are occurring? How satisfied are participants with the software that supports the community?

Metrics also are needed, to enable community developers and managers to assess activity in their communities. Studies of mass communication systems (Whittaker, Terveen, Hill, & Cherny, 1998) such as UseNet News (Smith, 1999) and the demography of lurkers (Nonnecke & Preece, 2000) are leading the way, but more work must be done on this important topic.

Summary

As in real life, online communities have different goals, based on their makeup and purpose; the user tasks are different and users themselves are different (Hagel & Armstrong, 1997). For example, student communities need motivation and support, as do members of an e-commerce community, but of a different sort (see *Chapter 4*).

Communities of practice, professional communities composed of lawyers, doctors, teachers, software developers, and so on, all have individual specialist needs (Figallo, 1998). Developers need ways to help them better understand the specific requirements of different types of communities, so that they can customize sociability and usability for each. Privacy, security, and trust, for example, are important to health, education, and e-commerce sites alike, but how these issues impact them varies.

To answer basic questions about online community and culture, teams of social scientists will have to investigate what we can learn from physical communities that will enable us to develop better online communities. Codes of behavior well understood in the physical world are far from being established online. What kinds of behavioral rituals and codes of conduct lead to successful online communities?

Ethical issues and universal access must be addressed by online community activists. For example, how to visually notify users about unencrypted or encrypted traffic, how to ensure privacy and encourage appropriate development of trust. More far-reaching is that digital technology is impacting cultural diversity, environmental concerns, and the standard of living worldwide. In the future, research will be necessary to inform national and international agencies so that they can deploy resources appropriately. Ensuring universal access for all people is, perhaps, the most important long-term goal.

In practice, sociability and usability are closely integrated. Knowledge of social interaction directly informs sociability planning and indirectly influences much usability design. Consequently, research will help developers learn to better represent online behavior in real time; to record histories of behavior; to store communication and knowledge; to track topics of discussion; to confirm the number of people participating; and to define relationships among participants. Concomitantly, scalability is a research priority for online community developers. With an increasing number of people all over the world joining online communities, we must learn how to develop software and guide social processes appropriate to very large communities.

In the future, carefully guided sociability and skillfully designed usability will help shape thriving online communities. Already, online communities are connecting seniors with children; enabling culturally diverse groups to explore their differences in a safe environment; disseminating knowledge and offering support. Yes, there are dangers, in these communities, as in their real-world counterparts, but with the concerted efforts of the public and professionals to harness this technology, we can shift the balance to ensure a positive outcome.

Further Reading

"Human-centered Computing, Online Communities, and Virtual Environments" (Brown et al., 1999a), and "Special Report on Human-Centered Computing, Online Communities, and Virtual Environments" (Brown et al., 1999b)
These reports present the findings of a joint National Science Foundation and European Commission Workshop to identify the future key strategic research directions in the areas of human-centered interaction, online communities, and virtual environments.

Frontiers of Human-Centered Computing, Online Communities, and Virtual Environments (Earnshaw, Geudj, van Dam, & Vince, 2000)

Like the previous entry this volume also relates the results of a joint National Science Foundation and European Commission Workshop set up to identify the future key strategic research directions in the areas of human-centered interaction, online communities, and virtual environments. This book, however, proposes a research agenda for each area, in addition to offering a more detailed discussion of the topics reviewed.

Falling through the Net: Defining the Digital Divide (National Telecommunications and Information Administration & U.S. Dept of Commerce, 1999)

The report indicates that, in the US, the differences between the well educated and the poorly educated, high- and low-income population, correlates with Internet access, which is beginning to stimulate much needed political discussion.

"User Population and User Contribution to Virtual Publics: A Systems Model" (Jones & Rafaeli, 1999)

This paper provides a thoughtful review of empirical research into the discourse that occurs in cyberspace.

"Internet Paradox: A Social Technology that Reduces Social Involvement and Psychological Well-being" (Kraut et al., 1998)

This paper discusses results of a longitudinal study of 73 households (169 people total) who were provided with Internet access. The researchers show that increased online communication among participants was associated with a decline in offline social contact with family and friends.

"Bowling Alone: America's Declining Social Capital" (Putnam, 1995)

This thought-provoking paper is very well written. The combination of authoritative quantitative research with scholarly interpretation make it a joy to read. The content may, however, be unsettling. Pessimists will take away from it how the Internet will compound loss of social capital. Optimists will argue that the Internet will empower local community activists by enabling them to more effectively communicate and mobilize supporters.

References

Abercrombie, N. E. A. (1988). *Penguin Dictionary of Sociology*. Middlesex, Penguin Books.

Ackerman, M. & Starr, B. (1995). Social activity indicators for groupware. *IEEE Computer*, *29*(6), 37–42.

Ackerman, M. (1999). Verbal communication. Talk on nuance in information systems, University of Maryland, College Park.

Alexander, C., Ishikawa, S., Silverstein, M., Jacobson, M., Fiksdahl-King, I., & Angel, S. (1977). *A Pattern Language: Towns, Buildings, Construction*. New York: Oxford University Press.

Anderson, R. H., Bikson, T. K., Law, S. A., & Mitchell, B. M. (1995). *Universal Access to Email: Feasibility and Societal Implications*. Santa Monica, CA: Rand.

Atkinson, P. & Hammersley, M. (1994). Ethnography and participant observation. In N. K. Denzin and Y. S. Lincoln (Eds), *Handbook of Qualitative Research*. London: Sage.

Axelrod, R. (1984). *The Evolution of Cooperation*. New York: Basic Books.

Baldwin, W. (1998). Spam killers. *Forbes*, pp. 254–255.

Bartle, R. (1996). Hearts, clubs, diamonds, spades: Players who suit MUDs. *Journal of MUD Research*, *journal.tinymush.org/vln1/bartle.html*

Basili, V., Caldiera, G., & Rombach, D. H. (1994). *The Goal Question Metric Paradigm: Encyclopedia of Software Engineering*. New York: John Wiley & Sons, Inc.

Baym, N. (1997). Interpreting soap operas and creating community: Inside an electronic fan culture. In S. Kiesler (Ed.), *Culture of the Internet*. Mahwah, NJ: Lawrence Erlbaum.

Benyon, D. E. A. (1997). Experience with developing multimedia courseware for the World Wide Web: The need for better tools and clear pedagogy. *International Journal of Human-Computer Interaction*, *47*, 197–218.

Berge, Z. L. (1992). The role of the moderator in a scholarly discussion group (SDG), *star.ucc.nau.edu/ star.ucc.nau.edu/~mauri/moderate/zlbmod.html*

Bertot, J. & McClure, C. (1996). Electronic surveys: Methodological implications for using the World Wide Web to collect survey data. Paper presented at the Proceedings of the 59th Annual Meeting of the American Society for Information Science.

Beyer, H. & Holtzblatt, K. (1998). *Contextual Design. Defining Customer-Centered Systems*. San Francisco, CA: Morgan Kaufmann Publishers, Inc.

Bhimani, A. (1996). Securing the commercial Internet. *CACM*, *39*(6), 31–35.

Borgatti, S. P., Everett, M. G., & Freeman, L. C. (1999). Ucinet 5 for Windows: Software for social network analysis. Natick: Analytic Technologies.

Branscomb, A. B. (1994). Jurisdictional quandaries for global networks. In L. M. Harasim (Ed.), *Global Networks*. Cambridge, MA: MIT Press.

Brown, J., van Dam, A., Earnshaw, R., Encarnacao, J., Guedj, R., Preece, J., Shneiderman, B., & Vince, J. (1999a). Human-centered computing, online communities, and virtual environments. *ACM SIGCHI Interactions*, 6(5), 9–16.

Brown, J., van Dam, A., Earnshaw, R., Encarnacao, J., Guedj, R., Preece, J., Shneiderman, B., & Vince, J. (1999b). Special Report on Human-Centered computing, online communities, and virtual environments. *ACM SIGGRAPH Computer Graphics*, 33(3), 42–62.

Bruckman, A. (1993). Gender swapping on the Internet. Paper presented at the Internet Society (INET '93) Conference, San Francisco, CA.

Bruckman, A. (1994). Panel: Approaches to managing deviant behavior in virtual communities. *CHI'94 Conference Companion*, Boston, MA.

Bruckman, A. (1998). Community support for constructionist learning. Computer supported collaborative work. *The Journal of Collaborative Computing*, 7, 47–86.

Card, S. K. (1991). *Presentation on the Theories of HCI at the NSF Workshop on Human Computer Interaction*. Washington, DC: National Science Foundation.

Card, S. K., Mackinlay, J. D., & Shneiderman, B. (1999). *Readings in Information Visualization: Using Vision to Think*. San Francisco, CA: Morgan Kaufmann.

Carroll, J. M. & Kellog, W. A. (1988). Interface metaphors and user interface design. In M. Helander (Ed.), *Handbook of Human-Computer Interaction*. Amsterdam: North-Holland.

Carroll, J. M. (1990). Infinite detail and emulation in an ontologically minimized HCI. Paper presented at the Empowering People, CHI '90 Conference, Seattle.

Carroll, J. M., Kellog, W. A., & Rosson, M. B. (1991). The task-artifact cycle. In J. M. Carroll (Ed.), *Designing Interaction: Psychology at the Human-Computer Interface*. Cambridge: Cambridge University Press.

Carroll, J. M. (1995). *Scenario-Based Design: Envisioning Work and Technology in System Development*. New York: John Wiley & Sons, Inc.

Carroll, J. M. & Rosson, M. B. (1996). Developing the Blacksburg Village. *Communications of the ACM, 39*(11), 69–74.

Clark, H. H. & Brennan, S. E. (1991). Grounding the communication. In L. Resnick, J. M. Levine, & S. D. Teasley (Eds), *Perspectives on Socially Shared Cognition*. Washington, DC: APA.

Clark, H. H. & Brennan, S. E. (1993). Grounding in communication. In R. M. Baecker (Ed.), *Readings in Groupware and Computer-Supported Cooperative Work*. San Mateo, CA: Morgan Kaufmann Publishers.

Cohill, A. M. & Kavanaugh, A. L. (1997). *Community Networks: Lessons from Blacksberg, Virginia*. Norwood, MA: Artech House.

Collins, M. P. & Berge, Z. L. (1997). Moderating online electronic discussion groups. Paper presented at the 1997 American Educational Research Association (AREA) Meeting, March 24–28, Chicago, IL.

Constant, D., Sproull, L., & Kiesler, S. (1996). The kindness of strangers: The usefulness of electronic weak ties for technical advice. *Organization Science, 7*(2), 119–135.

Corry, D., et al. (1997). User-centered design and usability testing of a Web site: An illustrative case study. *ETR&D, 45*(4), 65–76.

Coste, R. (2000). Fighting speech with speech: David Duke, the Anti-defamation League, online bookstores, and hate filters. Paper presented at the 33rd Annual Hawaii International Conference on System Sciences, Maui, HI.

Coyle, A. (1995). Discourse analysis. In G. M. Breakwell, S. Hammond, & C. Fife-Schaw (Eds.), *Research Methods in Psychology*. London: Sage.

Cranor, L. F. & LaMacchia, B. A. (1998). Spam! *Communications of the ACM, 41*(8), 74–83.

Culnan, M. J. & Markus, M. L. (1987). Information technologies. In F. M. Jablin, L. L. Putnam, K. H. Roberts, & L. W. Porter (Eds), *Handbook of Organizational Communication: An Interdisciplinary Perspective*. Newbury Park, CA: Sage.

Culnan, M. J. & Milberg, S. J. (1999). Consumer privacy. In M. J. Culnan, R. J. Beis, & M. B. Levy (Eds), *Information Privacy: Looking Forward, Looking Back*. Washington, DC: Georgetown University Press.

Curtis, P. (1997). MUDding: Social phenomena in text-based virtual realities. In S. Kiesler (Ed.), *Culture on the Internet* (pp. 121–142). Mahwah, NJ: Lawrence Erlbaum.

Czaja, S. J. (1997). Computer technology and the older adult. In M. G. Helander, T. K. Landauer, & P. V. Prabhu (Eds), *Handbook of Human-Computer Interaction*. Amsterdam: Elsevier.

Daft, R. L. & Lengel, R. H. (1986). Organizational information requirements, media richness and structural design. *Management Science, 32*, 554–571.

Davis, R. & Miller, L. (1999). Net empowering patients. *USA Today*, pp. 1A–2A.

Denzin, N. K. & Lincoln, Y. S. (1994). *Handbook of Qualitative Research*. London: Sage.

Denzin, N. K. (1999). Cybertalk and the method of instances. In S. Jones (Ed.), *Doing Internet Research: Critical Issues and Methods for Examining the Net*. Thousand Oaks, CA: Sage Publications.

DeSanctis, G. & Gallupe, R. B. (1987). A foundation for the study of group decision support systems. *Management Science, 33*(5), 589–609.

DeSanctis, G., Poole, M. S., Dickson, M. S., & Jackson, M. (1993). Interpretive analysis of team use of group technologies. *Journal of Organizational Computing, 3*(1), 1–30.

Dix, A., Finlay, J., Abowd, G., & Beale, R. (1998). *Human-Computer Interaction (Second Edition)*. London: Prentice Hall Europe.

Dumas, J. S. & Redish, J. C. (1999). *A Practical Guide to Usability Testing (Revised Edition)*. Exeter, UK: Intellect.

Earnshaw, R. A., Geudj, R. A., van Dam, A., & Vince, J. A. (Eds.). (2000). *Frontiers of Human-Centered Computing, Online Communities, and Virtual Environments*. Amsterdam: Springer-Verlag.

Eason, K. D. (1988). *Information Technology and Organisational Change*. London: Taylor Francis.

Eisenberg, N. & Strayer, J. (1987). Critical issues in the study of empathy. In N. Eisenberg & J. Strayer (Eds), *Empathy and Its Development*. Cambridge, UK: Cambridge University Press.

Eisenstadt, M. & Vincent, T. (1998). *The Knowledge Web: Learning and Collaborating on the Net*. London: Kogan Page.

Ellis, B. J. & Bruckman, A. S. (1999). Building a community of history. Paper presented at the CHI '99 Senior CHI Development Consortium, Pittsburgh, PA.

Ellis, C. A., Gibbs, S. J., & Rein, G. L. (1991). Groupware: Some issues and experiences. *Communications of the ACM, 34*(1), 38–58.

Erickson, T. (1996). Social interaction on the the Net: Virtual community as participatory genre. Paper presented at the 30th Hawaii International Conference on System Sciences, Maui, HI.

Erickson, T., Smith, D. N., Kellog, W. A., Laff, M., Richards, J. T., & Bradner, E. (1999). Socially translucent systems: Social proxies, persistent conversation, and the design of Babble. Paper presented at the CHI '99 Human Factors in Computing Systems, Philadelphia, PA.

Etchegoyen, R. H. (1991). *The Fundamentals of Psychoanalytic Technique*. New York: Karnac Books.

Feenberg, A. (1989). The written word: On the theory and practice of computer conferencing. In K. R. Mason & A. Kaye (Eds), *Mindweave: Communication, Computers and Distance Education*. Elmsford, NY: Pergamon Press.

Feenberg, A. (1993). Building a global network: The WBSI experience. In L. M. Harasim (Ed.), *Global Networks: Computers and International Communication* (pp. 185–220). Cambridge, MA: MIT Press.

Ferguson, T. (1996). *Health Online*. Reading, MA: Addison-Wesley.

Fernback, J. (1999). There is a there there. Notes toward a definition of cyber-community. In S. Jones (Ed.), *Doing Internet Research. Critical Issues and Methods for Examining the Net* (pp. 203–220). Thousand Oaks, CA: Sage Publications.

Figallo, C. (1998). *Hosting Web Communities*. New York: John Wiley & Sons, Inc.

Fiske, J. (1994). Audiencing: Cultural practice and cultural studies. In N. K. Denzin & Y. S. Lincoln (Eds), *Handbook of Qualitative Research*. Thousand Oaks, CA: Sage.

Fowler, C. J. H. & Mayes, T. (1997). Applying telepresence to education. *BT Technology Journal, 14*(4), 188–195.

Fox, S. (1996). Listserv as a virtual community: A preliminary analysis of disability-related electronic listservs. Paper presented at the Speech Communication Association, San Diego: CA.

Friedman, B. (1997). *Human Values and the Design of Computer Technology*. Cambridge: Cambridge University Press.

Friedman, T. L. (1999). *The Lexus and the Olive Tree*. New York: Farrar, Straus and Giroux.

Fukuyama, F. (1995). *Trust*. New York: Free Press Paperbacks, Simon & Schuster.

Gaines, B. R., Chen, L. J. L., & Shaw, M. L. G. (1997). Modeling the human factors of scholarly communities supported through the Internet and the World Wide Web. *Journal of the American Society of Information Science*, *48*(11), 987–1003.

Garton, L., Haythornthwaite, C., & Wellman, B. (1999). Studying online social networks. In S. Jones (Ed.), *Doing Internet Research*. London: Sage Publications.

Gates, W. H. (1995). *The Road Ahead*. New York: Viking.

Goleman, G. (1995). *Emotional Intelligence*. New York: Bantam Books.

Granovetter, M. (1973). The strength of weak ties. *American Journal of Sociology*, *78*, 1360–1380.

Granovetter, M. (1982). The strength of weak ties: A network theory revisited. In P. M. N. Lin (Ed.), *Social Structure and Network Analysis* (pp. 105–130). Beverly Hills, CA: Sage.

Greenbaum, J. & Kyng, M. E. (1991). *Design at Work: Cooperative Design of Computer Systems*. Hillsdale, NJ: Lawrence Erlbaum.

Hackos, J. & Redish, J. C. (1998). *User Analysis and Task Analysis for Interface Design*. New York: John Wiley & Sons, Inc.

Hagel, J. I. & Armstrong, A. G. (1997). *NetGain: Expanding Markets through Virtual Communities*. Boston, MA: Harvard Business School Press.

Harasim, L. M. (1993). *Global Networks. Computers and International Communication*. Cambridge, MA: MIT Press.

Harasim, L. M. (1994). Networks as social space. In L. M. Harasim (Ed.), *Global Networks: Computers and International Communication*. Cambridge, MA: MIT Press.

Harasim, L., Hiltz, S. R., Teles, L., & Turoff, M. (1995). *Learning Networks*. Cambridge, MA: MIT Press.

Harper, B., Slaughter, L., & Norman, K. (1997). Questionnaire administration via the WWW: A validation and reliability study for a user satisfaction questionnaire. Paper presented at the Proceedings of WebNet 97: International Conference on the WWW, Internet, and Intranet.

Hawking, S. (1998). *A Brief History of Time (Revised Edition)*. New York: Bantam.

Haythornthwaite, C. (1996). *Media Use in Support of Communication Networks in an Academic Research Environment*. Ph.D. Thesis, University of Toronto.

Haythornthwaite, C., & Wellman, B. (1998). Work, friendship, and media use for information exchange in a networked organization. *Journal of the American Society for Information Science*, *49*(12), 1101–1114.

Haythornthwaite, C. (2000). Online personal networks: Size, composition, and media use among distance learners. *New Media and Society*, *2*(2), 195–226.

Haythornthwaite, C., Guziec, M. K., Robins, J., & Shoemaker, S. (2000). Community development among distance learners. Temporal and technological dimensions. *Journal of Computer-Mediated Communication (under review)*.

Herring, S. (1992). Gender and participation in computer-mediated linguistic discourse: ERIC Clearinghouse on Languages and Linguistics (October).

Hillery, G. J. (1955). Definitions of community: Areas of agreement. *Rural Sociology*, *20*, 111–122.

Hiltz, S. R. (1985). *Online Communities: A Case Study of the Office of the Future*. Norwood, NJ: Ablex Publishing Corp.

Hiltz, S. R., Johnson, K., & Turoff, M. (1986). Experiments in group decision making: Communication process and outcome in face-to-face versus computerized conferencing. *Human Communication Research*, *13*, 225–252.

Hiltz, S. R. & Turoff, M. (1993). *The Network Nation: Human Communication via Computer (Revised Edition)*. Cambridge, MA: MIT Press.

Hiltz, S. R. (1994). *The Virtual Classroom: Learning without Limits via Computer Networks*. Norwood, NJ: Ablex Publishing Corporation.

Hix, D. & Hartson, H. R. (1993). *Developing User Interfaces: Ensuring Usability through Product and Process*. New York: John Wiley & Sons, Inc.

Hodges, S. D. & Wegner, D. M. (1997). Automatic and controlled empathy. In W. Ickes (Ed.), *Empathic Accuracy*. New York: The Guilford Press.

Hoffmann, D. (1978). *Frank Lloyd Wright's Fallingwater. The House and Its History*. New York: Dover Publications, Inc.

Hutchins, E. L. (1995). *Cognition in the Wild*. Cambridge, MA: MIT Press.

Ickes, W. (1993). Empathic accuracy. *Journal of Personality*, *61*, 587–610.

Ickes, W. (1997). *Empathic Accuracy*. New York: The Guilford Press.

Isaacs, E., Morris, T., Rodrigues, T. K., & Tang, J. C. (1995). A comparison of face-to-face and distributed presentations. Paper presented at the CHI '95 Conference: Human Factors in Computing Systems, Denver.

Jacko, J. A., Sears, A., & Borella, M. S. (2000). Toward a characterization of the usability of distributed multimedia documents. *Behaviour and Information Technology* (in press).

Jefferies, R. (1997). The role of task analysis in the design of software. In M. G. Helander, T. K. Landauer, & P. V. Prabhu (Eds), *Handbook of Human-Computer Interaction*. Amsterdam: Elsevier.

Johnson, S. (1997). *Interface Culture. How New Technology Transforms the Way We Create and Communicate*. San Francisco, CA: HarperSage.

Jones, Q. (1997). Virtual-communities, virtual-settlements and cyber-archaeology: A theoretical outline. *Journal of Computer-Mediated Communication*, *3*(3) December. *www.ascusc.org/jcmc/vol3/issue3/jones.html*

Jones, Q. & Rafaeli, S. (1999). User population and user contribution to virtual publics: A systems model. Paper presented at the Supporting Group Work (Group '99), Phoenix, AZ.

Jones, Q. (2000). Time to split, virtually: Expanding virtual publics into vibrant virtual metropolises. Paper presented at the 33rd Hawaii International Conference on System Sciences.

Jones, S. (1995). Understanding community in the information age. In S. Jones (Ed.), *CyberSociety: Computer-Mediated Communication and Community*. Thousand Oaks, CA: Sage Publications.

Jones, S. E. (1998). *Virtual Culture: Identity & Communication in Cybersociety*. London: Sage.

Jones, S. E. (1999a). *Doing Internet Research. Critical Issues and Methods for Examining the Net*. Thousand Oaks, CA: Sage Publications.

Jones, S. (1999b). Studying the Net: intricacies and issues. In S. Jones (Ed.), *Doing Internet Research. Critical Issues and Methods for Examining the Net* (pp. 1–27). Thousand Oaks, UK Publications.

Kahin, B. & Keller, J. (1995). *Public Access to the Internet*. Cambridge, MA: MIT Press.

Kapor, M. (1996). A software design manifesto. In T. Winograd (Ed.), *Bringing Design to Software*. Reading, MA: Addison-Wesley.

Kayany, J. M. (1998). Contexts of uninhibited online behavior: Flaming in social newsgroups on the UseNet. *Journal of American Society for Information Science*, *49*(12), 1135–1141.

Kendall, K. E. & Kendall, J. E. (1998). *Systems Analysis and Design*. Englewood Cliffs, NJ: Prentice Hall.

Kerr, E. B. & Hiltz, S. R. (1982). *Computer-Mediated Communication Systems: Status and Evaluation*. New York: Academic Press.

Kerr, E. B. (1986). Electronic leadership: A guide to moderating online conferences. *IEEE Transactions on Professional Communications, PC 29*(1), 12–18.

Kiesler, S. E. (1997a). *Culture of the Internet*. Mahwah, NJ: Lawrence Erlbaum.

Kiesler, S. S. L. (1997b). "Social" human-computer interaction. In B. Friedman (Ed.), *Human Values and the Design of Computer Technology*. Cambridge: Cambridge University Press.

Kim, A. J. (1998). Secrets of successful Web communities. *www.naima.com/articles/*

Kim, A. J. (2000). *Community Building on the Web*. Berkeley, CA: Peachpit Press.

King, S. (1994). Analysis of electronic support groups for recovering addicts. *Interpersonal Computing and Technology: An Electronic Journal for the 21st Century (IPCT), 2*(3), 47–56.

Kling, R. (1996). Social Relationships in Electronic Forums: Hangouts, salons, workplaces, and communities. In R. Kling (Ed.), *Computerization and Controversy: Value Conflicts and Social Choices (Second Edition)*. San Diego, CA: Academic Press.

Kling, R. (1999). What is social informatics and why does it matter? *D-Lib Magazine, 5*(1), January. *www.dliborg/dlib/january99/k/ing/01/ < lmg.html*

Kochen, M. (1989). *The Small World*. Norwood, NJ: Ablex.

Kollock, P. & Smith, M. (1996). Managing the virtual commons: Cooperation and conflict in computer communities. In S. Herring (Ed.), *Computer-Mediated Communication: Linguistic, Social, and Cross-Cultural Perspectives*. Amsterdam: John Benjamins.

Kollock, P. (1998a). The economies of online cooperation: Gifts and public goods in cyberspace. In M. Smith & P. Kollock (Eds), *Communities in Cyberspace*. London: Routledge.

Kollock, P. (1998b). Design principles in online communities. *PC Update, 15*, 58–60.

Kollock, P. (1999). The production of trust in online markets. In M. Macy, E. J. Lawlwer, S. Thyne, & H. A. Walker (Eds), *Advances in Group Processes*. Greenwich, CT: JAI Press.

Kollock, P., & Smith, M. (1999). Chapter 1. Communities in cyberspace. In M. Smith & Kollock, P. (Ed.), *Communities in Cyberspace* (pp. 3–25). London: Routledge.

Korenman, J. (1999). Email forums and women's studies: The example of WMST-L. In B. E. A. Pattanaik (Ed.), *CyberFeminism*. Melbourne, Australia: Spinifex Press.

Krackhardt, D., Blythe, J., & McGrath, C. (1994). Krackplot 3.0: An improved network drawing program. *Connections, 17*(2), 53–55.

Kraut, R., Scherlis, W., Mukhopadhyay, T., Manning, J., & Kiesler, S. (1996). HomeNet: A Field Trial of Residential Internet Services. Paper presented at the Proceedings of CHI '96, Vancouver, Canada.

Kraut, R., Patterson, M., Lundmark, V., Kiesler, S., Mukhopadhyay, T., & Scherlis, W. (1998). Internet paradox: A social technology that reduces social involvement and psychological well-being? *American Psychologist, 53*(9), 1017–1031.

Kreitzberg, C. (1998). *The LUCID Design Framework (Logical User-Centered Interaction Design)*. Princeton, NJ: Cognetics Corporation.

Lanzetta, J. T. & Englis, B. G. (1989). Expectations of cooperation and competition and their effects on observers' vicarious emotional responses. *Journal of Personality and Social Psychology, 56*, 543–544.

Larson, K. & Czerwinski, M. (1998). Web page design: Implications of memory, structure, and scent for information retrieval. Paper presented at the CHI '98, Human Factors in Computing Systems, Los Angeles.

Lazar, J. & Preece, J. (1998). Classification Schema for Online Communities. Paper presented at the 1998 Association for Information Systems, Americas Conference.

Lazar, J. & Preece, J. (1999b). Designing and implementing Web-based surveys. *Journal of Computer Information Systems, xxxix*(4), 63–67.

Lazar, J. & Preece, J. (1999a). Implementing service learning in an online communities course. Paper presented at the Proceedings of the 1999 Conference of the International Association for Information Management, 22–27.

Lazar, J., Tsao, R., & Preece, J. (1999). One foot in cyberspace and the other on the ground: A case study of analysis and design issues in a hybrid virtual and physical community. *WebNet Journal: Internet Technologies, Applications, and Issues, 1*(3), 49–57.

Lazar, J., Hanst, E., Buchwater, J., & Preece, J. (2000). Collecting user requirements in a virtual population: A case study. *WebNet Journal: Internet Technologies, Applications, and Issues (under review)*.

Lea, M. & Spears, R. (1991). Computer-mediated communication, de-individuation, and group decision-making. *International Journal of Man-Machine Studies, 34,* 283–301.

Lea, M., O'Shea, T., Fung, P., & Spears, R. (1992). "Flaming" in computer-mediated communication: Observations, explanations, and implications. In M. Lea (Ed.), *Contexts of Computer-Mediated Communication*. London: Harvester-Wheatsheaf.

Lehnert, W. G. (1998). *Internet 101: A Beginner's Guide to the Internet and the World Wide Web*. Reading, MA: Addison Wesley Longman, Inc.

Levenson, R. W. & Ruef, A. M. (1992). Empathy: A physiological substrate. *Journal of Personality and Social Psychology, 63,* 234–246.

Liebowitz, J. & Beckman, B. T. (1998). *Knowledge Organizations: What Every Manager Should Know*. Boca Raton, FL: St. Lucie Press.

Liebowitz, J. E. (1999). *Knowledge Management Handbook*. Boca Raton, FL: CRC Press.

Linden, T. & Kienholz, M. L. (1995). *Dr. Tom Linden's Guide to Online Medicine*. New York: McGraw-Hill.

Lynch, P. J. & Horton, S. (1999). *Web Style Guide (Preliminary Version)*. New Haven, CT: Yale University Press.

Markus, M. L. (1987). Toward a critical mass theory of interactive media: Universal access, interdependence, and diffusion. *Communication Research, 14,* 491–511.

Markus, M. L. (1990). Toward a critical mass theory of interactive media: Universal access, interdependence, and diffusion. In J. Funke & C. Steinfield (Eds), *Organizations and Communication Technology*. Newbury Park, CA: Sage.

Mason, R. & Kaye, A. (1989). *Mindweave: Communication, Computers, and Distance Education*. Oxford: Pergamon Press.

Mayer, R. E. (1997). From novice to expert. In M. G. Helander, T. K. Landauer, & P. V. Prabhu (Eds.), *Handbook of Human-Computer Interaction*. Amsterdam: Elsevier.

Mayhew, D. J. (1999). *The Usability Engineering Lifecycle*. San Francisco, CA: Morgan Kaufmann Publishers, Inc.

McGrath, J. E. (1984). *Groups: Interaction and Performance*. Englewood Cliffs, NJ: Prentice Hall.

McLaughlin, M., Goldberg, S. B., Ellison, N., & Lucas, J. (1999). Measuring Internet audiences: Patrons of an online art museum. In S. Jones (Ed.), *Doing Internet*

Research: Critical Issues and Methods for Examining the Net. Thousand Oaks, CA: Sage Publications.

McLuhan, M. (1960). Effects of improvements of communication media. *Journal of Economic History*, *20*, 556–575.

McMann, G. W. (1994). The changing role of moderation in computer-mediated conferencing. Paper presented at the Proceedings of the Distance Learning Research Conference, Covering the World with Educational Opportunities, Department of Educational Human Resource Development, Texas A&M University.

Mehta, M. D. & Plaza, D. E. (1997). Pornography in cyberspace: An exploration of what's in UseNet. In S. Kiesler (Ed.), *Culture of the Internet* (pp. 53–67). Mahwah, NJ: Lawrence Erlbaum.

Miller, D. P. (1956). The magic number seven plus or minus two: Some limits on our capacity for processing information. *Psychological Review*, *63*, 81–97.

Morris, M. & Ogan, C. (1996). The Internet as mass medium. *Journal of Communication*, *46*(1).

Morse, J. M. (1994). Designing funded qualitative research. In N. K. Denzin & Y. S. Lincoln (Eds), *Handbook of Qualitative Research*. Thousand Oaks, CA: Sage Publications.

Muller, M. J. (1992). Retrospective on a year of participatory design using the PICTIVE technique. Paper presented at the Proc. CHI '92 Human Factors in Computing Systems, Monterey, CA.

Mumford, E. (1983). *Designing Participatively*. Manchester, UK: Manchester Business School.

Murphy, E. F. (1978). *The Crown Treasury of Relevant Quotations*. New York: Crown Publishers, Inc.

Mynatt, E. D., Adler, A., Ito, M., Linde, C., & O'Day, B. (1999). Learning from Seniors in Network Communities. Paper presented at the CHI '99 Senior Development Consortium, Pittsburgh, PA.

National Telecommunications and Information Administration & U.S. Dept. of Commerce (1999). *Falling through the Net: Defining the Digital Divide*. Washington, DC.

Newell, A. F. & Gregor, P. (1997). Human-computer interaction for people with disabilities. In M. G. Helander, T. K. Landauer, & P. V. Prabhu (Eds.), *Handbook of Human-Computer Interaction*. Amsterdam: Elsevier.

Nie, N. H. & Ebring, L. (2000). *Internet and Society: A Preliminary Report*. Stanford, CA: The Institute for the Quantitative Study of Society.

Nielsen, J. (1993). *Usability Engineering*. Boston, MA: AP Professional.

Nielsen, J. & Mack, R. L. (1994). *Usability Inspection Methods*. New York: John Wiley & Sons, Inc.

Nielsen, J. (1995). A home-page overall. *IEEE Software, 12*(3), 75–78.

Nielsen, J. (1998). *Jakob Nielsen. www.useit.com/*

Nielsen, J. (2000). *Designing Web Usability: The Practice of Simplicity*. Indianapolis, IN: New Riders Publishing.

NIST (National Institute of Standards and Technology). *NIST Industry Usability Reporting Project (USA), www.nist.gov/iusr*

Noble, D. (1998). Digital diploma mills: The automation of higher education. *Educom Review, 33*(3).

Nonnecke, B. & Preece, J. (1999). Shedding light on lurkers in online communities. Paper presented at the Ethnographic Studies in Real and Virtual Environments: Inhabited Information Spaces and Connected Communities, January, 24–26, Edinburgh.

Nonnecke, B. (2000). *Lurking in Email-Based Discussion Lists*. South Bank University Ph.D. thesis: SCISM, London.

Nonnecke, B. & Preece, J. (2000a). *Lurker Demographics: Counting the Silent. Human Factors in Computing Systems*. Paper presented at CHI '00 The Hague, Holland.

Nonnecke, B. & Preece, J. (2000b). Persistence and lurkers: A pilot study. Paper presented at the HICSS-33 IEEE Computer Society, Maui, Hawaii.

Norman, D. A. (1986). Cognitive engineering. In D. Norman & S. Draper (Eds), *User-Centered Systems Design*. Hillsdale, NJ: Lawrence Erlbaum.

Ogan, C. (1993). Listserver communication during the Gulf War: What kind of medium is the electronic bulletin board? *Journal of Broadcasting and Electronic Media*, (Spring), 177–195.

Olson, G. M. & Olson, J. S. (1997). Research on computer-supported cooperative work. In M. Helander, T. K. Landauer, & P. Prabhu (Eds), *Handbook of Human-Computer Interaction (2nd Edition)* Amsterdam: Elsevier.

Olson, G. M. & Olson, J. S. (2000). Distance matters. *Transactions on Computer Human Interaction (TOCHI)*. In press.

Oppenheim, A. N. (1992). *Questionnaire Design, Interviewing and Attitude Measurement*. London: Pinter Publishers.

Ostrom, E. (1990). *Governing the Commons: The Evolution of Institutions for Collective Action*. New York: Cambridge University Press.

Parks, M. R. & Floyd, K. (1996). Making friends in cyberspace. *Computer-Mediated Communication, 4. ascusc.org/jcmc/roll/issue4/parks.html*

Patterson, S. (1997). Evaluating the Blacksberg Electronic Village. In A. Cohill & K. Cavanaugh (Eds), *Community Networks: Lessons from Blacksburg*. Boston, MA: Artech House.

Picard, R. (1997). *Affective Computing*. Cambridge, MA: MIT Press.

Pitkow, J. & Kehoe, C. (1996). GVU's WWW User Surveys. *www.gvu.gatech.edu*

Poole, M. S. & DeSanctis, G. (1990). Understanding the use of group decision support systems: The theory of adaptive structuration. In J. Fulk & C. W. Steinfield (Eds), *Organizations and Communication Technology*. Newbury Park, CA: Sage.

Preece, J. (Ed.). (1993). *A Guide to Usability. Human Factors in Computing*. Wokingham, UK: Addison-Wesley.

Preece, J., Rogers, Y., Sharp, H., Benyon, D., Holland, S., & Carey, T. (1994). *Human-Computer Interaction*. Wokingham, UK: Addison-Wesley.

Preece, J. & Rombach, D. (1994). A taxonomy for combining software engineering (SE) and human-computer interaction (HCI) measurement approaches: Towards a common framework. *The International Journal of Man-Machine Studies, 14*, 553–583.

Preece, J. & Ghozati, K. (1998a). In search of empathy online: A review of 100 online communities. Paper presented at the 1998 Association for Information Systems Americas Conference, Baltimore, MD.

Preece, J. & Ghozati, K. (1998b). Offering support and sharing information: A study of empathy in a bulletin board community. Paper presented at the Computer Virtual Environments Conference, Manchester, UK.

Preece, J. (1998). Empathic Communities: Reaching out across the Web. *Interactions Magazine, 2*(2), 32–43.

Preece, J. (1999a). Empathic communities: Balancing emotional and factual communication. *Interacting with Computers, 12*, 63–77.

Preece, J. (1999b). Empathy online. *Virtual Reality, 4*, 1–11.

Preece, J., Rogers, Y., & Sharp, H. (2001) *Interaction Design*. New York, NY: John Wiley & Sons, Inc.

Putnam, R. D. (1995). Bowling alone: America's declining social capital. *Journal of Democracy*, *6*(1), 65–78.

Rafaeli, S. & LaRose, R. J. (1993). Electronic bulletin boards and "public goods". Explanations of collaborative mass media. *Communications Research*, *20*(2), 277–297.

Rafaeli, S., Sudweeks, F., Konstan, J., & Mabry, E. A. (1998). Project overview. A collaborative quantitative study of computer-mediated communication. In F. Sudweeks, M. McLaughlin, & S. Rafaeli (Eds), *Network and Netplay: Virtual Groups on the Internet*. Menlo Park, CA: AAAI/MIT Press.

Ramsay, J., Barabesi, A., & Preece, J. (1998). A psychological investigation of long retrieval times on the World Wide Web. *Interacting with Computers*, *10*, 77–86.

Reid, E. (1993). Electronic Chat: Social issues on Internet Relay Chat. *Media Information Australia*, *67*, 62–70.

Report (1998). Hate Groups Top 500. *Intelligence Report*, Winter (93).

Resnick, P. & Varian, H. R. (1997). Recommender systems. *Communications of the ACM*, *40*(3), 56–58.

Rheingold, H. (1993). *The Virtual Community: Homesteading on the Electronic Frontier*. Reading, MA: Addison Wesley.

Rheingold, H. (1994). A slice of life in my virtual community. In L. M. Harasim (Ed.), *Global Networks: Computers and International Communication* (pp. 57–80). Cambridge, MA: MIT Press.

Rice, R. E. & Barnett, G. (1986). Group communication networks in electronic space: Applying metric multidimensional scaling. In M. McLaughlin (Ed.), *Communication Yearbook 9*. Newbury Park, CA: Sage.

Rice, R. E. (1987a). Computer-mediated communication and organizational innovations. *Journal of Communication*, *37*, 85–108.

Rice, R. E. (1987b). New patterns of social structure in an information society. In J. S. L. Lievrouw (Ed.), *Competing Visions, Complex Realities: Social Aspects of the Information Society*. Norwood, NJ: Ablex.

Rice, R. E. (1988). Task analyzability, use of new media, and effectiveness: Multi-site exploration of media richness. *Organization Science*, *3*(4), 475–500.

Rice, R. E. (1989). Issues and concepts in research on computer-mediated communication systems. *Communication Yearbook*, *12*, 436–476.

Rice, R. E., Grant, A. E., Schmitz, J., & Torobin, J. (1990). Individual and network influences on the adoption and perceived outcomes of electronic messaging. *Social Networks, 12*, 17–55.

Rice, R. E. (1993). Media appropriateness. Using social presence theory to compare traditional and new organizational media. *Human Communication Research, 19*(4), 451–484.

Rice, R. (1994). Network analysis and computer-mediated communication systems. In S. W. J. Galaskiewkz (Ed.), *Advances in Social Network Analysis*. Newbury Park, CA: Sage.

Rice, R. (1999). Personal communication.

Risjord, N. K. (1994). *Thomas Jefferson*. Madison, WI: Madison House.

Robinson, J. P., & Godbey, G. (1997). *Time for Life: The Surprising Ways That Americans Use Their Time*. University Park, PA: The Pennsylvania State University Press.

Robson, C. (1993). *Real-World Research*. Oxford, UK: Blackwell.

Robson, C. (1994). *Experimental Design and Statistics in Psychology*. Aylesbury, UK: Penguin Psychology.

Rogers, C. R. (1959). A theory of therapy, personality, and interpersonal relationship, as developed in the client-centered framework. In S. Koch (Ed.), *Psychology: A Study of a Science* (vol. 3). New York: McGraw-Hill.

Rogers, E. (1986). *Communication Technology: The New Media in Society*. New York: Free Press.

Rogers, Y. & Ellis, J. (1994). Distributed cognition: An alternative framework for analyzing and explaining collaborative working. *Journal of Information Technology, 9*, 119–128.

Ryer, J. C. (1997). *Health Net*. New York: John Wiley & Sons, Inc.

Sack, W. (2000). Discourse diagrams: Interface design for very large-scale conversations. Paper presented at the 33rd Annual Hawaii International Conference on System Sciences, Maui, HI.

Salmon, G. (2000). *E-moderating: The Key to Teaching and Learning Online*. London: Kogan Page.

Schmidt, W. (1997). World Wide Web survey research: Benefits, potential problems and solutions. *Behavior Research Methods, Instruments and Computers, 29*(2), 274–279.

Schoch, N. A. & White, M. D. (1997). A study of the communication patterns of participants in consumer health electronic discussion groups. Paper presented at the Proceedings of the 60th ASIS Annual Meeting, Washington, DC.

Schuler, D. & Namioka, A. E. (1993). *Participatory Design: Principles and Practices:* Mahwah, NJ: Lawrence Erlbaum.

Schuler, D. (1994). Community networks: Building a new participatory medium. *CACM, 37*(1), 39–51.

Schuler, D. (1996). *New Community Networks: Wired for Change.* Reading, MA: ACM Press and Addison-Wesley.

Sears, A., Jacko, J. A., & Dubach, E. M. (2000). International aspects of WWW usability and the role of high-end graphical enhancements. *International Journal of Human-Computer Studies* (in press).

Sellen, A. (1994). Remote conversations: The effects of mediating talk with technology. *Human-Computer Interaction, 10*(4), 401–444.

Sharf, B. F. (1999). Beyond netiquette: The ethics of doing naturalistic discourse research on the Internet. In S. Jones (Ed.), *Doing Internet Research: Critical Issues and Methods for Examining the Net.* Thousand Oaks, CA: Sage Publications.

Shneiderman, B. (1998a). *Designing the User Interface: Strategies for Effective Human-Computer Interaction (Third Edition).* Reading, MA: Addison-Wesley.

Shneiderman, B. (1998b). Relate-create-donate: A teaching philosophy for the cyber-generation. *Computers in Education, 31*(1), 25–39.

Shneiderman, B. (2000). To trust or not to trust: Design guidelines for enhancing cooperative behaviors online. *Communications of the ACM* (in press).

Short, J., Williams, E., & Christie, B. (1976). *The Social Psychology of Telecommunications.* London: John Wiley & Sons.

Smith, M. A. (1999). Invisible crowds in cyberspace: Mapping the social structure of the Internet. In M. A. Smith & P. Kollock (Ed.), *Communities in Cyberspace.* London: Routledge.

Smith, M. A. & Kollock, P. (1999). *Communities in Cyberspace.* London: Routledge.

Smith, M. A., Farnham, S. D., & Drucker, S. M. (2000). The social life of small graphical chat spaces. CHI 2000 Conference Proceedings. The Hague, Netherlands, 462–469.

Snow, C. P. (1969). *The Two Cultures.* Cambridge, UK: Cambridge University Press.

Spears, M., Russell, L., & Lee, S. (1990). De-individuation and group polarization in computer-mediated communication. *British Journal of Social Psychology*, *29*, 121–134.

Spears, R. & Lea, M. (1992). Social influence and the influence of "social" in computer-mediated communication. In M. Lea (Ed.), *Contexts of Computer-Mediated Communication*. Hemel Hempstead, UK: Harvester Wheatsheaf.

Spool, J. M., Scanlon, T., Schroeder, W., Snyder, C., & DeAngelo, T. (1997). *Web Site Usability: A Designer's Guide*. North Andover, MA: User Interface Engineering.

Sproull, L. & Faraj, S. (1997). The Net as a social technology. In S. Kiesler (Ed.), *Culture of the Internet*. Mahwah, NJ: Lawrence Erlbaum.

Sproull, L. & Kiesler, S. (1986). Reducing social context cues: Electronic mail in organizational communication. *Management Science*, *32*, 1492–1512.

Sproull, L. & Kiesler, S. (1991). *Connections: New Ways of Working in the Networked Organization*. Cambridge, MA: MIT Press.

Sudaweeks, F., McLaughlin, M., & Rafaeli, S. (1998). *Network and Netplay: Virtual Groups on the Internet*. Cambridge, MA: MIT Press.

Sudaweeks, F. & Simoff, S. J. (1999). Complementary explorative data analysis: The reconstruction of quantitative and qualitative principles. In S. Jones (Ed.), *Doing Internet Research: Critical Issues and Methods for Examining the Net*. Thousand Oaks, CA: Sage Publications.

Sumrall, A. C. (1992). *Write to the Heart: Wit & Wisdom of Women Writers*. Freedom, CA: The Crossing Press.

Tannen, D. (1990). *You Just Don't Understand. Men and Women in Conversation*. New York: William Morrow & Co. Ltd.

Tannen, D. (1994). *Talking from 9 to 5*. New York: William Morrow and Company, Inc.

Tech, G. (1998). GVU's Tenth WWW User Survey. *www.gvu.gatech.edu/user_surveys-1998-10/graphs/privacy/q01.htm*

Thach, L. (1995). Using electronic mail to conduct survey research. *Educational Technology*, 27–31.

Tnnies, F. (1955). *Community and Organisation*. London: Routledge & Kegan Paul.

Travis, D. (1991). *Effective Colour Displays*. New York: Academic Press.

Turkle, S. (1995). *Life on the Screen. Identity in the Age of the Internet*. New York: Simon & Schuster.

Turkle, S. (1999, Winter 1999/2000). Tinysex and gender trouble. *IEEE Technology and Society Magazine, 4,* 8–20.

Viegas, F. B. & Donath, J. S. (1999). Chat Circles. Paper presented at the CHI'99 Human Factors in Computing Systems, Philadelphia.

Vygotsky, L. (1978). *Mind in Society.* Cambridge: Cambridge University Press.

Vygotsky, L. (1986). *Thought and Language.* Cambridge, MA: MIT Press.

Wallace, P. (1999). *The Psychology of the Internet.* Cambridge: Cambridge University Press.

Walsham, G. (1993). *Interpreting Information Systems in Organizations.* Chichester, UK: John Wiley & Sons.

Walther, J. B. (1992). Interpersonal effects in computer-mediated interaction: A relational perspective. *Communication Research, 57,* 52–90.

Walther, J. B. (1993). Impression development in computer-mediated interaction. *Western Journal of Communications, 57,* 381–398.

Walther, J. B., Anderson, J. F., & Park, D. W. (1994). Interpersonal effects in computer-mediated interaction: A meta-analysis of social and antisocial communication. *Communication Research, 21,* 460–487.

Walther, J. B. (1994). Anticipated ongoing interaction versus channel effects on relational communication in computer-mediated interaction. *Human Communication Research, 20*(4), 473–501.

Walther, J. B. (1996). Computer-mediated communication: Impersonal, interpersonal, and hyperpersonal interaction. *Communications Research, 23*(1), 3–43.

Wellman, B. (1982). Studying personal communities. In P. M. N. Lin (Ed.), *Social Structure and Network Analysis.* Beverly Hills, CA: Sage.

Wellman, B. (1992). Which types of ties and networks give what kinds of social support? *Advances in Group Processes, 9,* 207–235.

Wellman, B. (1997). An electronic group is virtually a social network. In S. Kiesler (Ed.), *Culture of the Internet* (pp. 179–205). Mahwah, NJ: Lawrence Erlbaum.

Wellman, B. & Gulia, M. (1998). Virtual communities as communities: Net surfers don't ride alone. In M. Smith & P. Kollock (Eds), *Communities in Cyberspace.* Berkeley, CA: Routledge.

Wellman, B. & Gulia, M. (1999). Net surfers don't ride alone. In B. Wellman (Ed.), *Networks in the Global Village.* Boulder, CO: Westview Press.

Werry, C. (1999). Imagined electronic community: Representation of virtual community in contemporary business discourse. *FirstMonday.*

Whittaker, S., Issacs, E., & O'Day, V. (1997). Widening the net. Workshop report on the theory and practice of physical and network communities. *SIGCHI Bulletin*, *29*(3), 27–30.

Whittaker, S., Terveen, L., Hill, W., & Cherny, L. (1998). The dynamics of mass interaction. Paper presented at the ACM CSCW '98, Seattle, WA.

Whitten, J. L. & Bentley. D. (1998). *Systems Analysis and Design Methods (Fourth Edition)*. Boston, MA: McGraw-Hill.

Whitworth, B. & Turoff, M. (2000). Groupware: Old wine in new bottles. Unpublished draft and personal communication.

Williams, F., Rice, R. E., & Rogers, E. M. (1988). *Research Methods and the New Media*. New York: The Free Press, Macmillan, Inc.

Winner, L. (1995). Peter Pan in cyberspace. *Educom Review*, *30*(3).

Witmer, D. F., Colman, R. W., & Katzman, S. L. (1999). From paper-and-pencil to screen-and-keyboard. In S. Jones (Ed.), *Doing Internet Research: Critical Issues and Methods for Examining the Net*. Thousand Oaks, CA: Sage.

Wixon, D. & Wilson, C. (1997). The usability engineering framework for product design and evaluation. In M. G. Helander, T. K. Landauer, & P. V. Prabju (Eds), *Handbook of Human-Computer Interaction*. Amsterdam: Elsevier.

Zimmer, B. & Alexander, G. (1996). The Rogerian interface: For open, warm empathy in computer-mediated collaborative learning. *Innovations in Education and Training International*, *33*(1), 13–21.

Index

*Index compiled by Indexing Specialists,
Hove*